LET EVERY CHILD BE WANTED

LET EVERY CHILD BE WANTED

How Social Marketing Is Revolutionizing
Contraceptive Use Around the World

Philip D. Harvey

AUBURN HOUSE
Westport, Connecticut • London

Library of Congress Cataloging-in-Publication Data

Harvey, Philip D., 1938–
    Let every child be wanted : how social marketing is
revolutionizing contraceptive use around the world / Philip D.
Harvey.
        p. cm.
    Includes bibliographical references and index.
    ISBN 0–86569–282–3 (alk. paper)
    1. Contraceptives—Marketing. 2. Social marketing. 3. Birth
control—Government policy. 4. Family policy. I. Title.
HQ763.5.H38   1999
363.9'6—dc21   99–13697

British Library Cataloguing in Publication Data is available.

Library of Congress Catalog Card Number: 99–13697
ISBN: 0–86569–282–3

First published in 1999

Auburn House, 88 Post Road West, Westport, CT 06881
An imprint of Greenwood Publishing Group, Inc.
www.greenwood.com

Printed in the United States of America

The paper used in this book complies with the
Permanent Paper Standard issued by the National
Information Standards Organization (Z39.48–1984).

10 9 8 7 6 5 4 3 2 1

For Harriet Lesser,
who persuaded me to write this book
and for
Terry Louis (1934–1990)

Contents

viii   Contents

Illustrations

FIGURES

Acknowledgments

I am particularly grateful to Peter King and to Bob Ciszewski who contributed substantially to the content of this book. The early history of the world's first social marketing program in which King played a pivotal role and the massive Bangladesh program, which Ciszewski launched and managed, are particularly important components of the analysis that follows.

I am also most grateful to John Davies, Dana Hovig, Malcolm Potts, Kitty Thuermer, Judith Timyan, Renée Wessels, Bill Schellstede, and, especially, Steve Chapman for reviewing the manuscript and offering valuable suggestions, most of which have been incorporated. Dan Lissance was both a valued reviewer and a contributor.

Thanks also to Tim Black, Andy Piller, Craig Darden, Jim Myers, and Santiago Plata, who contributed lively and illuminating segments of this narrative. Sara Blackburn performed a superb job of editing, for which my special thanks are due. Thanks also to Michele Thorburn for exhaustive proofing and organizing of this book, and to Rebecca DeVost for typing and rearranging endless iterations and for creating many of the graphs and tables. Thanks also to Jason Finkle, Julian Simon and Lester Brown for their useful comments and suggestions and to Ron Schultz for his suggestions and invaluable help in finding the right publisher.

1

The Pioneers

It was early morning in Calcutta, March 1964. Peter King was walking the seven blocks from his apartment at number 2 Hungerfurd Street along Chowringee to New Market near the center of the city. Though it was only 6:30, already the air was stifling. King was perspiring heavily after just two blocks, but he was as oblivious to this as he was to the growing cacophony of sounds around him: the thousands of street-dwellers who live on Calcutta's sidewalks who were beginning their day with ablutions from fire hydrants and pots and pans; the thousands of rickshaws being pulled by barefoot men jogging and straining against the weight of their human cargos; the taxis—horns blaring—swarming along Chowringee, Calcutta's largest and busiest street, each fighting for advantage in the great and growing tangle of trucks, cars, bicycles, rickshaws, bullock carts, two-wheeled trundles, cargo carts, scooters, and other conveyances. Hawks circled overhead and crows cawed from the leafy foliage of Bodhi trees, competing with the cries of the hawkers, the jingling of the bicycle bells, and the deep growling of the trucks and buses. Peter King was oblivious to all this because an exciting idea was taking shape in his mind. King and his colleagues at the Indian Institute of Management, Calcutta, were conceiving a revolutionary approach to India's family planning challenge.

Peter King knew the Indian government was fully committed to family planning. Top officials were convinced that the astonishing growth in the population of India—more than twelve million people being added every year—seemed an impediment to the country's social and economic improvement that was overwhelming. But how to persuade people to use birth control, and how even to reach the widely dispersed 500 million citizens of India, most of them in deeply rural areas? Clearly, family planning that was administered only through doctors and clinics could never accomplish the job alone; India had far too few doctors and clinics, and most of these were concentrated in the major urban areas, away from the great mass of the country's population. So Peter King and his colleagues had begun to work on the idea of promoting and distributing condoms through *commercial* rather than medical networks.

The concept seemed simple enough. Condoms, after all, did not require a prescription or any medical supervision. They had a long shelf life. Physically, they could be distributed through retailers, just like tea or cigarettes and just as broadly, if it became economically feasible for a commercial distributor to do so. The government of India was already distributing free condoms through its public health network. But the government, like most nonprofit entities, lacked the marketing and advertising expertise to create a real demand for the condoms, and it certainly lacked the kind of distribution network required to make them widely available.

Peter King was in Calcutta as a visiting professor at the Indian Institute of Management, Calcutta (IIMC), one of three professors from MIT's Sloan School of Management who had come to India to help establish one of the two executive development centers that the government of India was setting up with Ford Foundation support. The second school, the Indian Institute at Ahmedabad, had a collaboration arrangement with the Harvard Business School.

The institute's students were middle managers in their thirties, attending a twelve-month MBA program; senior managers attending specialized one-month courses; and regular MBA students just out of college. Brainstorming new approaches to the family planning problem by using commercial management and marketing techniques fit perfectly into the curriculum.

Condoms had been sold in India since the 1940s, but in 1964 they were being stocked by only a few hundred drugstores and other retail outlets that offered high-priced, specialty goods to the wealthy in large cities. Market prices were equivalent to those prevailing in the United States or Europe, and total consumption was very low. Nevertheless, four small- and one large-scale private manufacturer had gone into production a few years earlier, but they were unable to generate any expansion in consumer sales.

To marketing specialists, none of this was surprising. India's per-capita income was, and is, about 2 percent of that of the United States. To aim for the median-income consumer, a condom manufacturer would have had to price its product below the cost of production, an obviously untenable proposition. So the first thing apparent to King and his team was that a mass-marketed condom would have to be priced below—way below—the level of condoms on the commercial market.

Two other components also had to be addressed: distribution and communications. The IIMC planners hoped that experienced distributors could be enlisted to perform the entire condom distribution operation at normal percentage margins. Brooke Bond Tea, for example, sold directly to about 600 thousand tea shops and grocery stores utilizing some 3,600 regularly employed salesmen and a vast network of transportation, storage, and credit and collection facilities.

Imperial Tobacco sold its cigarettes in more than one million outlets, most of which received daily visits from bicycle-riding salesmen of the wholesalers in the company's hierarchical network of independent distributors, stockists, and wholesalers, each compensated by receiving a percentage of its sales revenue.

King and his colleagues believed that a small central marketing organization would be able to rapidly execute a professionally managed, nationwide sales campaign without any direct costs of personal selling, transport, or warehousing, as these functions could all be performed by commercial distributors. The distributors would pay an agreed-upon percentage of their sales to the central project team.

This prospective income stream provided the final piece in the planning puzzle—how to fund the kind of professional advertising and sales promotion campaign that the project would require if it were to create demand for the product and market it successfully. If the product could be provided at no cost to a central marketing organization, the planners figured, perhaps 70 percent of its sales revenue could be spent on advertising.

To marketers this is an unheard-of figure. Large advertisers typically spend 2 to 5 percent of sales on advertising. An expenditure for promotion of 70 percent is impossible for a commercial company because sales revenue must normally first pay the factory's costs of production. But, from the government's point of view, government programmers being accustomed to giving things away for free, this aspect of a marketing program would be a real budget stretcher.

The income stream, however, would become significant only after the program reached substantial sales volume. Initially, revenue would be a trickle, and that was just when efforts at creating demand should be at a maximum. In other words, a substantial start-up investment in advertising and sales promotion (and marketing research) would have to be provided.

As these issues were addressed and resolved, the document that King had been assembling from his notes and his students' suggestions began to fill out. As an academician, he was tempted to publish an article on what was now becoming a full-fledged "marketing plan," but he knew that if the idea of marketing subsidized contraceptives as part of a family planning program were believed to have originated with a foreigner—and a foreign academic at that—it would likely take its place among the thousands of public papers that languish on bookshelves all over the world without ever inspiring action. King understood that this idea had to become the possession of Indians, of the government or of other Indian sources, so that it could be taken up by Indians as their own and championed by Indians as a concept especially suited to their populous and impoverished country.

At last the document was ready, and King presented it on April 25, 1964, prefacing it with a memorandum from the "secretary of the study group," a group of ten persons—IIMC professors, Indian businessmen, and Ford Foundation population experts. It was anticipated that, after some refinement, the document would be circulated to interested parties including Indian government officials. As "secretary," Peter King was merely passing along the ideas and concepts that had grown out of the normal activities at the IIMC, an Indian institution in a very Indian city.

The 150-page document was called "Proposals for Family Planning Promotion: A Marketing Plan" (Indian Institute of Management, 1964) and it contained all of the essential ideas for the social marketing of contraceptives—contraceptive social marketing (CSM), as it is now somewhat ungrammatically called—in India and, as it turns out, throughout the world. These were:

Consumer research. The document reviewed available research, including the finding that most Indian couples wished they could limit their family size and that, contrary to common belief, husbands were nearly as eager to do so as wives. Consonant with the much later findings in Bangladesh (see Chapter 6) the document pointed out that by far the largest number of couples cited economic reasons rather than health reasons or other factors for wishing to restrict the size of their families—a fact that social marketers have had to relearn again and again. The marketing plan did not call for much additional market research, but it suggested that the commercial companies—advertising agencies and distributors—would and could conduct appropriate research as the project progressed.

Source of product. The marketing plan called for a high-quality, well-packaged condom and sales targets of as many as 400 million condoms per year. A good deal of attention was paid to where such a large supply might be obtained and at what price. In 1964 a requirement of 400 million additional condoms was sufficient to stretch the capacity of worldwide production. Since "foreign exchange" was a major preoccupation of the Indian government in those days, the necessity of acquiring condoms outside of the country appeared a formidable obstacle. Local Indian capacity at the time was only four million condoms a year, and even that had been interrupted because of quality control problems.

Despite these drawbacks, the plan contemplated that an adequate supply could be obtained at a cost of about U.S. 1 cent each. The project was to be phased in over a period of at least three years, which would give international manufacturers enough time to gear up. Note that the long-term sales target of 400 million condoms per annum very closely approximates one condom per capita (India's population was just under 500 million), precisely the same guideline target described later in this book (Chapter 9), which was set on the basis of an additional thirty years of experience. In other words, using an entirely different set of calculations, with no other CSM program in the world to guide them, Peter King and his colleagues arrived at a sales target that has proved over time to be entirely feasible in several other countries, including neighboring Bangladesh. Had this target been achieved in the late 1960s, King calculated that it would translate to contraceptive protection for about 9 percent of all couples in India.

Branding and packaging. A number of brand names had been suggested and a short list of recommended names was included in the marketing plan. These included Nirodh (meaning "protection"), which had been suggested by an IIMC student and was the name finally chosen; Anand, meaning joy; and Madan, Ratiraja, and Kamaraja, all names of Hindu gods of love. (The plan took care to note, puckishly, that Kamaraja must be carefully spelled so the project would not be accused of pandering to the then chairman of India's dominant political party, the Congress, whose name was Kamaraj.) Good-quality packaging was considered a must, and could be produced in India.

Advertising and promotion. Targeted at a population greater than that of Europe, North Africa, and the Middle East combined, the marketing and sale of the new Indian condom was to constitute perhaps the biggest new product introduction in the history of the world. The authors of the plan believed very strongly that effective advertising in at least fifteen different Indian languages would be essential for the condom's success. To have the desired impact, every available advertising medium would have to be utilized, sometimes to the maximum amount available for procurement. The project, just like social marketing projects today, could not succeed on a small scale, and a media blitz was essential to make it a genuinely large-scale undertaking.

Seventy-five percent of the advertising and promotional budget was to be devoted to "films"; these were envisioned as two- to three-minute advertisements to be shown during cinema intermissions, a medium that was considered the best possible way to present effective motivational messages to hundreds of millions of young Indian males, since there was no television except for a test station in Delhi. Radio advertising was another major component of the plan; the government-owned All India Radio was expected to donate air time. The press would also be used, as would posters and billboards. Folders and leaflets were to be distributed at stores and provided to medical professionals, including nurses and midwives. The campaign would also use mobile exhibits and outdoor metal signs to be affixed above shop entrances ("Nirodh for sale here"), and retail dispenser information and "show" cards.

Distribution. Following the conventional commercial wisdom of the day (and of our day as well), the authors noted that multiproduct distributors like Mueller & Phipps, a national distributor of pharmaceutical products, herbal soaps, and dental products manufactured by other companies (as well as its own), might be persuaded to cooperate. Also identified were Parry's, and TTK. The plan stated: "These firms have large direct selling organizations which are needed, not only to sell to middle men, but also to ensure effective operations throughout the wholesale distribution system. Our information indicates that a sufficient number of such reputable houses would be willing to undertake condom distribution on a commission basis."

The authors also identified what they called "a second class of distributors," which turned out to be very important. These were companies that ordinarily marketed only their own products, but it was suggested that "one or two" might be induced for "a small percentage commission to distribute family planning products as a social service." The marketing plan continued: "The large tea companies sell directly to over 600,000 retailers through their own salesmen and warehouses. A recent Brooke Bond [tea] company newspaper advertisement showed a camel moving across the desert in Rajasthan ladened with tea destined for retailers. We don't think a small case of condoms would have broken that camel's back."

In addition to Brooke Bond and Lipton Tea companies, the document identified Hindustan Lever and Tata Oil Mills (competing manufacturers of cooking oil and bath soap), Imperial Tobacco, and National Tobacco as six firms that might be induced to add condoms to their distribution networks. This turned out to be the cornerstone of the program—except for National Tobacco, all ended up participating, as did Union Carbide, a manufacturer and distributor of flashlight batteries.[1]

The use of manufacturer/distributors rather than multiproduct distribution specialists would turn out to be unique to the Indian program. Since that time, dozens of social marketing organizations, including both Population Services International (PSI) and Social Marketing for Change (SOMARC), have attempted in numerous countries to piggyback contraceptives onto these kinds of consumer goods—for example, Coca-Cola and cigarettes—but, outside of India, it has never succeeded. Coca-Cola has wanted no association with a product like a condom, and that has generally been the case with cigarette manufacturers as well. The latter are inclined to remark that cigarettes are controversial enough already without another controversial product like the condom to cause more problems. To the best of my knowledge there is no social marketing program anywhere in the world today that relies for its distribution function on a company that distributes primarily its own (noncontraceptive) products rather than products of other companies.

Nevertheless, in India in 1964, these companies seemed eager for a way to contribute to the solution of a major national problem. Part of the reason, no doubt, was that the socialist policies of the Indian government created a climate in which all major corporations working in India were anxious to please the government in any way they could, as their continued existence as private entities was always uncertain. But multinational corporations, in those days especially, wanted to show that the business sector was socially responsible. And King reports that India's senior corporate executives, "top businessmen," were genuinely eager to be of service to their nation and to demonstrate that private corporations could provide a useful service.

Pricing.[2] The marketing plan called for the condom to be priced at about one-fifth of normal commercial prices in India at that time. It recommended a consumer price of Re.0.05 (5 paisa) per condom, which happened, purely by coincidence, to be the same as the anticipated FOB price of condoms, purchased in large bulk quantities. At 1965 exchange rates, this was about 1 U.S. cent, a price well within the guidelines discussed in Chapter 8.[3]

Cost-benefit analysis. A substantial final section of the marketing plan contained a sophisticated cost-benefit analysis to demonstrate to the government of India that the costs of a large-scale social marketing program would be offset many times over by the government's consequent savings in social services. A series of formulaic suppositions concluded that the government's investment in the subsidized contraceptive marketing project would result in returns of 7 to 75 times the cost of the program in societal savings. This is the only area of this otherwise astonishingly prophetic marketing plan that experience has demonstrated to be less than prescient.*

*What we have subsequently learned is not a more sophisticated way to calculate the social cost of a pregnancy prevented or a birth averted (King suggests a "minimum" value of a birth averted in India in 1964 at 600 rupees [U.S. $120]). Rather we have learned that such a figure simply cannot be calculated. Short-term saving to a family for preventing or postponing a birth may be calculated (schooling, clothing, and health care), but these do not represent societal costs, nor do they tell us about the longer-term economic value of additional human beings. There are just too many variables involved, including such intangibles as the fact that parents tend to work harder when they have more children, thus increasing the gross national product.

Otherwise, here in Peter King's 1964 outline, are virtually all of the elements that we have learned and relearned in the thirty years since then, from research to product to branding, pricing, advertising, and distribution. That King and his colleagues could have come up with a target of just under one condom per capita (0.8), at a price equivalent to 0.5 to 0.8 percent of per capita GNP is quite humbling to those of us who have reached similar conclusions by traveling different paths and with much more information. We owe King and his IIMC colleagues a debt of gratitude for establishing the framework, both intellectual and practical, within which social marketing of contraceptives has been successfully carried out.

FROM BLUEPRINT TO REALITY

It would be four-and-a-half years from the first publication of this marketing plan until the Nirodh nationwide condom marketing program actually got under way. There were several reasons:

• As elsewhere, condoms were still highly controversial in India;
• The number of condoms needed for a full-fledged program exceeded the number any government or other donor had ever purchased before; and
• Establishing a privately managed, commercially oriented project as a major component in what had previously been entirely an Indian government program presented numerous political and other obstacles.

Despite these obstacles, the idea itself encountered remarkably little resistance. Copies of the proposal were circulated to the faculty and board members of the two management institutes. The latter included many of India's top private and public sector executives as well as senior government officials, such as the Secretary of Education and the Chief Ministers of the states of West Bengal and Gujarat, who were the chairmen of their respective institutes (Calcutta is in West Bengal, Ahmedabad is in Gujarat). K. T. Chandy,[4] director of the IIMC, personally walked the halls in New Delhi explaining the marketing idea to high government officials, including the deputy prime minister, and to political leaders of all persuasions. The "proposals" spread back to business and management science circles in the United States through MIT's Sloan School of Management and Harvard Business School connections. Through the Ford Foundation, the proposals quickly reached major donors and population study centers, to whom Ford was often the major donor.

Bernard Berelson, president of the Population Council in New York, edited and published an abbreviated version of the marketing plan in 1965 (Indian Institute of Management, 1965).*

The reaction to the plan was highly favorable in India and abroad. But any action toward implementation had to be done by or with the cooperation of the government of India, and specifically with the Ministry of Health, in whose jurisdiction family planning fell. Col. B. P. Raina, a public health physician, headed the ministry's small family planning branch in 1964 and he was closely assisted by Dr. Moye Freyman, also a public health physician and the population expert at the Ford Foundation in New Delhi. Colonel Raina supported the plan but neither he nor anyone else felt that his office would be an appropriate base to actually carry out the program envisaged.

In 1965 the picture changed. The government of India raised the family planning program to highest priority. The Ministry of Health became the Ministry of Health and Family Planning with a Minister of State for family planning. Some of India's top civil servants, including Govind Narain who was appointed secretary of the renamed ministry, were brought in to strengthen administration. To provide technical direction, a Commissioner of Family Planning, Lt. Gen. Shiv Bhatia, formerly head of the Indian Army Medical Corps, was appointed along with a large staff. While this was going on in Delhi, the fifteen major state government health administrations were reorganized and strengthened to increase the capacity of the states to plan and execute a substantial expansion of the sterilization programs and also the introduction of the IUCD program,[5] all conducted through the tens of thousands of hospitals, clinics, primary health centers, and subcenters that comprise India's extensive public health service, the largest in the developing world.

Donors, too, were gearing up during this period to greatly expand their support to family planning. The Ford Foundation and USAID each brought about a dozen foreign advisers to India. Colonel Raina was transferred from the ministry to become head of a new Ford Foundation–supported institute, the multidisciplinary Central Family Planning Institute (CFPI), based in New Delhi.

Peter King returned to MIT in 1964, but two months later he was asked by the Ford Foundation to rejoin the Ford team in New Delhi at the CFPI.

---

*In a move of extreme self-effacement, King apparently persuaded Berelsen to remove his (King's) name from the published list of study group members who were cited as collective authors of the plan. Also removed from the group list were Moye Freyman and Katherine Kuder, the two other foreign members of the IIMC team. Even allowing for the political and cultural sensitivities carried over by the fact that India had become independent from Great Britain only eighteen years before, it seems patronizing and untruthful to have expunged from the list of authors of this remarkable document the very person most responsible for its creation. Dharam Gupta, Nirodh's first executive, agrees: "I am amazed and disappointed that other members of the IIMC team agreed to the deletion of the names of Peter King et al." (Gupta, 1996).

He was soon transferred to the Ministry of Health and Family Planning to serve as manager/consultant in the office of the Commissioner of Family Planning, mainly to help with the hectic IUCD introduction program.

These many moves created the officially approved administrative base from which the planning and negotiation that eventually led to the introduction of Nirodh began. From the outset, support began to coalesce throughout the ministry. The new Commissioner of Family Planning, Col. Depak Bhatia (formerly head of the Punjab State Health Services); K. N. Srivastava, joint secretary; Secretary Govind Narain, and the health minister, Dr. Sushila Nayyar, who had been Gandhi's personal physician, all came to support the "Nirodh" idea.

Support was also building outside the government. Colonel Raina, in his new position at the CFPI, was able to play an important role, as did Dr. Moye Freyman and Robert L. Blake, Ford Foundation consultants assigned to the CFPI. Blake, the CFPI's communications expert, agreed that condom promotion would be an appropriate way to start his efforts. Accordingly, a test project was designed and carried out in Meerut district, northeast of New Delhi, in 1966–1967.

Part of the purpose of the pilot project was to gauge the reaction of the trade, to see if shopkeepers could be persuaded to buy, display, and openly sell condoms. There was particular concern that retailers would simply refuse to carry them or that consumers would react adversely if they did. Condoms were procured on the open market and stickered over with the Nirodh name and the special low price. Advertising and promotion were confined to local newspaper advertisements and point-of-sale material.

The pilot project went off without a hitch. Retailers proved perfectly willing to stock condoms, but, on the other hand, sales were very slow. It was clear that heavy advertising and promotion would be crucial components of a successful program.

While the market test was proceeding, progress was being made on both the distributor and the advertising fronts. Ministry officials and distributors' executives were meeting together and working out a myriad of details.

Six distribution companies agreed to participate. Union Carbide, India Tobacco Company (ITC), Hindustan Lever, Brooke Bond Tea, Lipton Tea and Tata Oil Mills. Each company was given responsibility for operations in a specific geographic territory; collectively they covered the entire country.

On the advertising front, there was an important development in 1967. Doubtless at the urging of the distribution companies that had agreed to participate in the program (particularly ITC), the J. Walter Thompson (JWT) advertising agency in Calcutta prepared and presented a detailed proposal for the new advertising campaign, complete with dozens of pieces of finished art for all media, including several film storyboards and proposed packaging designs in fifteen languages. It was the planners' intention, in part, to demonstrate to the government how different such an advertising campaign would be from the usual drab government publicity campaign and to clearly show what was really needed. Government publicity was the responsibility of the Ministry of Information and Broadcasting and, particularly, the Directorate of Advertising and Visual Publicity (DAVP) in that ministry. The experience of the DAVP had centered around poster campaigns for general health issues, agricultural information, leafleting in support of government programs, and similar kinds of promotion. Advertising a branded product was quite alien to the DAVP and to the government generally, consumer goods advertising being outside the scope of government activities anywhere.

The "private-sector" proponents of the Nirodh project hoped that JWT's campaign, which was presented in the conference hall of the ministry's family planning section where some of the artwork was left on display, would convince senior government officials that this advertising should be executed by a private advertising agency rather than by the government. Tense negotiations followed, but the government insisted on retaining control.

One underlying problem was the funding mechanism: who was going to pay, and how? Private advertising agencies in India, as elsewhere, were typically compensated by the media, not the advertiser, and usually received 15 percent of the value of ads placed. But the Government of India paid no advertising agencies; DAVP was the government advertising agency and it placed all government advertising, receiving the 15 percent media discount. And DAVP was in the Ministry of Information and Broadcasting (Indira Gandhi's former ministry), not the Ministry of Health and Family Planning. Arguing that it had no legal authority to make such payments, the government refused to pay J. Walter Thompson for any work.

Finally, to break the impasse, ITC, which was a major client of J. Walter Thompson for its tobacco products, itself agreed to pay JWT for the initial design and artwork and for completing the few materials actually used in the initial launch campaign. The Department of Family Planning agreed to reimburse the DAVP for the cost of advertising and the printed materials it purchased.

By the time this decision was reached, the planned program launch was nearing, but plans for the important cinema component of the campaign had to be scrapped because time had run out. Despite this acute disappointment, project proponents were at least satisfied that the other parts of the advertising campaign had been designed by private-sector professionals with the requisite commercial experience. The DAVP was satisfied because it remained in financial control of the actual implementation of the campaign, buying the newspaper and magazine advertising (using JWT's materials) and buying the printed materials, the metal shop signs, and other point-of-sale items. These were delivered to the central warehouses of the distribution companies, to be moved with the condoms for placement at the retail level.

GETTING THE CONDOMS

In 1968 pressure to launch the program was building, for a huge shipment of condoms was on its way. USAID (United States Agency for International Development) and SIDA (Swedish International Development Agency) had been persuaded to provide the initial shipments, totaling more than 400 million condoms.

The condoms were produced by six manufacturers, three in the United States, two in Japan, and one in Korea. All were packaged identically: the box contained three condoms. The gold and red aluminum-foil inner pack featured Indian-designed printing.

USAID and SIDA were involved in many of the project's other early negotiations as well. Indeed, aware of the problems with organizing the advertising program, USAID arranged to fund the advertising-agency and copy-testing costs of the second advertising campaign in 1969, this time contracting with the Clarion-McCann agency in Bombay. The fact that Chester Bowles, the former head of Benton & Bowles, a major U.S. advertising agency, was the U.S. Ambassador to India at the time was helpful.

MANAGING THE PROJECT

King and his colleagues had specified from the beginning that the project should be managed by a separate entity, perhaps a "government corporation" as opposed to the Health Ministry. Early in 1968, the Ford Foundation funded an Arthur D. Little study of the organization problem, and it reached the same conclusion: an independent corporate entity with some form of government oversight should be created to run the project. Social marketing of contraceptives in the private sector is simply inimical to the way governments operate—from official discomfort with paying commissions to salespeople to government doubts about the necessity for professional advertising and marketing.

The early organizers of the Nirodh program had consistently stressed the need to establish a small, but highly skilled management team that had the authority to plan, execute, and control such a large and unique program. Yet at the time the Nirodh program was launched, not a single person had been designated to be responsible for its management; authority was diffused throughout the Ministry of Health and Family Planning.

Table 1.1
Sales of Nirodh Condoms by Distribution Company, 1968–1974 (millions)

Brooke Bond (tea)	43.6	(12%)
Hindustan Lever (cooking oil, soap)	60.0	(17%)
India Tobacco Co. (cigarettes)	98.5	(27%)
Lipton (tea)	11.1	(3%)
Tata Oil Mills (cooking oil, soap)	17.9	(5%)
Union Carbide (batteries)	128.0	(36%)
Total	359.1	

Source: Gupta, 1974.

LAUNCH OF THE NIRODH PROGRAM

Despite the absence of a designated management team and the loss of the cinema advertising considered so vital to project success, the program was launched early in 1968.

The initial stocking of retailers went surprisingly well, even though few retailers (and hardly any consumers) had any idea what the product actually was or what it was for. Initial sales were relatively easy because the packaging looked good, the price was low, and the salesmen were allowed to sell on consignment, promising to take the product back if it did not sell.

All six distribution companies took part and all, during the period 1968–1974, contributed significantly to Nirodh sales and distribution. (See Table 1.1.) But sales to consumers in these early days were very poor, especially in smaller towns and villages. Hindustan Lever conducted a sales analysis in West Bengal and found that one-third of the retailers stocking Nirodh had not sold a single condom in the first six weeks after the launch. To deal with this, key ministry officials and the distributors' marketing executives met in Delhi in mid-1968 and agreed to stop the expansion of the number of retail outlets being stocked and to restrict distribution to cities larger than 25 thousand until the hoped-for massive cinema campaign could be developed and executed.

ENTER THE MARKETING EXECUTIVE

In July 1968, Dharam Gupta was hired as the Marketing Executive for the Nirodh project; he was employed by the government's Ministry of Health and Family Planning. While the idea of a separate managing corporation or other independent (or partially independent) entity would be raised again subsequently, it had become clear that the project's early years would have to unfold under the direct supervision and management of the Indian Government. Nevertheless, those who stressed the importance of private-sector skills and techniques for the project had obtained at least one concession: the person in charge would have a background in the private sector and in marketing. Gupta came from the Bombay office of the Swiss pharmaceutical firm Sandoz, where he had been a marketing specialist for the company's pharmaceutical products. He assumed his government post with some misgivings but with optimism and great hope that his work would be of service to the country.

The problems that were by now familiar to the planners continued to dog Gupta throughout the early years. The government's support for the project's advertising budgets was desultory; as King and others had learned, bureaucracies find it all too easy to slash budgets that are not considered "vital" to cope with politically sensitive exigencies, and the project suffered accordingly. Sales were way below projections; Gupta believed those projections had been far too optimistic. The forecasts had been based on what seemed like reasonable sales assumptions for each of the many hundreds of thousands of retail outlets being served by the six distributors. It was assumed that these distributors would get Nirodh into essentially every retail outlet where their own products were sold and that, backed by heavy advertising, each of these retailers would sell at least a few dozen condoms per year.

Both of these assumptions turned out to be optimistic. By 1970 the project managers were faced with a substantial glut in supply. Cumulative sales in the first two years were only about one-third of the 400 million condoms initially supplied. A massive campaign of "sampling" was therefore undertaken to dispose of the excess, raising objections from private condom manufacturers that the giveaways were undermining private commercial demand. Gupta pointed out to them, correctly as it turned out, that the Nirodh campaign would so increase overall demand for condoms in India that everyone, including even the highest priced commercial manufacturers, would see sales increases within a reasonable period of time. Experience since then has confirmed that when social marketers create a demand for their subsidized products, they normally stimulate demand for higher priced commercial contraceptives as well.

A government program to distribute Nirodh condoms free of charge was taking place simultaneously. The free condoms were packaged differently, in blue and white paper foil as opposed to the gold and red of the socially marketed Nirodh. The free condoms were made available through government health and family planning clinics and other non-commercial outlets, and their distribution paralleled the social marketing sales effort well into the 1990s. The giveaways, while helping to increase condom use overall, made it that much more difficult to increase sales of the socially marketed red and gold Nirodh. Even though the free distribution made his job more difficult, Gupta endorsed the giveaway program:

Free distribution of condoms was meant to cater to a different segment of the market, those who could not afford to pay even the low, subsidized price of commercial Nirodh. It was known at that time that there were people who walked two or three miles to save bus fare of 10–15 paise [2–3 cents], and for whom, therefore, even the subsidized price of Nirodh was probably more than they could afford. In this sense, there was a place for free condom distribution even though it affected the sales of commercial Nirodh. While being "wasteful" to some extent, free distribution of condoms helped remove "shyness" about a product which at that time was associated primarily with prostitution and illegitimate sex. It therefore indirectly helped sell Nirodh by legitimizing the project. (Gupta, 1996)

Like so many subsequent large-scale contraceptive social marketing programs, the Nirodh project was also plagued by pressure to increase prices. In the mid-1970s, the price of a three-pack was raised from 15 paise to 25 paise (roughly 3 cents to 5 cents), as government officials and other "experts" were convinced that the higher amount was still so low as not to present an obstacle to sales[6] Predictably, sales of Nirodh came down throughout the last half of the 1970s and did not recover to the 1973–1974 peak until 1981. Figure 1.1 shows the twenty-seven-year record of Nirodh sales expressed in terms of the Couple Years of Protection (CYPs) provided by those sales.*

Despite desultory advertising, price increases, competition from give-aways, and other problems (including the fact that the distribution companies found their role increasingly onerous and expensive), the Nirodh program quickly became the world's largest social marketing effort and remained so until 1994 when, as its own sales declined, those in adjacent Bangladesh continued to grow and surpassed the Indian program.

While Nirodh was the world's social marketing volume leader for more than twenty-five years, its prevalence levels have not matched those of other early programs. At least five major programs have done better (in addition to Bangladesh, those in Colombia, Egypt (1985–1993), Jamaica, and Nigeria (1994–1995)). But, given the pioneer status of India's project, the fact that it has remained under government management throughout its history, and the fact that its marketing budget has been periodically decimated, it has perhaps performed as well as could be expected.

In the early 1990s an oral contraceptive (OC) was added to India's social marketing program. By the late 1990s sales of the OC, called Mala-D, grew to more than 15 million cycles per year. (Compare sales of OCs in the Bangladesh CSM of 12 million cycles/year in a market one-eighth as big.)

In 1995 the government of India accelerated the privatization of con-

---

*A CYP is defined as the provision of an adequate supply of contraceptives (or the provision of a contraceptive service), sufficient to protect one couple from pregnancy for one year. (See Chapter 9.)

Figure 1.1
Nirodh Condom Social Marketing Program, Couple Years of Protection (CYPs) Based on 100 Condoms per CYP, 1969–1996

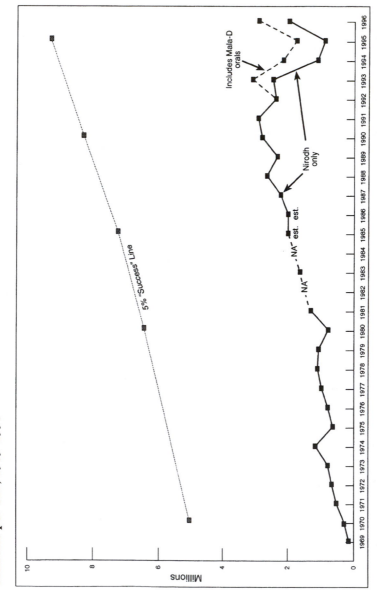

Notes: The 5 percent success line represents sales equivalent to 5 percent of estimated eligible couples, enough to have a significant impact in any country. See Chapter 9. NA = not available.

Sources: Directorate of Advertising and Visual Publicity, Government of India, Kuldip Press, "Nirodh Programme/A Pioneering Social Marketing Project in India." 1981; Social Marketing Forum; DKT sales statistics.

traceptive social marketing in India. Increasingly, distribution has been taken over by family planning organizations, including PSI/India and two affiliates of DKT International. The commercial distribution firms, meanwhile, have gradually pulled out. Of the original six commercial distributors, only Brooke Bond was still active as late as 1995, and they, too, were out of the program by 1997.

It would be another four years after the Nirodh launch until the next social marketing project was started, an interval that seems lengthy in retrospect, especially after the rapid acceleration in CSM start-ups that has taken place in more recent years. But in fact, given the resistance to the CSM idea in other countries and the complete novelty of this approach to donors, the interval was probably pretty short. Among other such tasks, for example, USAID, when it funded the next projects, had to provide entirely new accounting mechanisms to deal with the income generated by product sales. No other form of grant assistance had ever produced even small amounts of income from the sale of products before.

KINGA IN KENYA, WITH A PERSONAL PREAMBLE

Using the Nirodh idea, and convinced that the Nirodh project designers had been right about the importance of private management, Tim Black, a British doctor I had met at the University of North Carolina in 1969, and I joined in an effort to demonstrate that social marketing of contraceptives, managed entirely in the private sector, could succeed under differing circumstances and on different continents.

I came to the conviction about the importance of birth control from working on food supply programs; I had spent five years in India with the relief organization CARE during the same years that Peter King and his colleagues were designing Nirodh. Each year we had been supervising the import of ever increasing amounts of fortified foodstuffs to supply nutritious school lunches to hundreds of thousands of school children throughout India. This was a well-meaning and, in many respects, worthwhile effort. But every year as we expanded the program we had to admit that we were falling further behind as the number of school children and preschool children in India continued to grow faster than our ability to keep up. It gradually became clear to me that over time, feeding programs had only a limited impact on children, and they were accompanied by potentially troublesome side effects including the fact that our imported free foodstuffs inevitably competed to some degree with locally grown foods.

Something else happened to me in India that began my journey toward family planning. Part of my job with CARE was to make sure that emergency relief food supplies reached their intended beneficiaries. In 1968

I escorted a truckload of food to a badly flooded village in the northern state of Punjab. As we stood about discussing logistics, a woman in a ragged sari, carrying a baby, walked over to me, knelt down, and touched my feet. I was upset, confused, and instinctively repelled by this gesture. I sensed that there was something deeply wrong in any situation that so divided the benefactor from the "beneficiary." Why should this woman, struggling for her existence and her children's, a woman whose life probably exemplified many of the virtues we most admire, be "grateful" to a privileged young man who had it easy? This was not the way helping people should work.[7]

I knew then, and came to understand later, that I would never be comfortable providing help to people in ways that suggested they should express gratitude. I found such relationships (outside of close personal and family relationships, of course) demeaning, and, yes, immoral. Family planning, and, as it later turned out, social marketing particularly, provided a solution to this conflict.

Tim Black arrived at his conclusions about birth control along a different path. He had served as a physician in the jungles of New Guinea and in rural Nigeria and tells the following story:

As a physician committed to a full-time career in fertility control I am often asked the question: When did you first become interested in family planning? I can quote the year, the month, the day.

I was visiting an aid post in a rural, remote jungle area of New Guinea. Towards the end of a long day, a thin woman of about 30, in a grass skirt, shyly laid a small crying baby on the crude bamboo table which served as an examination couch. The baby, a three-month-old boy with a distended abdomen, had a small hernia. He was dehydrated and like many babies in that region, underfed, for mothers are often unable to obtain the adequate protein diet so necessary for a good flow of breast milk. Besides, she was still suckling another child of about two-and-a-half years.

I reduced the size of the hernia, but it was obvious that if it was not operated on it would recur and eventually strangulate. In that case, unless the mother was able to walk the 10 miles or so to the river and then bring the baby by canoe to the hospital, or unless a doctor or nurse was traveling in the area, the baby would die.

As I handed back the baby and the little bundle of rags which passed for nappies, I gently explained to the mother the need to perform a small operation at our little district hospital; otherwise the swelling would return and the child might die. In Pidgin English, the *lingua franca* of New Guinea, the phrase for death has a brutal finality about it: "Pikinin belon' you'e die pinish"—die finish.

Without emotion the mother began to tell me of her troubles. She had four young children and her husband had recently died. She was unable to spend enough time fishing or preparing sago, the staple diet of the area, and the sale of copra from her few coconut trees did not raise enough cash to meet the meager needs of her family. She ended her sad monologue of tragedies by saying that she could not leave the family to take this baby to a distant hospital.

I pleaded, cajoled, even threatened, but she was adamant. She would not leave her other children, nor would she let me take the baby down the river with me to the hospital. Eventually we compromised. I would perform the operation right there in the crude village dispensary.

The operation went well despite my inexperience in this field and the primitive conditions. We anaesthetized the infant with ether and gauze. The wound was neat, bleeding had not been a problem, and we finished before the evening swarm of mosquitoes had become unbearable.

I was deeply satisfied and success had released the tension of the operation. Proudly I carried the limp and still sedated baby out to the mother, who was squatting in the shade of a tree with her children. As I handed her the baby and she saw he was still alive her face fell in obvious disappointment.

My shock was absolute. My immediate reaction was one of utter indignation. The gulf separating my life experience and that of this pitifully poor native woman was complete. She had wanted the baby to die—not live—during the operation.

I suddenly realized that I had presented her not only her baby, but with another mouth to feed—another dependent human being to whom she could offer nothing: no father, no education, no future—merely the cruel ritual of bare survival.

It was at that moment that I began to realize that preventing a birth could be as important as saving a life. (Black, 1977: 159)

In recent years it has often been argued that social marketing might be more appropriately used to bring family planning to those who can afford to pay enough for their contraceptives so that a major part of programmatic costs may be recovered, rather than to those at the lowest end of the economic scale. Because of experiences like mine and particularly Tim's, I have always disagreed strongly with this position. Those who are better off can generally fend for themselves. Those who urgently—even desperately—need subsidized, affordable contraceptives are the clients we should serve, and social marketing is an excellent way to do it.

THE NEXT PROJECT

In 1972 after an agonizing approval process, Tim Black and I received a grant from USAID to conduct an experimental social marketing project in Kenya. Unlike Nirodh, this would be entirely a private-sector effort (though funded by USAID), with no government involvement in the day-to-day operation of the program. We hoped to demonstrate that social marketing worked, that it was cost-effective, and that mass media advertising for branded contraceptives would not cause serious controversy even in conservative religious cultures.

We had thought that the funding process would be relatively easy, but it never is. Our rationale for optimism seemed sound: in the early 1970s, a substantial and rapidly growing amount of U.S. government money was available for international family planning, and there were few good projects to absorb those funds. Furthermore, we were, as Tim enthusiastically put it, "selling enterprise to enterprise." As an Englishman, Tim may have been a bit naive about the free-enterprise credentials of U.S. government employees, but the United States was and is at least reasonably committed to free-market economics, and we were almost certain that selling a "commercial" model to the U.S. government aid agency would be pretty straightforward. In fact, the government financing of anything is a political process, and it usually has little to do with overarching ideology. We learned this the hard way.

The funding took us a year and a half. Tim had done some pretty vigorous investigative work in both East and West Africa. Our proposal was walked through the USAID Mission in Kenya, and we lobbied hard for it in Washington, D.C. But this perspective was new, and there were no precedents. "Waivers" had to be obtained. Because Tim was British, for example, that meant securing a waiver to use a "third country national" to operate the project. So we worked and waited. At the end, I remember leaving the contracts office at USAID in Washington, clutching our new contract under my jacket, phoning Tim from a telephone booth in National Airport and weeping with joy. We had our first project! No grant or contract for a social marketing program, or anything else, since that day in Washington has ever induced in me such intense pleasure as the final signature on that first document.

We had decided on a division of labor for those early days of Population Services, Inc. (PSI), which was what we were calling our young enterprise.[8] I was to stay behind and manage the fledgling business that was growing out of our experiments in mail-order condom sales in the United States, which we had begun as part of our course work as students at the School of Public Health at the University of North Carolina. Replete with his credentials as a physician and his passion for non-physician family planning, Tim would implement the African project. We were determined that it would be only our first of many social marketing projects, and about that, at least, we were right.

Tim designed and conducted the Kenya project in such a way as to provide the only research-based proof of the effectiveness of social marketing that, to my knowledge, has ever been conducted, using carefully defined test and control populations. A control group is like the "placebo group" in the test of the efficacy of a new drug. In order to be sure that your program is the cause of certain changes, you select a group that will be deliberately *excluded* from your program, just to be sure that similar changes are not taking place generally in a society for independent reasons. So Tim elected to do our test marketing program in the Meru district of Kenya and to establish a control district in Kirinyaga, an area of Kenya with similar demographic characteristics to Meru, but with a different language; this meant that the Kirinyagans would not hear, or would not understand if they did hear, our radio advertisements. No promotion or selling work would be done in Kirinyaga.

Meru had a population of about 600 thousand, largely rural. Fifty-seven percent of its households had an annual income of less than US$142 and only 10 percent earned more than $275 per annum. No more than 22 percent had completed primary education. Our selection of this relatively low-income, low-literacy area was deliberate. We did not want anyone to be able to say we had picked an "easy" part of Kenya to conduct this test marketing program.

The situation with family planning services in Meru at the time typified the problem with clinic-based service delivery in the 1970s, and indeed up to this day. There were fourteen part-time "official" family planning clinics, but most of them were seldom open. Three clinics purported to be open weekly (that is, one day per week), three on just two days each month, and the rest only one day each month. How any facility that is open only one day per month can straight-facedly call itself a "clinic" is beyond me, but this was (and still is) not unusual.

Tim performed assiduous baseline research in both Meru and Kirinyaga on key variables, which included people's knowledge and attitude about family planning, about specific contraceptive methods, and about using condoms. Follow-up surveys would be conducted in both districts after six and twelve months of marketing in Meru.

The baseline pre-surveys revealed generally positive attitudes. Sixty-six percent of the respondents in both districts were aware of family planning and approved of it, despite the fact that about one-third of the population in both districts identified themselves as Roman Catholic. Only 23 percent of the Meru sample and 19 percent of the Kirinyaga sample had heard of condoms.

The brand name Kinga was chosen for the condom to be marketed (Kinga means "protection" in Swahili). The condoms, supplied from U.S. sources by USAID, were packed three to a package in bright pink, blue, and white containers that could be easily seen from some distance away. Shelf space in the shops was severely limited and it was therefore decided to use cardboard dispensers that could be tacked or taped on vertical shelf supports.

Kinga was priced at 50 Kenyan cents for a three-pack, or about U.S. 2 cents per condom. The single-coin purchase price (50 cents) was expected to facilitate consumers' transactions.

An advertising agency was asked to design a promotional campaign, and a complete advertising campaign was developed to generate awareness of the name, nature, availability, price, and especially the quality of the Kinga condom; to create awareness of the general benefits of child spacing; and to encourage trial and repeated purchase of the product through positive promotion (no mention of venereal disease). The campaign centered around the Swahili theme: "Kinga: items/things for men to plan their families with." Messages advocating both the health and economic benefits of child spacing went out in the form of leaflets, radio (a weekly fifteen-minute question-and-answer program, "The Kinga Doctor"), a sixty-second spot at commercial village cinema shows, metal Kinga shop signs and "day-glow" shelf signs, and mobiles in the stores.

Within a year 138 thousand condoms had been sold in Meru, representing 0.2 pieces per capita, compared to commercial sales of 0.005 prior to the program. Would our surveys confirm a substantial increase in condom use? We believed they would. Tim states other important things he learned about the men and women who actually sold the condoms:

The great majority of Duka (shop) owners were highly receptive to the program. Many shop owners appeared to enjoy the prestige that their role of resident family planning expert gave them in their community. The potential importance of the man behind the counter in family planning is substantial: shopkeepers are virtually ubiquitous in nearly all countries and their apparent pleasure at being part of a program is noteworthy. (Black and Harvey, 1976: 103)

Tim also notes that this shopkeeper support was our key to surviving a severe public relations crisis:

About three months after Kinga appeared on the market, an influential physician who operated four private clinics in Meru strenuously attacked the program for allegedly selling to children. We felt the charges were politically motivated and largely groundless. Nonetheless, when a family planning field educator from another district joined in [against Kinga], it took several conciliatory meetings, threats by our attorneys, and communications with the shopkeepers stocking our condoms before the rumpus subsided.

Yet Kinga sales were largely unaffected. We postulate that was because the product was being distributed by local shopkeepers. Understandably, the shopkeepers reacted strongly to the implication that they had done something wrong. Thus, they became vocal advocates of the project. There is little doubt that had it not been for the shopkeepers' vested interest in the sale of Kinga and their role as the village family planning expert, the project would not have survived such an attack. (Black and Harvey, 1976:103)

Table 1.2 gives the complete breakdown of knowledge, attitude and practice indicators on certain key questions before and after the campaign in both the test district and the control district, and confirms the success

Table 1.2
Knowledge, Attitude, and Practice of Family Planning in Test and Control Areas Before and After the Twelve-Month Kinga Campaign (in percents)

Parameter	Before	After	Significance of change	Before	After
		Test area		Control area[a]	
Awareness of family planning	64	81	xx	71	73
Methods known by those aware					
Pill	51	60	x	72	72
Condom	23	57	xx	19	18
IUD	50	61	x	42	44
Injection	21	29		16	19
Attitude toward family planning					
Disapprove	8	5		13	13
Approve	88	94	x	81	81
No comment	4	1		6	7
Currently contracepting by method					
Pill	6	6		9	13
Condom	4	15	xx	1	1
IUD	8	8		3	1
Not specified/ other	3	6		7	4
All methods	21	35	xx	20	19
Number of respondents	506	499		350	350

Notes: xx significant at a 99 percent level of confidence; x significant at a 95 percent level of confidence;[a] no significant change over the period.

of the experiment.

In Meru survey respondents claiming to be currently using a contraceptive method rose from 21 percent of the fertile population prior to the program to 35 percent twelve months later. By contrast, practice levels in Kirinyaga showed little change. Awareness of condoms went from 23 percent to 57 percent in Meru, and remained unchanged in Kirinyaga. Current condom use went from 4 percent to 15 percent in Meru, and did not change in Kirinyaga.

Success! We were elated. Now that we had demonstrated conclusively that this approach worked, and that it was effective even in a very poor rural area of East Africa, we were sure that donors would come flocking to our door. Tim summed up the implications in 1976:

[The project] offered further indication of the potential for contraceptive social marketing—an approach that appears to provide a significantly new psychological, physical, and technical avenue toward effecting a voluntary reduction in human fertility. The concept is a fundamental departure from traditional preoccupation with the contraceptive-acceptors-are-patients idea (a notion that all too often has been allowed to obscure the fact that the sexual act is not a disease to be controlled by medical discipline but is a normal and extremely gratifying human function of which pregnancy is by no means always the desired outcome).

The project has also confirmed the Indian Nirodh experience in demonstrating that commercial marketing represents a highly significant nonmedical resource that can be effectively mobilized to supplement clinical family planning programs. As we have pointed out elsewhere, there is no reason why contraceptive promotion and delivery need be restricted by shortages of medically trained personnel. The advertising man, the distributor, and the village shopkeeper are willing and able, provided the terms are attractive, to make contraceptives both desirable and readily available, virtually throughout the world. (Black and Harvey, 1976: 106)

We learned very quickly that proving the point was not enough. While our project had demonstrated the effectiveness of social marketing, no one seemed interested in proceeding further. This astonished and baffled us. We found that cautious politicians in the Kenyan government were opposed to the expansion of the program there, partly out of tribal concerns. Worse, we had a falling-out with USAID about what strategy to pursue. Instead of being expanded, the project was terminated.[9]

Tim went back to London to start his own family planning clinic organization in the United Kingdom (Marie Stopes International) and, had it not been for Malcolm Potts, who was Medical Director of the International Planned Parenthood Federation (IPPF) in London, that might have been the end of the line for PSI social marketing. But the IPPF had an overstock of condoms in Sri Lanka, and Malcolm Potts thought we should try selling them through CSM. And a particularly skilled and enthusiastic manager was available to take on that new assignment.

NOTES

1. Union Carbide was "fired" as a condom distributor a year or so after the tragic accident at Carbide's fertilizer plant at Bhopal in 1984.

2. This completed the "Four P's" so often referred to in (social) marketing literature: Product, Price, Promotion, Place.

3. Per-capita GNP in India in 1965 was about $130 (in 1973 $), at the projected seventy-two condoms per couple per year the cost came to 70 cents per year, or 0.5 percent of per capita GNP. At the more realistic rate of one hundred condoms per year the consumer cost would come to 0.8 percent of per capita GNP, essentially identical to the recommended guideline given in Chapter 8.

4. Mr. Chandy, the project's most influential proponent, had very nearly been taken out of the game before it began. An out-of-control Indian Air Force Caribou aircraft nearly beheaded him at the IIMC compound in Barakpur north of Calcutta where Chandy, King, and their colleagues were meeting during the early days of

their collaboration in 1964. The plane crashed into the Hooghly River, killing all 12 Indian airmen on board. One of the few people around with a working aqualung, Peter King took on the grizzly task of extricating the bodies from the swamped airplane.

5. In India, the IUD (intra-uterine device) is still referred to as the IUCD; the "c" stands for contraceptive.

6. The lesson has been learned over and over again since that time. Substantial *percentage* increases like the 67 percent increase in this case, are always dangerous, even on a very low base amount. (See Chapter 8.)

7. An interesting treatment of this issue is "The Dysfunctionality of Unrequited Giving," Chas. A. S. Hynam (1966).

8. We had meant for the "Inc." to suggest the businesslike orientation of the organization, but it succeeded too well. Everyone, including potential supporters among private foundations, assumed that we were a for-profit company. So "Inc." was changed to "International," in 1973.

9. I am happy to report that, after a ten-year hiatus, PSI returned to Kenya in 1989, restarted social marketing, and was selling condoms nationwide there in the late 1990s.

2

Social Marketing: How It Works

I have never known much good done by those who affected to trade for the public good.

—Adam Smith

Like many effective ideas, social marketing has many fathers. The term was probably first used by Philip Kotler in 1971; he subsequently wrote a book on the subject (Kotler and Roberto, 1989), as have others (Manoff, 1985; Andreasen, 1995). But as we have seen, the first social marketing program predates the coining of the term.

As the Nirodh and Kinga experiences demonstrated, the fundamental principle of social marketing is to use marketing and other such time-refined business techniques to achieve social or otherwise beneficial objectives. A more formal definition by Alan Andreasen states:

Social marketing is the adaptation of commercial marketing technologies . . . to influence the voluntary behavior of target audiences to improve their personal welfare and that of society of which they are part. (Andreasen, 1995)

This definition encompasses such campaigns in the United States as the Smokey the Bear forest fire prevention advertising (much of which was inexplicably run on the New York subway system), and more recently, scores of anti-smoking campaigns. It describes the media efforts by the Australian and Canadian governments to grapple with alcohol abuse and nutritional problems, campaigns to increase the use of seat belts, and media programs to persuade parents to inoculate their children.[1]

Most social marketing consists of mass-media efforts to persuade people to behave differently without reference to a product; contraceptive social marketing (CSM) is tied to specific products with brand names. Like media-only campaigns, it seeks to change behavior—and in a very specific and measurable way. By informing people about the advantages of birth control, describing specific methods, and offering low-priced contraceptive brands, CSM programs increase contraceptive use.

It is an idea that has worked remarkably well. In 1997 CSM programs were serving more than 16 million couples in 55 countries. Over 900 million condoms, 50 million cycles of oral contraceptives, and 500 thousand IUDs were sold this way in 1997 (DKT International, 1998). Also sold through social marketing are injectable contraceptives and vaginal spermicides. The programs that sell these products normally create local brands, establish prices that are affordable even to the poorest segments of society, and advertise the branded contraceptives along with information about how to use them. These projects have provided efficient and cost-effective birth control services in a wide variety of cultural and economic environments. The cost of providing full contraception to one couple for one full year through social marketing mechanisms averages about U.S.$8, a remarkably small figure for what it accomplishes.*

WHY BIRTH CONTROL?

In 1989, building on our experience with PSI in Kenya and other countries, I founded DKT International, an organization that also specializes in the social marketing of contraceptives. Its three board members—Tim Black, Bob Ciszewski (who designed and managed the Bangladesh CSM project for eight years)—and I, sit down every year or so and go back to square one, asking ourselves if the provision of the means for voluntary fertility control (birth control) is still the most important thing we can be doing to assist people in low-income countries. All three of us have been working in this field for more than twenty years, which is why we must repeatedly question whether, if we started all over again, we still would focus on this area. So far, every time we revisit the issue we conclude that birth control represents the highest priority for humanitarian and developmental assistance to people in low-income countries—at least within the realm of what we are able to do.

The ability to plan and space pregnancies and births has a remarkable impact on people's lives (See Appendix 3 for a brief survey of birth con-

*All program costs and costs per CYP cited in this book represent net total donor costs, including the cost of contraceptives.

trol methods). Throughout the world and at every income level, a desired pregnancy can be one of life's greatest joys; but an unexpected pregnancy or an unplanned birth can have a devastating impact on family life, on the family budget, and on the health of mothers and children. In poor countries especially, repeated childbearing, with babies born at close intervals, has a massive health impact. High rates of infant death and illness, and maternal mortality—mothers dying in childbirth or for reasons related to childbirth—are much more common when birth intervals are short.

The scope of the problem is enormous. In 1990 an estimated fourteen million children under the age of five died. Over 500 thousand women die each year of causes related to pregnancy and childbirth (WHO, 1995). Birth spacing can save many of these lives.

Research on the subject has been both substantial and definitive. The Population Reference Bureau publication "Family Planning Saves Lives" reports:

On average, babies born less than two years after their next oldest brother or sister are almost twice as likely to die as those born after at least a two year interval. . . . At the same time, the older child is, on average, one-and-a-half times, more likely to die.

The report concludes that in many countries, "spacing births at least two years apart could prevent 20 percent of infant deaths" (1991: 4, 8).

That means that the dissemination and availability of affordable and convenient contraceptives, by itself, could prevent the deaths of more than two million infants and young children around the world each year. And indeed, because the use of contraception is becoming ever more widespread, many such deaths are already being prevented through this means.

The impact on family economics is also dramatic. If pregnancies and births can be planned and spaced there will be more food, shelter, and other material benefits for all family members. Educational opportunities for planned children are also likely to be significantly better than they are when families experience frequent unplanned and unexpected births. The World Health Organization observes:

By providing a means for couples to have smaller healthier families, family planning helps reduce the economic . . . burden of parenthood. Families with fewer and healthier children can devote more resources to providing their children with adequate food, clothing, housing, and educational opportunities. (WHO, 1995: 13)

Having briefly made the case for the importance of family planning, and for its ranking as a "high-need" charity, I must add that it also has relatively low appeal to donors. There is just nothing about providing contraceptives to healthy adult couples, even if those couples are very poor, which gives us a warm glow as philanthropists. When family planning is successful, something unwanted does not occur, an outcome that simply does not have the emotional tug of more popular charitable causes. That is all the more reason why we should support family planning, because relatively few others will do so. It is a "low-appeal" cause, yet one with remarkable humanitarian impact.

THE BEST INTENTIONS

One important issue to bear in mind when presuming to be useful to other people is how often good intentions have backfired. There are some notorious examples of well-intentioned, even well-designed "benevolent" programs doing more harm than good. In a valuable way, Malcolm X was right when he observed that "Doing good is a hustle too."

A few examples will suffice to clarify this melancholy point. Food assistance provided by the United States to India on a massive scale in the 1960s benefited American farmers, but it had the effect of most dreadfully undermining Indian agriculture. Because the imported food made it impossible for Indian farmers to get good prices for their own crops, India remained dependent on food imports for many years longer than it need have. When the subsidized shipments were discontinued and the Indian government permitted prices for local crops to rise to their natural market levels, Indian farmers quickly demonstrated that even with the rapidly growing population, with the help of the high-yielding seed varieties of the "green revolution," they could provide virtually all the food India needed. By the early 1990s India was actually exporting some food grains.

Government-to-government foreign aid has additional deleterious effects, including propping up bloated bureaucracies, keeping tyrants like Zaire's Mobutu in power (and adding to his personal wealth), and helping put off badly needed social and economic change. Economist Steve Hanke and others have pointed out that foreign aid increases the power of local politicians at the expense of the private sector, thus undermining economic progress.

So when we presume to provide assistance to poor people in developing countries we must be careful. This is one more reason why voluntary fertility control through the private sector continues to be such a good investment: It appears to have virtually no negative consequences.

Here the word "voluntary" must be stressed. The coercive measures adopted on many occasions by the Chinese government and briefly during the "emergency" period by the Indian government in the 1970s have had numerous adverse consequences, beginning with the deprivation of liberties and human rights of the people so coerced. In democratic India, the overzealous implementation of policies to meet sterilization targets was a principal reason for the downfall of Indira Gandhi's government in 1977. In China pressures to limit couples to have no more than one or two children have led to coerced abortions and even the sterilization of unwilling women and men. This is a fundamental violation of basic human rights and should be categorically condemned by all those who love liberty. But the provision of subsidized contraceptives that users must buy with their own money—even if the amount is very small—cannot ever be coercive.

WHY CHARGE ANYTHING AT ALL?

If lower prices mean that more people will use contraceptives, why not set the lowest possible price—and charge nothing at all? The reason it is essential to charge a price for contraceptives under CSM is that a social marketing program cannot exist without the participation of retailers, and the only way to get retailers involved is by providing them a profit. The whole social marketing system rests on the fact that we can take advantage of already existing commercial infrastructures—the system of wholesaling, distributing, and retailing that exists in every country of the world and that, with astonishing efficiency, makes available Coca-Cola, salt, beer, and hundreds of other needed and desired consumer products. In order to piggyback onto this extraordinarily complex yet highly efficient network, the customer must pay some price to the retailer or we will not have the participation of the commercial system. Indeed, the customer must pay enough to reimburse not only the retailer but any other middlemen in the wholesaling and distribution system, of which there are normally (but not always) two.

Three other reasons why it is desirable to charge a price are wastage, control, and measurability.

Wastage

When products are given away, they frequently are wasted. This is just as true of contraceptives as anything else. When there is no financial discipline in the system—when contraceptives are given away—they are subject to overstocking at every stage, whether in the homes of those field-workers paid to distribute them, in "beneficiaries' " homes, or in warehouses. Field-workers have been known to throw away contraceptives and simply claim that they have been "distributed." Additionally, products given away free, particularly by governments, are almost universally considered to be of poor quality by potential users. This further denigrates the products in the minds of consumers and increases the likelihood of wastage.

Other misuse of contraceptives is also far more likely when they are given away free. Condoms have been used to make and repair sandals and repair vehicle radiator hoses in India. Condoms have been used as balloons in both Egypt and Bangladesh (and, I suspect, elsewhere). While this also can happen with very low-priced contraceptives, it is much more likely to occur with giveaways.

Control and Measurement

The fact that the sale of contraceptives through the social marketing system is backed by and can be tracked by a flow of cash from consumer to retailer to distributor to project headquarters injects a discipline in the system that is essential to adequate control. When things are given free by party A to B to C, no control of any kind exists except for records that can be easily altered. When money changes hands, control is dramatically improved. Financial records are auditable; they are more difficult to falsify than non-financial records, and most important of all, the correct amount of cash must, at the appropriate time and at an agreed-upon schedule, be returned to project management, an event that will not occur for very long if consumers are not paying at least the agreed-upon price at the other end of the pipeline. Put another way, the trade will not go on paying the project for contraceptives if they themselves are not regularly paid by retailers who, in turn, will not buy unless the level of consumer purchase is satisfactory.

Finally, charging a price permits program managers a high degree of accuracy in measuring their program success. Sales are an excellent proxy for the number of couples being served by the program, and thus for the ultimate outcome desired by family planning programmers: increased contraceptive prevalence. Salespeople's performance can be measured by how many contraceptives they sell, and they can receive commissions on those sales. Managers can be held accountable for sales performance, and program problems can be spotted (and corrected) quickly.

In short, when customers pay for contraceptives, we have every reason to believe that wastage will be minimal; we can engage the ubiquitous and efficient retail trade; and we can have a high level of confidence that the contraceptives will be used for the purpose intended. When contraceptives are given away there are no assurances or control.

Social marketing, therefore, is an unusually effective way of enabling couples to space, plan, and prevent pregnancies:

• It can reach very large numbers of people with information and contraceptives in a very short period of time.

- It can make contraceptives available in widely dispersed rural as well as urban areas, providing convenient access for entire populations.

- With the use of donor funds to subsidize the price, contraceptives in social marketing programs can be sold at low enough prices to be affordable to even the poorest segments of today's poorest societies and still provide a sufficient income stream so that retailers and other businesspeople, essential participants in a CSM program, will be interested in selling these products.

The CSM models developed in the 1960s and 1970s have proved to be very good designs. An effective contraceptive social marketing project sells subsidized contraceptives through already existing commercial networks, backed by mass media advertising. (For variations on the subsidy issue see Chapter 8 and Appendix 1.) Because no new infrastructure needs to be created, all that is normally required is a small centralized project staff with adequate expertise, experience, and autonomy to make marketing and sales decisions on a day-to-day basis, to contract for research and advertising, and to keep the project on target. To accomplish these things, an adequate budget is essential.

More specifically, these are the necessary components for a CSM program:

1. Market research. Skillful research guides the project's management on fundamental decisions about branding, pricing, "positioning" of the product (for example, whether to market it as an "upscale, lifestyle" commodity or a "family economics" product), and other such critical variables.

2. A national distributor. Successful social marketing distributors have included companies that handle products from shoe polish to analgesics to prescription drugs. When no distribution company is available, this function can be carried out by direct-hire project staff.

3. Mass media advertising. A professional advertising campaign creates brand awareness for the contraceptives, educates people about the availability of contraceptives and their characteristics and use, and persuades people of the desirability of using these products to plan their families.

These three functions are contracted and coordinated by the CSM management team. In a successful program, contraceptives can be made available in tens of thousands of retail outlets, accessible to millions of people, within just a year or two of program start-up.

In this process, contact by the project staff with its "beneficiaries" is minimal. This can be an advantage because it means that social marketing is never patronizing and is essentially immune from issues of class, tribe, race, or ethnicity. Anyone can participate if they participate in the local economy, as virtually all people in the world do. The service "provider" cannot be condescending about the "help" he or she is providing to the client (as often happens in clinics); indeed, the shopkeeper is highly motivated to accommodate his or her clients—to be open during times of day when clients need service, to be polite and helpful in making products available, and to otherwise serve the customers' needs.

The immediate impact on the lives of project clients may seem a small one. If I am a member of the Baldev family in rural India, the availability of a contraceptive at a nearby shop does not have the same potential impact on the lives of my family members as would the availability of a well-equipped clinic staffed by trained and motivated physicians. Baldev family members might go to such a clinic when seriously ill, to deliver a baby, to get their children inoculated, and to otherwise avail themselves of important primary health care services. Those who do provide such comprehensive services to poor people in developing countries deserve our accolades and our applause. God bless them. But they are necessarily constrained in reaching the masses of people who require their services by the sheer number of hours in the day.

Social marketing occupies quite a different part of the spectrum. By making possible what seems a relatively small difference in people's lives—access to affordable contraceptives and the information needed to use them correctly—we can provide services to millions of people at very low cost. Moreover, we can do this work with very few project staff. Most of the work is done by retailers and wholesalers who are "paid" by the consumer through margins on the product. This means that only twenty or thirty people might be needed as project staff to serve a half-million clients, a fact that does wonders for cost-efficiency.

And, by making birth spacing possible and accessible, social marketing saves lives. (For calculations on the life-saving benefits of contraceptives, see Appendix 4.)

OTHER ATTRIBUTES OF SOCIAL MARKETING

We have already noted that social marketing can reach large numbers of people in a short period of time, and that it relies on already-existing infrastructures and time-tested commercial techniques. Another important asset of CSM is its measurability. (See Chapter 9.) CSM is also:

- Coercion-proof. Because each client pays a small amount of his or her own money to get the product, no one can be forced into participating. A person who purchases a product with his or her own money is, by definition, engaging in a voluntary transaction. This is a very important characteristic of social marketing. Other methods of providing family planning have been occasionally subject to abusive practices and require extra care for that reason. In the case of social marketing, no extra care is needed. Notwithstanding the objections of those who dislike advertising, one cannot be coerced into buying a product.

- Fun to manage. It is gratifying to take part in a program that employs practical commercial techniques and at the same time achieves a useful social objective. The creative process of putting together packaging and brands and themes, shooting television spots, recording radio spots, and designing newspaper ads is enjoyable work. It is also gratifying to quickly develop a CSM program and see it have a substantial impact in a relatively short time. The feedback from sales statistics gives one a sense of accomplishment. While social marketing managers seldom get to spend more than 50 percent of their time actually running their projects—the other 50 percent goes to donor and government relations, red tape, and fund raising—the project time is usually very enjoyable.
- Quick. Projects can be started and contraceptives made available nationwide within a year (or even less) of funding.
- Mass-applied. Millions of consumers can be reached through tens of thousands of outlets in short order.
- Cost-effective. Clients can be served for as little as $3 or $4 per couple per year. The average is around $8. This is an astonishingly low figure for what it provides.

TRADITIONAL SOCIAL MARKETING VERSUS THE "NEW BREED"

Since the 1980s, those who support and operate social marketing programs have had more than one vision of its proper role. The debate has centered primarily on whether social marketing should focus on reaching the largest possible number of lowest-income consumers, as it has traditionally, or whether its role is to act as a catalyst for private-sector entities, usually for-profit companies, to improve their marketing and distribution of contraceptives.

While it is quite possible for both kinds of programs to operate in the same markets and, indeed, both approaches are in fact being used simultaneously in a few countries today, these visions of social marketing are, nevertheless, generally opposed to each other. The vision I share is that our primary obligation is to help the citizens of poor societies, people whose near-subsistence living standard gives them first call on our available resources. Thus focused, we arrive very quickly and unambiguously at the conclusion that social marketing should be designed to reach the largest number of lowest-income people possible, to provide contraceptives to people who need them desperately, most especially to avert high rates of infant death. This means following the traditional, or "Bangladesh," model of social marketing, an approach fully described in Chapter 6.

In the other corner of the ring is a view of social marketing that focuses on entirely different variables. Its proponents start with the recognition that international assistance funding is very limited, and that the ability of the industrialized countries to be of assistance to peoples of the third world is circumscribed and temporary. Because foreign assistance must be treated as a temporary intervention with a realistic "exit strategy," social marketing should properly be regarded as a catalytic process in which "experts" can go work with already-existing private-sector companies, make some changes, and get out. This approach has been called the "New Breed" of social marketing program, and it is also referred to as the "manufacturer's model" or "third/fourth generation" social marketing.

One good example of the new breed is the Blue Circle/Gold Circle project in Indonesia, where foreign assistance was provided to four Indonesian contraceptive manufacturers in the form of advertising and promotion budgets, in exchange for which the four companies kept their prices low. Schering Indonesia (an affiliate of the big pharmaceutical company in Berlin) sold its Microgynon pills throughout Indonesia for $1 per cycle, backed by advertising and promotional support paid for by foreign assistance. Similarly the distribution of IUDs, condoms, and Upjohn's injectable Depo-Provera, all produced by Indonesian companies, was assisted by foreign funds in the form of advertising, promotion, and research. The plan assumes that when foreign assistance ends, the marketing and selling of contraceptives by the four companies will continue, and that no further external support will be required.

This is a compelling vision. It is also a vision that some USAID professionals and perhaps others in the British Department for International Development (DFID) may have felt required to assume for political reasons; working under policies that demand exit strategies, they may have felt bound to arrive at a programmatic design that has a visible ending. To this extent I am sympathetic with this view, and I understand the process by which it was developed. When contraceptives are highly subsidized, as they are in the traditional (or Bangladesh) model, the success of the program achieves the humanitarian and developmental objectives of its supporters, but costs rise as the program grows. There is no exit strategy. Not only is there no clear path to a cessation of outside funding, but the inertial forces of such programs are to make them bigger, and as they become bigger, they become ever more expensive. Thus, USAID saw the Bangladesh social marketing program rise in cost from $2 or $3 million a year in the late 1970s to nearly $10 million a year by 1992. People began asking, not unreasonably, "How do we get out?" This (and other forces) led to the focus on the "new breed" version.

On a theoretical basis, the new breed has more appeal than the traditional approach. It conforms with the practice of providing temporary "technical assistance"—a respected and time-honored way of providing foreign aid. Philosophically, it affirms the Western world's emphasis on free-market economics because it assists for-profit companies in the private sector. It has a certain intellectual appeal as well: there are many design variations (as we shall see) and the theoretical applications of the new-breed model are fundamentally more interesting (because they are new, varied, and sometimes more complex) than setting up a program of the time-tested model, which closely imitates, at least in its structure, previous programs. The "new breed" approach is exemplified by most of the programs supervised by the SOMARC organization, in the 1980s and 1990s, under its mandate from USAID. That mandate reflects a policy that favors foreign assistance as a temporary catalyst with a visible exit strategy.

The problem is that, on a large scale, these new-approach programs simply do not deliver the goods and, most particularly, they do not deliver the goods to very poor people in the world's lowest-income countries. The only social marketing programs that have consistently delivered contraceptives at a level equivalent to 5 percent contraceptive prevalence or greater over a period of five years or more have been programs designed pretty much along the lines of the Bangladesh model.* (See also Chapter 6 and Appendix 1.) The *best* "new-breed" programs are either very small in absolute terms, small relative to the markets where they operate, short-lived, or all three.

The traditional "Bangladesh" approach (which in turn is similar to its predecessor in Kenya) is the one most often used by PSI and DKT International. This approach is supported by numerous USAID overseas missions where the view of foreign assistance is more apt to focus on the urgency of present need than on the necessity for an articulated exit strategy. PSI and DKT are also supported in this approach by the German KfW (Kreditanstalt für Wiederaufbau), by the Dutch government, by the British DFID, and several other governments and private foundations.

But how do those of us who believe in the time-tested model answer the officials who so legitimately ask: How do we get out? Where is the exit strategy? The answer is that the appropriate exit strategy for foreign assistance by the rich countries to the poor countries is the economic development of the poor countries themselves. As countries like Ethiopia and Vietnam—today's poorest large countries—develop economically, their citizens will gradually become more able to pay the full cost of contraceptive products. Foreign governments should do everything they can to accelerate this process, through open trade policies and encouragement of free enterprise and democracy, trends that seem well under way in most of the world today. When Ethiopia catches up with Colombia

---

*As noted in Figure 1.1, I have set this level as the definition of success for a CSM project. This "success line," or 5 percent prevalence equivalent means that roughly 5 percent of the eligible couples in a given population are using the brand or brands described. The number of eligible couples is calculated by taking 80 percent of women aged 15–49, it being assumed that 20 percent of all couples are pregnant, sterile, desirous of becoming pregnant, or not sexually active. Eleven of the fifty-four CSM programs achieved this 5 percent success level in 1995. Two, Bangladesh and Colombia, achieved 10 percent.

on the basis of per-capita GNP, it will be possible to have a social marketing program in Ethiopia that is financially self-sufficient, just as Colombia's is already. Meanwhile, foreign assistance should be directed at the poor. If we let the desire for an exit strategy take precedence over prioritizing the most deserving beneficiaries, we will have undermined the whole purpose of providing assistance to developing countries.

BECOMING (TOO) RESPECTABLE

There is still something about a contraceptive—its sexual connotations, its role as a preventer of pregnancy—that makes the subject controversial. Accordingly, those of us who work in family planning—in actually providing services—have a touch of rebelliousness, a certain crusader's zeal.[2] At the organizational level, this enthusiasm too often gets replaced by a certain ossification that tends to inhibit effective service delivery. As an organization grows, it builds interests. Its donor list broadens. It gets "respectable." In this way, organizations lose their zest for risk-taking, even become risk-averse. Tim Black has referred to this tendency as "the evolution of a bureaucratic dinosaur, which must consume vast resources to maintain its metabolism, is slow in response and generates prodigious amounts of wind" (Black, 1972: 45).

I remember when Tim Black and I consulted two lawyers at the Planned Parenthood Federation of America, on a lofty floor of a high-rise office building in midtown New York. It was 1970, and we were planning to experiment with selling condoms through the mail as part of our course work at the School of Public Health at the University of North Carolina. In 1970, sending condoms through the mail was illegal. Under an 1873 "Comstock" law, named for its progenitor Anthony Comstock (who tried to expunge everything sexual from American life), contraceptives, and all information about birth control and abortion, were "obscene" and therefore unmailable. The penalty for being convicted for this offense was a maximum of five years in jail and/or a $5,000 fine.

At the time, this was not a rigorously enforced law. We had asked the postal authorities if they intended to enforce it and they had carefully instructed us that they could not tell us they would *not* enforce it, but that, with the federal government spending millions of dollars on family planning, prosecuting legitimate mailers of nonprescription contraceptives would probably not be very high on their priority list. So we were inclined to go ahead. But Planned Parenthood's lawyers viewed our enterprise with some concern and spoke darkly of the length of our possible jail terms, turning Tim's thoughts to his wife and two pre-school daughters. The lawyers succeeded in scaring both of us pretty thoroughly.

To maintain perspective here, it is useful to recall that Planned Parenthood was inspired by, and founded on, the work of Margaret Sanger, a genuine crusader. Because she believed passionately in a woman's right to birth control, she was not intimidated, even though she was thrown in jail on a number of occasions. The threat of jail did not stop her.

But by 1970, Planned Parenthood was big and "respectable." They were providing valuable services but their culture had become risk-averse. What we were planning was illegal, might rock the boat, could invite lawsuits, and might interfere with Planned Parenthood's status quo. So they tried to discourage us.

Two years later we wanted to sue the State of New York on a right-to-birth-control issue. New York's law forbade the sale of contraceptives to minors (even married minors), the sale of contraceptives outside of pharmacies (the vestige of successful lobbying by the pharmacy interests), and any display or advertisement of contraceptives in any manner. The law was clearly discriminatory and almost certainly unconstitutional. It was inhibiting access to contraceptives by people who badly needed them. We were ready to sue.

Once again, Planned Parenthood tried to discourage us, this time with some vehemence. Such a lawsuit might threaten the carefully crafted ways that Planned Parenthood doctors in clinics then counseled minors. If we lost, it might make it *harder* for clinics to provide birth control. These were not frivolous arguments, but they reflected a fearful, cautious mindset.

This is a danger that all organizations that seek to change society for the better must guard against. If we want to make change we must take risks and behave in ways that are controversial. George Bernard Shaw once remarked that reasonable people accommodate themselves to society, that unreasonable people attempt to make society accommodate to them, and that all progress therefore depends upon unreasonable people.

In Planned Parenthood's case, I am pleased to report an almost complete organizational resurgence under its then new president Faye Wattleton in the 1980s. Under Wattleton's leadership Planned Parenthood charged into the vanguard of the abortion-rights battle—an entirely new undertaking for the national organization. As this risky new crusade got under way the organization regained much of its energy, zeal, and capacity to take risks for the sake of change. It became "unreasonable." While this created many tensions inside the organization, it also made it effective and dynamic.[3]

I am also happy to report that our efforts at selling condoms through the mail not only turned out well, incurring no indictments, but went on long enough to see the elimination of the law that had made condoms by mail illegal. In 1971 President Nixon, in one of his least known legislative actions, signed most of the Comstock law out of existence. Further, our lawsuit against the state of New York went forward and we won.

On June 9, 1977, by a 7 to 2 vote, the U.S. Supreme Court struck down New York's anticontraceptive law. The advertisement of contraceptives in New York, the sale of contraceptives by retailers other than pharmacists, and the sale of contraceptives to minors have been legal ever since.

Another matter of "respectability" is just as paradoxical. Social marketing programs that sell contraceptives have always existed in a gray nether world, straddling the zones of the commercial private sector and the public/social service sector.

It has sometimes been an awkward posture. These two worlds—commercial and "social"—have always regarded each other askance. Government officials and foundation representatives are inclined to view the private sector and those who make their living in it with a combination of awe and disregard. Those who work in the world of commerce are not perceived as creating the wealth that makes government and foundation work possible; rather they are seen as vaguely magical experts in esoteric fields like manufacturing and marketing who are at the same time both inappropriately profit-driven and socially uninformed. In turn, government bureaucrats and others engaged in pursuing the social good are viewed by most commercial managers as wasteful, inefficient, and inimical to the commercial activity that creates the wealth and pays the taxes that make "social" programs possible. There is just enough truth in these clichéd views to keep the stereotypes alive.

Those who conduct contraceptive social marketing programs must straddle these two worlds and work effectively in both. Social marketing managers must speak the language of governments, donors, and foundations. They must also speak the language of business as they deal with commercial contractors and contraceptive manufacturers and as they conduct social marketing programs that closely follow the commercial model. This is a special challenge that many social marketing managers enjoy. For some, however, these two views of the world are too difficult to reconcile.

NOTES

1. The list is a very long one. Manoff (1985) adds: oral rehydration therapy in Honduras, a Philippine program to increase rice production, a Tanzanian radio campaign on men's health, and a breast-feeding campaign in Trinidad and Tobago. In Australia, social marketing campaigns have included exercise promotion, sun-protection messages, safe sex, and injury prevention.

2. Abortion service providers need more than zeal, at least in the United States. They need both physical and moral courage. At least seven abortion service workers have been murdered in recent years and countless others have been harassed in their homes, at work, or while otherwise going about their daily lives.

3. See Wattleton's autobiography, *Life on the Line* (Wattleton, 1996).

3

Sex, Contraception, Religion, and AIDS

Because birth control has to do with sex, it has always provoked controversy. The interrelationship between sex and contraception, however, has been loaded with paradoxes. At an earlier time in history conservative thinking generally held that procreation was good and sex was bad. At the end of the twentieth century we have arrived at a general consensus that too much or inappropriate procreation is bad and that, at least in some circumstances, sex may not be quite as "bad" as we thought it was. Most people would agree, for example, that procreation by very young girls is bad; that procreation consisting of very closely spaced, health-draining births is bad, and that sexual relations between mature married couples is good. It is a valued and pleasurable component of an intimate relationship.

There is yet another massive paradox in the family planning movement. Family planners have worked almost incessantly for three decades to disassociate birth control from sexuality. This somewhat bizarre movement was nicely analyzed by J. Mayone Stycos twenty years ago:

Just as modern advertising has spent the last half century infusing the subject of sex into [other] areas . . . family planners have been busily eradicating sex from the one place where it uniquely belongs. The accommodation of the professionals and the desexualization of the birth control message have combined to give family planning communications the typically sterile, slightly prudish and somewhat dated tone which may reassure the older generation but which alienates . . . the young. By failing to face up squarely and honestly to its revolutionary contribution to human sexuality, the [birth control] movement may have given away the most precious of its early possessions. (1977:292)

Why have family planners eschewed sex? Because, says Stycos, "respectability" was essential for family planners, and sex has never been respectable. To get the support of the medical community, birth control had to be the purview of physicians. The rationale had to be health oriented. Latin American doctors, for example, began to embrace contraception as a way to prevent the dire consequences of unsafe abortion. No sex in that equation. At one point, seeking help from conservative establishment opinion, the American birth control revolutionary Margaret Sanger even cozied up to the eugenecists, who sought to discourage excessive breeding among the "dysgenic" populations—the poor and others thought to be genetically less desirable.

Then along came the "population" movement. Here were demographers, economists, scholars of all stripes, addressing issues of world population. No sex there! Everyone agreed that contraceptives were needed to defuse the "population bomb," although there was no "bomb." (See Chapter 12.) Here was yet another "respectable" approach to the problem that was entirely free of sexual taint. The conspiracy to keep sex out of birth control was (and is) still going strong.

Stycos points out that,

from the dawn of history, the fundamental reason for using contraception has never varied in the slightest for the billions of couples who have practiced it. *Contraception is practiced in order to enjoy sexual relations without suffering the consequences of unwanted reproduction.* . . . [t]he part of the equation which never varies refers to the enjoyment of [sex]. (1977:287)

So contraception is not only about sex. Even worse, it is about the enjoyment of sex! By the enjoyment of sex, I (and I believe Stycos) mean more than the purely sensual pleasures of sexual congress. Sexual pleasure includes those very deep satisfactions associated with the sexual expression of intimacy between partners who know each other well and trust each other fully. Indeed much of the best modern expert analysis on sexuality stresses that the most electrifying sexual relations are often enjoyed by couples whose trust in each other has become so profound that they are able to risk exposure of their most intimate emotional and sexual selves during intercourse or other forms of sexual activity.

But the pleasures of sexual intimacy have not been part of the family planning paradigm, except in the earliest days of the movement. The early revolutionaries, brave women like Marie Stopes in England, Margaret Sanger in the United States, and Ingrid Ottensen-Jensen in Sweden, had the courage to step forward and assert women's rights to sexual pleasure at the same time that they were demanding women's right to fertility control. Margaret Sanger went so far as to assert that "the magnetism of [sex] is health giving, and [it] acts as a beautifier and a tonic" (Kennedy, 1970, cited in Stycos, 1977:288). For these women the idea of sexual liberation automatically included access to information about birth control and contraceptives. If couples were to have the liberation of sexual expression, they had to have contraceptives. Otherwise, women would continue to be tyrannized by continuous pregnancy.

CONTRACEPTION AND RELIGION

The connection with sex is also a big part of the reason that contraception is controversial as a religious issue. All the modern methods of contraception are condemned by the Roman Catholic Church, though they are generally as widely used by Catholics as by others. Some very conservative Muslim societies oppose birth control, though there appears to be nothing in Islam per se that opposes contraception. Many Protestant denominations, as well as Roman Catholics, oppose abortion, often vehemently, but Protestants do not generally oppose contraception. (This may be changing for the worse. A temporary cut-off in funding for international family planning by the U.S. Congress in 1996 apparently reflected the views of Conservative (Protestant) Christian constituents.) Judaism, Buddhism, and Hinduism are neutral or supportive of birth control.

In Roman Catholic dogma the purpose of sex is procreation; all "artificial" methods of birth control are held to be sinful. It is argued that Roman Catholicism must maintain this position because so much of that religion's power derives from its capacity to forgive sin, and, since sexual "sins" are the most universally and regularly practiced, they constitute the forgiveness of which the Catholic Church cannot do without. If Catholicism fully acknowledged the acceptability of sex as a mode of expression of intimacy as well as a means of procreation, its ability to induce guilt (and hence the need for forgiveness) among its faithful would be drastically curtailed, as would that considerable part of the Church's power that derives from its capacity to forgive sexual errancy.

It has been argued too that the Catholic Church wants to see an increase in the numbers of their flock, an objective facilitated by proscribing birth control among the faithful.

Whatever the reason, Roman Catholicism remains the only major religion that explicitly and regularly condemns modern contraception. This does not seem to make much difference to Roman Catholics. In the United States, for example, Catholics have followed virtually identical patterns of contraceptive practice as the rest of the population, paying virtually no attention to the various encyclicals that from time to time remind Catholics of the Church's contraceptive strictures. Indeed, there are only two countries where Roman Catholic dogma on birth control seems to have affected public policy or the practice of contraception— Ireland and the Philippines—and of these two, the impact in the Philippines has been desultory. Family planning was aggressively pursued by the national government under Ferdinand Marcos and resumed under the Protestant president, Fidel Ramos. Only during the presidency of Corazon Aquino (between Marcos and Ramos) was the influence of the Catholic Church, in the person particularly of Philippine Cardinal Jaime Sin, clearly reflected in government policy on birth control. Despite her unquestioned leadership in the revolutionary "People Power" movement, Mrs. Aquino apparently owed substantial political favors to the Church and she felt compelled, as president, to follow Church teachings on the subject of birth control.

Even today, however, it cannot be gainsaid that Cardinal Sin and his colleagues exercise a powerful influence on this aspect of Philippine life. The Catholic establishment in the Philippines is virulently anticondom, even in the age of AIDS. In the face of massive evidence to the contrary, Church leaders continue to insist that condoms don't work. To oppose the use and the dissemination of condoms in the face of AIDS is, to me, deeply immoral. It constitutes the deliberate withholding from a fellow human being of the means by which a person may save his or her own life and save the lives of others. Yet the Church condemns condom use even as the number of Filipinos infected with HIV continues to climb, approaching twenty thousand in the mid-1990s. Cardinal Sin has described the government's anti-AIDS program as "intrinsically evil." According to the *New York Times*, "Church leaders have been known to set boxes of condoms on fire at anti-government demonstrations" in the Philippines (*New York Times*, 1996b:A8). And there is little doubt that church propaganda about condoms has been persistent and effective. One video produced by Human Life International in the United States and shown at church group activities in the Philippines claims that condoms contain "pores" big enough for the HIV to pass through, "as easily as rain passes through a broken window"—a deliberate falsehood. This kind of church-sponsored propaganda has resulted in a widespread belief, particularly among men in the Philippines, that condoms are ineffective.*

For the record, condoms are highly effective in preventing HIV transmission. The scientific evidence developed both by governmental and

*The Roman Catholic position on condoms has a long history. In an 1826 proclamation that forbade the use of condoms, Pope Leo XII approvingly called syphilis God's way to "punish sinners by striking them in the member with which they had sinned." (*Civilization*, 1995:37) Alas, 175 years have seen little change in this vulgar position.

independent academic researchers is that "undamaged condoms provide an effective physical barrier against HIV" (Rietmeijer et al., 1988:1851). The research has concluded that "sperm and disease-causing organisms cannot pass through an intact latex condom" (Johns Hopkins University, 1990:7). The U.S Centers for Disease Control and Prevention (CDC) concluded that "latex condoms are highly effective for preventing HIV infection and other STDs when used consistently and correctly" (Centers for Disease Control and Prevention, 1993:590).

Public policy in Ireland has also been deeply influenced by the Catholic Church. Only in 1995 was divorce made legal by referendum in that country. Irish women seeking abortions have for years been forced to journey to England. Condoms were made available over the counter only in the 1990s.

But outside of these two countries, the Church position on birth control seems to be widely ignored. Roman Catholic Italy has the most liberal abortion laws in Europe; Catholic Latin America has generally progressive policies on contraception (though generally restrictive abortion laws); French laws on birth control and abortion are quite liberal; American Catholics seek abortion at rates comparable to non-Catholics.

Similarly, Islam appears to offer very little resistance—at least as expressed through public policies—to the promulgation of birth control. Muslim Indonesia has one of the most progressive (and successful) birth control campaigns in the world. So does Muslim Bangladesh. And, while India's Muslims have complained that the Hindu majority promotes birth control among India's 100 million Muslims more aggressively than among its Hindus (there is no evidence of this), these disagreements have tended to be more political than religious. In any event, they have not affected India's support of a wide variety of birth control programs, including the government's massive sterilization program and a very liberal policy on early trimester abortions. Even conservative Iran is liberalizing its policies on family planning, and Muslim Egypt has been pro–birth control for years. The Grand Mufti of Egypt has stated: "God asked to always plan our lives and family planning is certainly a form of structuring our lives. . . . [Family planning is] one of the personal matters that belong to husbands and wives only" (Population Institute, 1995:1).

SEX AND THE POWER OF THE STATE

Sexual intercourse is the single most creative act of the human species; without it we could not exist. But depictions of this creative act are more feared, condemned, and proscribed than are depictions of the most horrifying and vicious human crimes, right on down to decapitation and disembowelment.

We are mystified by sex; we are afraid of it. Sex is revolutionary, yet utterly conventional. It has been an integral and necessary part of every society since the dawn of (human) time but, especially in modern centuries, a topic unfit for polite discussion. We pass laws against many kinds of sexual practices, yet often advocate those practices through other societal institutions. We are seduced by sex; we are repulsed by it. We love it and we hate it. Modern marriage counselors and sex therapists, for example, advise couples to pursue pleasurable sexual practices in a variety of ways. An active sex life is advocated as an important component of a healthy marriage. Couples in their seventies, eighties, and nineties are encouraged to maintain active sex lives. A variety of sex practices is encouraged. If a middle-aged or elderly man is having erection problems, today's sex therapists will usually counsel the couple to try oral sex. Yet oral sex, even between husband and wife, is illegal in nearly half the states in the United States! Our sex therapists are thus prescribing a felony. The fact that these "sodomy" laws are largely ignored, particularly with respect to heterosexuals, is further proof of our ambivalence about our sexuality: we would rather pass bad laws (which imply that we can all be "good") and ignore them (when people, absolutely predictably, are not "good") than remove such laws from our books. Laws against adultery and fornication are similarly overlooked and occasionally overturned. For example, in 1993, the police in several Connecticut towns were urged to enforce that state's adultery laws by several disaffected partners in divorce actions. Some police began indicting adulterous spouses. The Connecticut legislature was so appalled that it promptly rescinded the adultery law.

Scholars have pondered humans' ambivalence about sex for many centuries. Perhaps, some suggest, there is a primordial imperative for procreation that imbues males with an incessant urge to inseminate, and females with an instinct for creating appropriate environments for the raising of offspring. This tension makes us afraid of sex, afraid of the conflict inherent in our different procreative roles. Others have suggested that in our sexuality we fear loss of control; after all, we must relinquish control over our bodies at least briefly to achieve sexual climax, the peak moment of sexual pleasure. Such unstructured paroxysms, they argue, if permitted to take place too often, or with the wrong partners, could lead to a loss of control in our societal institutions. If we permit that form of anarchy in the bedroom that makes sexual lives richer—relinquishing control for the sake of orgasm—we may be inviting societal anarchy. President Richard Nixon, referring to "pornography," asserted that a permissive attitude about sex "would contribute to an atmosphere condoning anarchy in every other field—and would increase the threat to our social order as well as our moral principles" (Strossen, 1995:177).

Sexologist Marty Klein states:

Authentic sexuality is ultimately revolutionary. It challenges gender roles by depicting women as lusty without being bad. It enfranchises us all as sexual beings—but for who we are, not for what we do. It returns to us the right and means to own and evaluate our own sexuality, rather than referring us to social definitions of what is "normal." It challenges the role of monogamy and the nuclear family as the exclusive source of emotional comfort. It undermines traditional religions by refusing to make procreation the primary purpose of sex. . . . It trusts people to take care of themselves and others during sexual encounters. Finally, it sees sex as a positive force we can use to explore and expand our human horizons, rather than as a negative force we must control and restrict to protect ourselves.(1990:17)

Those who fear sex the most want to restrict its expression by others. No nudity, please! No bare breasts. Children must be protected from the sight of those glands from which, as infants, they first drew life. Sex must be banned from our books and movies. Prostitutes must be thrown in jail (but not for very long, of course). "Pornography" must be suppressed. One legal scholar suggests, I think with much wisdom, that these urges reveal something about our sexual selves that some of us would rather not know, or at least not address directly. Sexual imagery "threatens to explode our uneasy accommodation between sexual impulse and social custom—to destroy the carefully-spun social web holding sexuality in its place" (Tribe, 1988:919).

As noted, birth control and particularly the deliberate promotion of contraception, presupposes that sex without procreation is okay, that sex, for its own sake, is a positive human good. That makes it controversial.

IS CONTRACEPTION MORE CONTROVERSIAL THAN SEX?

Indeed, contraception can be more controversial than sex. I submitted a mail order ad for condoms to the *New York Times* in 1986 and was told that that august newspaper would carry the ad only if it contained no mention of pregnancy prevention. We made the necessary alterations and ran the ad, which stressed the "health" benefits of condom use, mimicking almost ludicrously Mayone Stycos's point about sex and birth control. Condoms are okay, but not as contraceptives![1]

This bears an eerie parallel to an event in 1877, when England's solicitor general explained why Charles Knowlton's *Fruits of Philosophy* should be suppressed; he referred to it as a filthy book that would "enable persons to have sexual intercourse and not to have that which in the order of Providence is the natural result of that sexual intercourse" (Fryer, 1965; cited in Stycos, 1977:287).

WHAT ABOUT SEX ITSELF?

On the matter of improved sexuality communication, the otherwise prudish United States has shown some progress.* Sex education has become an accepted part of the curricula of most American high schools and even some elementary schools. The American Association of Sex Educators, Counselors, and Therapists has nearly two thousand members, credentialed experts who help people solve sexual problems so they may lead more pleasurable and satisfying sexual lives. Articles and broadcasts on legitimate sexual subjects from libido problems to postmenopausal sexuality are very common. Sex education videos that combine educational material with explicit demonstrations have sold by the millions.

Furthermore these noncontraceptive sexuality products are promoted with sexual themes. Unlike the efforts to "desex" family planning, there seems to have been no attempt to camouflage their purpose by trying to describe them as something else. Indeed the most successful mail order ads for adult sex education videos seem to be those that appeal directly and explicitly to people's desire for sexual pleasure. (See Figure 3.1.)

Major contributions to increased sexual knowledge and to the discussability of sex have come from books published in the 1980s and the 1990s. These include Alex Comfort's *The Joy of Sex*, David Schnarsh's *Passionate Marriage*, Ruth Westheimer's *Sex for Dummies*, and Sandra Scantling's *Ordinary Couples, Extraordinary Sex*. Advertisements for these books have appeared in virtually all mainstream American media. Even explicit ads like those in Figure 3.1 have appeared in such publications as the *New York Times* (no mention of birth control!), the *Ladies' Home Journal*, *Popular Science*, and *U.S News and World Report*.

WHAT ABOUT CONTRACEPTIVE ADS?

Have we seen a "resexing of birth control"? Mayone Stycos wrote his article in 1977. Has there been real progress in the ensuing twenty years? Some, but not much. The idea that contraceptives are for pleasure without pregnancy is still bounded by constraints, and contraception advertising—in social marketing as well as all other family planning programs—still stresses themes of responsible parenthood and better health. An early social marketing headline from Sri Lanka was "Until You Want Another Child, Rely on Preethi." That is still typical of the themes

*Yes, the United States is among the more prudish of modern societies. Automobile and jeans advertising notwithstanding, American media are among the most skittish in the world about contraceptive advertising and often about sexuality advertising as well. This is especially true of the broadcast media, most especially television. The major networks assert that their advertising must meet the standards of their most conservative viewers, even as program content gets more steamy.

Figure 3.1

Ads for adult sex education videos often appeal directly to people's desire for sexual pleasure. Reproduced courtesy of Sinclair Intimacy Institute, 1829 East Franklin Street, Suite 1014, Chapel Hill, North Carolina 27516.

used in family planning advertising in the developing world. Even though we were able to advertise later in Sri Lanka that Preethi condoms are "gossamer fine for marital happiness," this is still about as far as most ads go more than twenty years later.

The reasons for this are natural enough. Margaret Sanger's successors needed the funds and establishment support that only respectability can bring, and this is still a powerful force in the conduct of human affairs. In Pakistan or Indonesia or Egypt we would not be likely to gain approval for any contraceptive advertisement stressing sexual pleasure. Indeed, in Pakistan, for the first few years of the Sathi condom social marketing project, PSI was not even permitted to mention the name Sathi or the word "condom" on television; the best we could do was put the orange and white logo—of two stylized birds silhouetted against the sun—on the screen with a voiceover about the (vague) virtues of family planning. Nevertheless, some sexual messages have begun to creep into contraceptive advertising, mostly in condom ads.

THE PHALLIC CONTRACEPTIVE

The fact that condoms are shaped like a penis—and an erect penis at that—makes it a little difficult to disassociate condoms from the sex act. Indeed, the intended use of a condom is necessarily a part of sexual activity and, while this has long been considered a disadvantage of this method, it may also have facilitated the tendency to keep condoms and sexuality closely paired.

Messages promoting the use of condoms have tended to have considerably more sexual content than messages promoting the use of any other family planning methods. Condoms promoted for disease prevention, including AIDS prevention, tend to be promoted with more sexual content than condoms promoted for birth control. See for example Figure 3.2. The ad on the left is a Trust condom family planning ad produced by the DKT social marketing project in the Philippines. It is a straightforward approach to condom promotion that, in this case, suggests that condoms are a normal everyday product and that adults of all ages and both sexes should feel comfortable buying them. The Panther ad, on the other hand, which was produced by the same DKT project staff and the same ad agency, promotes the use of the Panther condom in the context of AIDS prevention. It is unabashedly sexual and erotic.

Another example, Figure 3.3, shows an especially imaginative condom promotion. This deliciously provocative poster is from PSI's project in Bolivia promoting Pantera (Panther) condoms. The sly and slightly threatening but clearly sensual animal is actually composed of eyes drawn on a photograph of a woman's buttocks.

In India, the box covers of dozens of imported condom brands flaunt

Figure 3.2

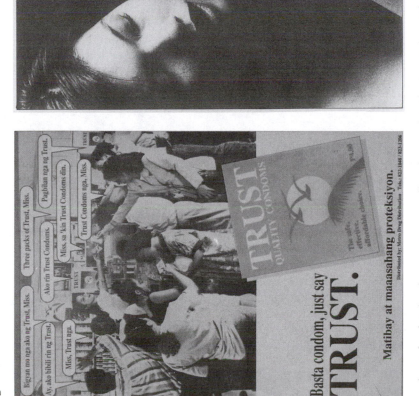

Condoms for family planning are usually advertised without any hint of sexual pleasure (Trust). Condoms marketed for AIDS prevention are much more likely to be overtly sexual, like this Panther ad.

Figure 3.3

This slightly threatening but clearly sensual beast promotes a socially marketed condom in Bolivia. It is composed of eyes drawn on a photograph of a woman's buttocks. Reproduced courtesy of PSI.

images of bare-breasted provocatively posed women. These condoms are produced in Malaysia or other Southeast Asian countries expressly for the Indian market.

India's *Kama Sutra* has also been used to provide the theme for that country's sexiest condom, which is made locally. (See Figure 3.4.) The nude and near-nude couples used on the Kama Sutra brand package and in much of its advertising is an astonishing anomaly in India. True, the *Kama Sutra* itself is an ancient Hindu book on sexual love, and India has an abundance of erotic art (particularly temple carvings) from earlier centuries. But modern India can be very prudish. In ever popular traditional Hindi films, the hero and heroine are rarely even allowed to kiss. Yet here are two attractive and sexy models promoting condoms in India in 1995 without the suggestion of a blush. And the slogan? "For the Pleasure of Making Love."

Figure 3.4

"Prudish" India is home to one of the world's sexiest condoms.

WHY ARE CONDOMS SEXIER THAN PILLS OR IUDS?

Birth control pills and IUDs are more effective than condoms as contraceptives and theoretically should go even further toward permitting the enhanced sexual pleasure that may be realized with freedom from fear of pregnancy. Indeed, these more modern contraceptives arguably permit greater sexual pleasure by removing the need for a layer of latex between the penis and vagina. Sex is more natural, more sensational. Yet the fact remains that, overwhelmingly, erotic contraceptive ads are ads (or other messages) for condoms. Why? There is the phallic shape, of course, and the fact that condom use is part of the sex act itself—not true of most other contraceptives. Too, most condoms are sold to men, and men traditionally respond to erotic images more readily than women.

Others speculate that condoms are associated with illicit sex and that illicit sex is somehow "sexier" than marital sex. Is sex outside marriage really more erotic than sex within marriage? Not in my view. But perhaps the association is real all the same. Here is a plausible hypothesis: since illicit sex—in most cultures any sexual activity outside of marriage—is by definition improper, extralegal, not "respectable," we are not bound by the same rules for advertising and promotion as we are when it comes to family planning. While family planning has exchanged the sexuality of contraception for the respectability required for acceptance by the estab-lishment, the promotion of condoms for protection in illicit sexual en-counters is under no such constraint. Since sex with prostitutes, for example, is, by definition, not "respectable" anyway, those of us who advertise condoms for use during such encounters are under no obliga-tion to try to make it so. We are free to infuse as much sexuality as we choose into our messages for condom use in those kinds of situations.

It should be noted that these erotic condom ads are by no means typical of condom ads generally. When condoms are promoted for family planning, they usually fall back into the "respectable" pattern of pill, IUD, and other contraceptive consumer advertising. Figure 3.5, a condom ad from Kenya, shows a creative mixture. The ad is unerotic, but promises pleasure and sensitivity.

I have noted that oral contraceptive ads are seldom sexy. In an excep-tion that may prove the rule, some early television ads for Microgynon pills in the Dominican Republic featured a well-known and sensual ac-tress, Vickianna, disappearing suggestively into her bedroom, confident of not becoming pregnant, and equally confident of enjoying a satisfying sexual encounter. The ad was extremely successful in launching the Mi-crogynon campaign in the Dominican Republic, but turned out to be so controversial that it had to be pulled off the air. Figure 3.6, from the television spot, is Vickianna showing us her "little secret" for enjoying love, the tiny oral contraceptive in her fingers.

FEMINISM AND FAMILY PLANNING

Whether they called themselves feminists or not, courageous pioneers like Margaret Sanger and Marie Stopes paved the way for the birth control movement, revolutionized it, went to jail for it, and deserve the gratitude of all of those of us who have benefited from their work and are honored

Figure 3.5

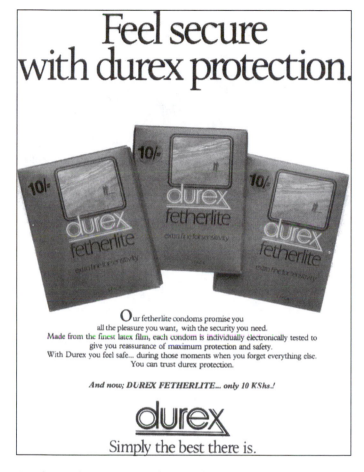

Condom advertisements frequently avoid mentioning either family planning *or* disease prevention. This ad from Kenya is a good example.

to help spread the family planning message. In more recent times, we have noted that women like Fay Wattleton, president of the Planned Parenthood Federation of America from 1978 to 1992, have carried on the tradition of the pioneers. In Wattleton's case this meant plunging Planned Parenthood into the abortion debate and bringing her organization solidly behind women's right to safe and legal abortion. She, and Planned Parenthood, incurred many risks along the way.

In sharp contrast to these tough, liberty-loving women, a new and re-

Figure 3.6

In a highly controversial television ad from the Dominican Republic, actress Vickianna shows us her "little secret" for a successful love life: an oral contraceptive pill.

actionary strain of feminism has appeared that is patronizing and ostensibly "protective." Feminists in this camp take the position that women are victims (especially of men) and that they must therefore be protected from everything from pornography to injectable contraceptives and even to abortion under circumstances that may be "inappropriate."

In family planning, the "protective" strain of feminism has manifested itself in occasional movements to outlaw or limit the availability of oral contraceptives because they affect women's bodies in potentially adverse ways, and most recently to suppress or make unavailable injectable contraceptives. In India, Brazil, and a few other countries, this opposition has greatly impeded the introduction of injectables and deprived thousands of women the right to use this safe and very effective method. Some "protective" feminists also oppose the availability of abortion unless it is accompanied by mandatory extensive counseling, whether such counseling is desired by the client or not. This group also tends to argue that all family planning be delivered in the context of obstetric and gynecological health care rather than "just" family planning:

While a majority of feminists still regard the promotion of access to contraceptive supplies and counseling as a worthwhile objective, increasing numbers are questioning the delivery of family planning services that are independent of comprehensive health services and that are provided without medical supervision. A growing radical wing disapproves the use of long-term, surgical, or hard-to-reverse methods on the grounds that they diminish women's control of their reproductive lives. A tendency exists in some women's organizations to adopt absolutist standards to measure the impact of hormonal methods on women's health. This stance is opposed to the "scientific" view that the correct standard is the relative risk as compared with the risk of pregnancy and childbearing in many less developed countries. (Finkle and McIntosh, 1994:269)

The point about an absolutist standard for hormonal contraceptives is particularly telling. To deprive or even impede women's rights to hormonal contraceptives on the ground that it could harm a small percentage is unreasonable and cruel. Such a policy is equivalent to condemning vaccination programs that save thousands of lives because, in a relatively large population, a few children will die from the vaccine itself. Public health policy has long recognized that some limited risks must be accepted in order to prevent virulent epidemics. Similarly, to ignore the lifesaving benefits of hormonal contraceptives and focus only on their risks is a grave mistake. In countries like Sierra Leone and Nepal, where nearly 2 percent[2] of women die agonizing deaths in childbirth and where the spacing of births could substantially reduce the number of such deaths, to withhold or impede injectables or orals or sterilization procedures, or any other safe and effective contraceptive method, is morally indefensible. With more than 500 thousand women dying in childbirth worldwide each year, such a policy should not be countenanced, and those of us who believe in women's rights should not be intimidated by the "moralizing" of those feminists who would withhold from others the lifesaving benefits of birth control.

Similarly, to suggest that contraceptives should not be made available except in the context of reproductive health or other general health programs is to deprive millions of people—women and men both—of contraceptives they need and want now. Comprehensive health services are expensive. They require face-to-face contact between trained health providers and their patients. Contraceptives, on the other hand, as clearly exemplified by the programs described in this book, may be made available over the counter by retailers, passed out in villages by community workers, and otherwise made available conveniently. Social marketing programs and other programs that make contraceptives easily available bear a clear responsibility, especially in the case of oral contraceptives, to provide adequate information to those who use their products so that they will be used effectively and so side effects may be appropriately considered and dealt with. This can be done through a combination of package inserts, pharmacist training, leafleting, and information provided via the broadcast media, such as "Ask the Doctor" programs. Given such efforts, it is retrograde and irresponsible to suggest that family planning cannot be provided by itself, independent of other health interventions (See Harvey, 1996).

So to those patronizing persons who contend that they know what is right for all women everywhere (especially, usually, poor women) and who therefore wish to impede women's access to hormonal contraceptives or sterilization, I would point out that those of us who are working to make contraceptives widely available to millions of women and men are saving maternal and infant lives. We applaud the efforts of those who provide comprehensive health services, including reproductive health services. But we disagree most vehemently with those who would impede access to contraceptives on the grounds that poor people must be "protected." Poor people are just as capable of deciding their own reproductive needs as anyone else. They should be treated as autonomous adults, given adequate information, and provided with their choice of whatever widely used contraceptives are available today.

THE POLITICS OF AIDS

In some parts of the world aggressive promotion of contraceptives was not possible until the impact of AIDS began to be felt. Sub-Saharan Africa has been the region lagging furthest behind in adopting birth control, and AIDS has struck this area especially hard. Africa is also behind in economic development, and in such indices of human well-being as infant mortality and life expectancy. Contraception contributes substantially to improvements in such measures, but African governments resisted aggressive family planning programs, including social marketing programs, during the 1960s and 1970s when most Asian and Latin American countries were moving quickly ahead with family planning services. Fear of neocolonialism was cited, as were references to racial genocide—deliberately slowing the growth of Black populations. There was little evidence of any such motivation and such accusations were seldom meant (or taken) very seriously, but African governments, nonetheless, resisted family planning, especially programs sponsored by outsiders.

Then came the scourge of AIDS. As more and more sub-Saharan African governments were forced to come to grips with the rapid spread of HIV among their general populations, and as it became widely known that use of condoms was the only effective way of inhibiting the sexual spread of this infection, other than abstinence or faithful monogamy,[3] these governments began to accept the idea of condom social marketing programs as an appropriate response to the epidemic.

The politics of AIDS is also important for its impact on donors and social marketing organizations. The threat of AIDS has an immediacy that even the necessity for family planning cannot match; preventing AIDS directly saves lives, whereas the lifesaving effects of family planning are less immediate and less dramatic. In fact, birth spacing with condoms saves as many—or more—lives than the HIV-prevention effect of condom use in most contexts, but the urgency is less apparent. Rough calculations of the lifesaving impact from condom use for AIDS prevention and from the point of view of pregnancy prevention suggests that the impacts are roughly comparable when HIV prevalence in the general population is in the 1 to 3 percent range (see Appendix 4). About two hundred lives are saved through birth spacing for every million condoms sold in a social marketing program in a representative developing country (infant mortality = 73 per 1,000 live births). Roughly the same number are saved by the HIV transmission effect from the sale of one million condoms where HIV incidence is 1 to 3 percent. The two effects are probably additive at least in part. This makes condom social marketing particularly cost-effective because the use of one condom can prevent, simultaneously, two undesired events.

I recognize that there are large differences in these impacts from one society to another, and in differing circumstances. A million condoms sold as a result of promotion in brothels and nightclubs in a society where 10 percent of adults are HIV positive will save far more lives by preventing AIDS. A million condoms sold in rural areas in a country of low HIV prevalence will have more impact from conception prevention, especially where infant mortality is high.

The lifesaving impact of condoms used for AIDS prevention is more dramatic than the family planning impact. Part of the reason is because the lives saved by the contraceptive effect are overwhelmingly the lives of infants and young children who tend to be relatively anonymous and relatively unproductive. One can maintain, as a matter of moral (or religious) belief, that every human life is equal, as I do, and still recognize that a society will be more impacted by the loss of educated, trained adults than by the loss of a comparable number of infants.

AIDS is also an unusually democratic disease. This is conspicuous in sub-Saharan Africa. Indeed, AIDS tends to strike better-off urban populations more often than poor rural populations that have been traditionally the most affected by life-threatening diseases. Unlike malaria, which overwhelmingly affects the poor, especially in fatal cases, AIDS disproportionately affects the middle class, particularly those in cities and therefore people likely to be known or related to government officials.

As these countries' leaders have come to know, often through members of their own families, how dreadful this disease is, it is only natural that more liberal policies toward condom marketing would begin to evolve, as indeed they did in the early 1990s. From just three sub-Saharan social marketing programs in 1988, the number had mushroomed to twenty-two by 1996, just eight years later.

NOTES

1. A nice counterpoint: *The Times of India*, a newspaper which is as prestigious in that country as the *New York Times* is in the United States, would never have turned down a condom ad, *especially* one that stressed family planning. Such ads were (and are) endorsed by the government and are widely accepted as "good" in Indian society.

2. Really more than 2 percent. In the late 1990s there are eighteen maternal deaths per one thousand live births in Sierra Leone, which means that after several pregnancies the average woman has a better than 4 percent chance of dying in childbirth. A 1996 UNICEF report, *Progress of Nations*, reveals that an appalling one out of thirteen sub-Saharan African women will die of causes related to pregnancy and childbirth.

3. The control of other sexually transmitted diseases has also been found to be a major factor in slowing the spread of AIDS. Condoms are, of course, one of the best ways to reduce the incidence of these diseases as well. See "STD Control for HIV Prevention—it works!" *The Lancet*, 1995.

4

Players in the Game: Donors, Governments, Family Planning Associations, and Others

---

DONORS

Family planning programs cost money. This is as true for social marketing as for any other kind of family planning effort. Those who provide the funds for such programs are normally called donors, and the largest donors are governments or groups of governments, like the United Nations. Their funds and their policies have made much of social marketing possible and have done much to shape the form and location of social marketing programs.

By far the most important supporter of social marketing programs in developing countries has been the U.S. Agency for International Development (USAID). USAID has invested more than $500 million (including the provision of contraceptives) in at least forty social marketing programs. It supported the first social marketing program in India and it paid for the Kinga program in Kenya in 1972. It has substantially supported the International Planned Parenthood Federation (IPPF), which funded the Sri Lanka social marketing program in 1973; and it provided massive funding for the important Bangladesh program (see Chapter 6) for more than twenty years, to name just a few.

More recently USAID has been virtually the entire source of support for the SOMARC project and, in the mid-1990s was providing more than $20 million a year in support of PSI-managed social marketing projects in at least twenty countries, as well as support to independently managed programs such as those in Nepal, Jamaica, and several Central American projects.

USAID is a decentralized agency; in most developing countries where the American government has an embassy, it also has a USAID office. That office is headed by an American citizen and frequently includes an HPN (health, population, and nutrition) officer who supervises American government support to in-country programs in those categories. The diffusion of decision-making power to the overseas USAID missions (as they are called) is one of USAID's great strengths. It means that individual country officers have the discretion to financially support activities according to priorities as they see them "on the ground," locally, and not necessarily in rigid conformity with the policies of USAID in Washington. This has been particularly important in the case of social marketing. While the decade 1985–1995 was characterized by USAID/Washington's emphasis on exit strategies and the "new breed" of social marketing programs as implemented through SOMARC, individual missions continued to provide very important and large-scale support for the time-tested social marketing programs as exemplified by PSI. When USAID/Washington first approved of social marketing in Bangladesh in 1975, for example, the agency would never have countenanced the prospect of continued large-scale funding for such a project through an intermediary organization like PSI over a period of twenty years. Yet, through a series of one-at-a-time decisions by USAID officers in Bangladesh, that is exactly what happened. One of the happy results has been that social marketing in Bangladesh, in close collaboration with a large-scale government program, has raised contraceptive prevalence in that very poor and low-literacy country from about 5 percent to more than 40 percent during the 1975–1995 period. Indeed, the combination of social marketing/government program in Bangladesh is perhaps the world's strongest proof that such programs, consistently sustained, can have a dramatic impact on contraceptive prevalence even while other indicators of economic and social development lag.

The Bangladesh case is described in Chapter 6. Here it is worth noting that Bangladesh has a "control" country which renders the family planning results in Bangladesh all the more credible and clear: Pakistan, of which Bangladesh used to be a part, and which has considerable advantages over Bangladesh in terms of gross national product per capita and literacy levels, has had no government family planning program and, until the late 1990s, only a desultory social marketing program. While Bangladesh was going from 5 percent to 40 percent contraceptive prevalence, Pakistan has continued to languish at around 10 percent or 15 percent throughout the same period.

Other important donors to social marketing programs have included, in the early days, the Swedish Aid Agency SIDA, which was one of the first governmental agencies to support family planning in the 1950s and 1960s, and, with USAID, a supplier of Nirodh to India in 1968. More recently, the German KfW, the German government's development bank, has become a major player with more than $100 million in commitments to social marketing programs beginning in the mid-1990s. Other significant supporters of social marketing have been the British government's Department for International Development (DFID), the Dutch government, and DKT International (which is also an implementing organization).

Both the World Bank and the United Nations Population Fund (UNFPA) are very substantial contributors to international family planning. But they have generally not supported social marketing because they insist on providing their resources to governments that, in turn, are reluctant to turn these resources over to private bodies for social marketing. Most attempts to bridge this chasm have been unsuccessful. In the late 1980s the World Bank earmarked $12 million for private-sector social marketing in India. As far as I know, those funds are still stuck with the Indian government, unspent. Similarly, funds were earmarked for social marketing as part of a major World Bank loan to Brazil in 1993, but by 1997 they still had not been deployed.

There have been a few bright spots. World Bank funds were used to support a small social marketing project in Guinea-Bissau in 1996. The UNFPA supplied a substantial number of condoms to PSI's Haiti program in 1995, and, in that same year it supported DKT's successful request to the Vietnam government for a supply of birth control pills. But mostly the United Nations and World Bank have been on the sidelines.

The IPPF acts as both a donor and donee. This multilateral federation receives very substantial family planning funding from many governments and foundations ($117 million in 1994) and uses those funds to support its affiliated private family planning associations (FPAs) in more than one hundred developing countries. Unfortunately, the IPPF restricts itself to a single affiliate in each country, a monopoly arrangement that greatly impairs its usefulness. To the extent that the IPPF has supported social marketing, which it has done most conspicuously in Colombia, Sri Lanka, and some small Central and South American programs, the governments that support IPPF have also supported social marketing. To the list above should therefore probably be added the Japanese government, which has been one of the largest contributors to the IPPF.

How to Be a Good Donor

The following suggestions are offered from the viewpoint of a private sector implementing organization. Having never worked in or for a government myself, I recognize that there is a good deal of presumption in offering advice to governments and multi-governmental organizations. Furthermore, that the donor governments are all democracies is not a coincidence and I am aware that, in democracies especially, political forces can be complex and unpredictable. Still, it seems useful to suggest a few guidelines that may serve to clarify and, I hope, strengthen the relationships between donor governments and those private organizations that carry out the programs they support.

Decide what you want to achieve. If the funding organization does not have a reasonably clear idea of its own objectives, it will create confusion with all concerned. Spell it out. If you want a social marketing program that will reach large numbers of low-income people, say so. If you want to conduct experiments in new approaches to social marketing irrespective of whether they reach a lot of people, say that.

Do not be reluctant to latch on to programs that already exist or programs that are or will be partially supported by other funders. While there is nothing wrong with a donor having a proprietary sense about particular project activities that it funds entirely itself, do not let that prevent you from accomplishing your objectives through organizations, arrangements, and programs where others are already investing. The trends are promising on this front. In the mid-1990s, the United States, Dutch, Swedish, British, and Norwegian governments had all supported the DKT social marketing project in Ethiopia. The German government saved the social marketing project in Pakistan when USAID was forced to pull out in 1993. The British DFID and USAID have been co-funders of the PSI social marketing project in Nigeria. And there are many other examples of donor collaboration in support of social marketing, reflecting the fact that it is more important to achieve mutual objectives than to be "donor-in-charge." Besides, when more than one donor supports a program, no donor has life-or-death control over what happens, and that is usually good for the project.

Pick your implementing organization and work with them to design a program they can run effectively. Do not put these kinds of projects out for bid; bidding for complicated service programs just does not seem to work. None of the most successful of the world's individual country CSM programs have been created as the result of a bidding process, while those country programs whose start-up has been put out for bid have had a very checkered history.[1] In addition, writing "Requests for Proposals" is a nightmare, as any donor representative who has ever written one can testify, partly because you do not have objective specifications as you do when inviting bids for physical items like generators, dams, or contraceptive products. The exact specifications of what you are seeking cannot be clearly stated in a bidding document. More important, when a social marketing project is put out for bid you virtually guarantee the loss of a very important project component: the proprietary zeal of the implementing organization about "its" project. Implementing organizations that have been part of the design process of a program, that have been involved either on their own or in collaboration with a donor from the beginning of a program, will work harder to achieve success because they have a vested interest in the program. Ask implementing organizations to bring their ideas and proposals to you, but not as part of a competition.

It will be argued that in some circumstances funding organizations are required to invite bids. If you must, you must. But recognize that it is likely to be a wasteful process. Historically, most bidding for these kinds of service programs has been done in situations where the winner is either predetermined or nearly so, and in such situations the bidding process is cynical and dysfunctional. Even those who are omitted from consideration will thank you for skipping the bidding process rather than putting them through a lot of unnecessary work.

Hold your implementing organization accountable. There is every reason for funders to insist that the companies and organizations with whom they contract deliver the goods. This means more than just surviving the financial audits (though that too is essential) and submitting reports. Quantifiable objectives should also be included and your implementing organizations should be held to them. If circumstances change and there are justifiable reasons why project objectives cannot be met, so be it. But do not let your contractors forget that they are expected to accomplish what you are providing the funds to accomplish.

Respect the beliefs and convictions of the organizations you hire. When you hire an organization that has a strong dedication—to social marketing and to family planning and to AIDS prevention, for example— do not expect them to be free from opinions, convictions, and policies of their own. They have such policies, and they should, so hire those organizations whose policies and convictions match, as closely as possible, the goals you seek to achieve in a particular situation, and treat them like the fellow professionals they are. Be prepared to compromise with your own convictions to a reasonable degree; you need the skills of the contractor as much as the contractor needs you, and in some situations you may have to split the difference over such issues as contraceptive retail prices, for example.

Do not be reluctant to implement your programmatic activities in incremental units. Donors are sometimes tempted to sweep an entire multi-million dollar package into one agreement, but this has caused much grief. Most conspicuously, USAID in India has twice encountered serious problems by trying to fold all of its family planning assistance into huge programs with multi-year budgets of many hundreds of millions of dollars rather than farming out smaller pieces of work to various implementing organizations. An unfortunate result has been maximum, highest-level scrutiny of these huge packages by the Indian government, by political as well as secretariat officials. The programs have become bureaucratized and encumbered by checks and balances so onerous that decision making becomes almost impossible.[2] Meanwhile several smaller programs, which could have continued or gone ahead without objection from the Indian government, have been stopped or have never gotten started. It may seen tempting to reduce workload by reducing the number of contracts and contractors, but if the result is the bottling up of everything you want to accomplish, it is clearly worth the extra effort to fund smaller individual programs with multiple agreements.

Minimize host government involvement. As long as host governments are kept fully informed about what is going on, there is no need for them to involve themselves in project operations, including funding flows. In the case of social marketing, the work is best performed in the private sector with only as much government oversight as is required to meet the host government's own demands. Most government officials are aware of this, I believe. When asked for their permission for a programmatic change, several have said to me, in effect, "Don't ask! If we get involved in all that, it will just slow things down." So donors should resist building in any more governmental involvement than projects genuinely require, freeing the implementing agency to work at its highest capacity.

Do not micro-manage. You have a fiduciary duty to see that funds provided by the taxpayers of your country are used as intended, to achieve agreed-upon objectives. But this does not extend to controlling the policies or day-to-day activities of your contractors. (Implementing organizations are referred to, under various circumstances, as contractors, grantees, and cooperating agencies.) One donor representative in an Asian country once became so possessive of contractor staff that she forbade a project director to travel inside the country or to even converse on program matters with representatives of other governments.

Celebrate success. As a key player in the game, you are not only entitled to join with your contractor/grantee in savoring successful moments, but the contractor will be delighted that you do. So many contacts between donors and implementing organization staff consist of complaints, problem solving, requests for permissions, and other negative paraphernalia that you will find contractors absolutely fawning on you if you congratulate them for a particularly successful month, an effective advertising campaign, or an unusually good report. I have seen contractor staff poring over USAID reports or cable traffic, for example, looking for even a crumb of recognition. When they find something that suggests they may be doing a good job, it gets instant circulation.

A special plea to the IPPF: Break the cold grip of affiliate exclusivity! By confining 100 percent of your support to a single affiliated organization in each country, you are wasting money in some places and missing opportunities almost everywhere. To support only a single (and, as it happens, rather small) organization in a country as vast as India, for example, is at the least highly impractical. And to support inefficient FPAs, who know they have a monopoly in their countries, is genuinely counterproductive. Change these rules and you will begin to see some healthy competition for your funds, and results will quickly improve.

GOVERNMENTS

The governments of the countries where social marketing projects are conducted are sometimes supporters of those programs, sometimes active players in them, and sometimes observers who provide the necessary permits and clearances. In the first and second categories, the governments of India and Jamaica have been active managers and supporters of social marketing programs themselves.

The government of India was one of the architects of the very first social marketing program, the Nirodh project, and the Indian government chose to manage the program itself. Similarly the government of Jamaica, after an initial period of social marketing management by Westinghouse Health Systems in 1974–1975, took over program management in that country and did a remarkably good job of it for more than a decade.

However, these are the only two governments to have actively managed social marketing programs, and India was moving quickly to privatize the whole process in the mid-1990s. The Jamaican program, too, is now largely privatized with the project in the hands of Grace/Kennedy, a company that deals in pharmaceuticals and food products.

Governments typically play less direct roles. The Vietnamese government has provided assistance in the form of contraceptives to the DKT-managed social marketing project in that country, for example. The Indonesian government has been active in social marketing through the parastatal organization BKKBN for more than a decade.

Governments have also played inhibitory roles. The government of Kenya in 1974 was extremely skeptical about social marketing and opposed it. That policy has happily been reversed. Other governments have been understandably skeptical of mass media advertising of contraceptives and, since the airwaves are generally closely controlled by governments in developing countries—indeed, they are controlled to an unfortunate degree by government everywhere—official strictures have in many cases inhibited the flow of information about social marketing products via radio and television. A notable example is Pakistan, where no specific contraceptive methods or brands could be mentioned on television until well into the 1990s.

But whether governments are enthusiastic supporters, part-time managers, facilitators, passive observers, or inhibitors, they are players in the game and must be included as partners to whatever degree they themselves desire.

How to Be a Good Host Government

If it is presumptuous of me to advise donor governments on matters relating to the implementation of the programs they fund, it is perhaps even more so to offer such advice to the governments of the countries where these programs take place. I do so in a spirit of respect, even humility. My special imprecations to the government of India are born of a deep affection for India and her people. The five years I spent there were among the happiest of my life.

If the social marketing of contraceptives is to serve—as I hope it does—to improve international relations and understanding among the peoples of the globe, those of us in private implementing organizations and representatives of both donor and recipient governments should speak frankly with one another about how we may better work together to achieve our common objectives. Here are a few suggestions for host governments:

- Welcome outsiders. The sanctity of sovereign nations is about as well established as any principle in the world today, and foreigners are no threat to it.

- Welcome outside ideas and outside money. Virtually all governments now recognize the importance of foreign investment for economic development, and social marketing programs represent one such investment. Additional capital comes in, people are employed—sometimes several hundred people in a single project—and a whole variety of businesses in your country will benefit as a result. Mass media will be enriched by substantial advertising that also serves a useful social purpose; market research organizations will have more work; distribution companies will get additional business; vehicle manufacturers or dealers will see their business increase, as will a number of ancillary business activities. In the case of social marketing projects, the fact that donor governments and implementing organizations choose to conduct them in the private sector is a reflection of the simple fact that they work better that way. Their representatives also do most of the work, which helps you. Insist that they obey all of the laws and regulations of your country, give them as much encouragement as you can, and let them get on with the project.

- Help them out. Implementing organizations, nongovernmental organizations, and others need help with routine matters like visas and import licenses. Make it as easy for them as you can. Complex registration requirements, Byzantine regulations for importing or testing imported products, barriers to bringing in funds, and high tariffs only get in the way of what you want to see accomplished.

So consider eliminating duties and taxes on such products and finding other ways to facilitate the flow of contraceptives. It can be a good investment.

- A special plea for the government of India. India contains nearly one-fifth of the world's population and its government has long recognized the need for family planning. But the Indian federal government has also been, sadly, unusually xenophobic. As an American, I often feel that it particularly suspects Americans and the American government, though I hope this is not so. Certainly, the dreadful U.S. policy on food grains in the 1960s and President Lyndon Johnson's inexcusable remarks about "keeping India on a short leash" made things worse. But it is surely time to get past this. No one patronizes India today. Indeed, India is widely admired for its fifty years of democratic governance, its agricultural successes, and its economic liberalization in the 1990s. That process has included greater foreign participation in Indian business, more trade, and more interdependence of India with the rest of the world. If the government would now do even moderately more to facilitate outside donor support of private family planning initiatives in India, private organizations could make a much greater contribution there.

FAMILY PLANNING ASSOCIATIONS AND OTHER LOCAL IMPLEMENTING ORGANIZATIONS

Funding: Getting More or Doing More?

In 1996 I attended a gathering at the home of a couple whose lifetime contributions to family planning around the world has been exemplary. Both individuals have worked hard to make access to contraception a reality and have taught the rest of us a great deal about our work in this field.

The meeting was about international family planning in the context of recently announced cutbacks in U.S. government funding for such programs. Representatives of USAID were on hand as were those of a half dozen major U.S. foundations that have been particularly supportive of international family planning.

The group included people who had worked for most of their careers in family planning services, research, training, and advocacy. It was a gathering that might have made note of the fact that birth rates were coming down all over the world, that family planning programs had demonstrated their value, and that we had learned much in the previous decade about how to make our programs more effective and how to serve more couples with limited resources.

But the conversation was almost exclusively about money, U.S. federal money. While this was admittedly the announced focus of the meeting, I was struck by the lack of creativity in the suggestions about how we should respond. Much of the U.S.-based family planning community has come to assume that the U.S. government is the only source of funds that "counts," that getting more money from it is not only our paramount objective but almost our exclusive one, and that there is only one response to such a reduction in funds: doing whatever it takes—through grassroots politics, contributions to key congresspersons, lobbying, or other activities—to restore these federal funds.

This strikes me as tunnel vision. It is true that the U.S. government has been the largest single contributor, by quite a lot, to international family planning in the last twenty years. But this is not likely to be true—certainly not to the same degree—over the next twenty years. European governments are contributing more, and so are the Japanese, the Australians, and others. We heard hardly a mention of these important donors at our meeting.

I have noticed a similar mind-set among U.S.-based clinics and other organizations. "Federal funds" are considered so crucial a component of every clinic, of every organization that has received any U.S. government support, that whatever else the organization does, it is assumed throughout its culture that its federal funds must be protected at all costs. Why? Many such organizations could survive without federal funds, and they know it. A reduction or cut-off would have many salutory effects on U.S. family planning clinics, including invigorating their boards of directors for fund raising and liberating their staffs from burdensome federal requirements. Yet this option is practically never considered; federal funding is considered sacrosanct.

The case of the International Planned Parenthood Federation provides a dramatic example of this point. The IPPF, which received a very substantial percentage of its funding from USAID up until 1984, was faced with a cut-off in USAID funding that year because, the Reagan administration contended, the organization supported abortion activities in some of its recipient countries. Despite the punitive animus behind it, the result was unexpectedly benign. Indeed, several senior IPPF managers will confirm (off the record) that the USAID cut-off in 1984 was one of the best things that had happened to their organization. The London headquarters had become hopelessly bloated and the cut-back, first of all, provided senior management with an opportunity to trim redundant staff, an action that should have been taken much earlier, but is very hard to accomplish without some kind of "crisis" to propel it. Additionally, the cut-off energized IPPF fund raisers and European government donors were quickly responsive; to them the crisis in U.S. funding was an opportunity to help a European organization in trouble. The result was that the IPPF made up the shortfall caused by the USAID cut-off within a year or two, ending up with as much funding as they had before, and a much more diverse resource base. Yet, at our meeting in March 1996, no one was even moderately inclined to address the issue of how a reduction in USAID funds might be compensated for by funds from other sources.

Even more baffling is the fact that at this meeting and many meetings like it, no one addresses the issue of how we can make our funds go further. The goal is always getting more money, not how we can better use what money we have. We know, for example, that sterilization and social marketing are among the most cost-effective ways of delivering family planning services (Huber and Harvey, 1989; Barberis and Harvey, 1997). Yet no one suggests, in the face of a funding reduction, how we might focus our funds more directly in these areas. No one suggests closing down less efficient programs or otherwise streamlining their organizations. The time has come to broaden this vision.

As noted earlier, the IPPF supports family planning associations (FPAs) in 140 countries. There is only one official IPPF "affiliate" organization in each country and only a few of them have been active in social marketing: The FPA PROFAMILIA in Colombia is the most notable example. PROFAMILIA has operated a successful social marketing program since 1975, an activity that is now financially self-sufficient. The Family Planning Association of Sri Lanka, also an IPPF affiliate, has operated the social marketing program in that country since the mid-1970s. The Costa Rica FPA, also called Profamilia, has run an excellent CSM program since the mid-1980s. Other family planning associations that have engaged in social marketing activities include Asociacion Demografica Salvadoreña (ADS) in El Salvador, and ASHONPLAFA in Honduras.

One important local implementing organization was Family of the Future (FOF) in Egypt, a nonprofit group created in affiliation with the Family Planning Association of Egypt but not actually a part of it. FOF started and operated the large Egyptian program from 1980 to 1992. (The large Egyptian and Colombian programs are more fully described in Appendix 2.) Other family planning organizations operating social marketing programs are APROPO in Peru, the Contraceptive Retail Sales (CRS) Corporation in Nepal, Profamilia in the Dominican Republic, IPROFASA in Guatemala, DANAFCO in Ghana, and PROSALUD in Venezuela.

How to Be a Good Local Implementor

To those family planning associations and other organizations that are attempting to perform an important service in family planning in their own countries but have yet to achieve an adequate degree of success, I urge you, above all else, to adopt a CYP-based set of goals against which you can measure your progress. The most useful and important step in moving from a merely acceptable performance to genuine accomplishment is to define your goals in measurable terms and then set out to achieve them.

To those outstanding organizations like Profamilia in Costa Rica and, especially, Colombia's PROFAMILIA, I say huzzah. You have inspired us all and we hope you will continue to do so. To those family planning associations and other groups that continue to operate moderately successful programs, I say set your sights higher. If you have been in business for more than seven years and have yet to achieve 5 percent prevalence, you should do better. This is true of a big group of organizations and includes the FPAs of Sri Lanka and El Salvador and the implementing organizations in Nepal, Guatemala, and Peru. There is no reason why social marketing in every country cannot achieve sales equivalent to 5 percent prevalence and then keep moving toward the 10 percent level. You cannot make 10 percent or even 5 percent prevalence if your contraceptives are overpriced, as they have been in several of these countries. Check your prices against the guidelines in Chapter 8. If necessary, reduce them. If you need financial help, you can probably get it. The IPPF is in pretty good shape financially. Both SOMARC and PSI are sometimes able to supplement local operating budgets and provide technical assistance in selected areas. If you keep your prices down and your media budgets up, you can do more.

Finally, like developing country governments, you should not be wary of outsiders. They usually bring money, which is nice. They can also be presumptuous and annoying, of course, but those characteristics can normally be kept within bounds. If outsiders offer useful advice without insisting that it be followed, welcome them. If they come in and try to tell you how to run your program, nod politely and wait for them to leave. This is not as difficult as it may seem.

INTERNATIONAL IMPLEMENTING ORGANIZATIONS

International implementing organizations have played a key role in social marketing; they are also referred to, under differing circumstances, as intermediary organizations, cooperating agencies, nongovernmental organizations (NGOs), and contractors. Primarily, these have been nonprofit organizations, but they have also included for-profit companies such as The Futures Group (SOMARC) and Westinghouse Health Systems. These implementing organizations have traditionally been U.S.-based and international in scope, covering many different countries. They work with donors and local governments, and sometimes with family planning associations, using funds supplied by donors and actively initiating or managing social marketing programs and/or providing technical assistance and advice to such programs.

For social marketing, the most important of these organizations historically, and in terms of contraceptive services provided, is Population Services International (PSI), which Tim Black and I founded in 1970. I resigned as executive director of PSI in 1978 but continue to support the organization and to serve on its board. PSI spearheaded the spread of social marketing after the launching of the Indian Nirodh program, first by implementing the project in Kenya, then by starting the national program in Sri Lanka (Chapter 5), and then starting, in collaboration with USAID, the prototype and probably most successful of all social marketing projects in Bangladesh. PSI is a nonprofit private organization based in Washington, D.C. It has started and/or supervised approximately thirty separate social marketing programs. PSI, headed by Dick Frank since 1987, is committed to the delivery of contraceptives through social marketing to the maximum possible number of lowest-income beneficiaries. Its policies favor the use of expatriate managers who follow the traditional design for social marketing: selling subsidized contraceptives through projects run by a local affiliate organization (or a branch of PSI) that exists solely for the purpose of managing the social marketing project, with concerns about financial self-sufficiency taking a back seat to meeting current needs.

A newer organization, DKT International, of which I serve as the executive head, funds some of its own programs and focuses on large markets, normally countries with populations of more than 50 million people. DKT's policies are otherwise similar to PSI's.

The other important international intermediary organization has been SOMARC, a consortium of private organizations headed by The Futures Group of Glastonbury, Connecticut. For twelve years consecutively SOMARC (and its predecessor at Futures, the International Contraceptive Social Marketing Program) were awarded the central Washington-based USAID social marketing contract.[3] Its activities centered on "new-breed" social marketing experiments that include the manufacturer's model described more fully in Appendix 1. SOMARC's focus, unlike PSI's, was to experiment with new approaches to social marketing, with somewhat less attention to reaching large numbers of beneficiaries. Under USAID's centralized (and firm) direction, SOMARC invested a good deal of effort in experimenting with "self-sufficient" models, a policy that has tilted it toward some of the more advanced developing markets, like Turkey, Mexico, and Morocco. SOMARC has also provided technical assistance to family planning associations such as the Sri Lankan FPA, and to the Contraceptive Retail Sales Company in Nepal. Through its consortium partner Porter, Novelli, SOMARC played a pivotal role in reorganizing and briefly reviving the project in Egypt in 1994.

In the mid-1990s, PSI was managing programs that provided contraceptive services to approximately six million couples; DKT and SOMARC were each managing programs that provided services to between two and three million couples.

Other intermediaries are Marie Stopes International, Tim Black's London-based charity that specializes in clinic-based services in the United Kingdom and in numerous developing countries, and that also has done important social marketing work in India and Uganda. International Family Health (London) also has performed some program design work for social marketing and has supplied assistance to other organizations working on social marketing programs.

Earlier, under contract to USAID in the 1970s, several organizations were instrumental in getting new social marketing programs started. These include Westinghouse Health Systems, a branch of Westinghouse Electric that started social marketing programs in Jamaica and Nepal; Juarez and Associates, which launched the project in Guatemala; Development Associates, Incorporated, which began the social marketing project in El Salvador; and Triton Corporation, which kicked off the Honduran program and served as the intermediary group in Egypt for several years.

Finally, mention should be made of the Swedish RFSU, the family planning and sex education organization based in Stockholm. The RFSU initiated several contraceptive marketing campaigns in Europe that have played a catalytic role in less-developed-country (LDC) social marketing. While they have generally sold their contraceptives on a for-profit basis, their innovative marketing efforts have inspired many imitators. A notable example of their success was the "Black Jack" condom ad campaign. Black Jack was a black condom that was represented by a cartoon penis character with a devilish grin; in animated cartoon form he was shown becoming erect and then pulling a condom down over his "body." The black color and the rakish demeanor of the Black Jack penis were wildly popular in Sweden and sparked social marketers and other family planners to enliven their campaigns. See Figure 4.1.

How to Be a Good International Implementing Organization

A few key steps can help ensure success for an implementing organization.

Measure your results and publish them. All family planning organizations should do this, and practically none does. If you publish your CYPs (couple years of protection), your costs, and your costs per CYP you will find it has a highly felicitous impact on what you actually accomplish, because everyone in the organization will know that these measurement yardsticks are important and will work to improve them.

The format does not matter. It is unimportant whether sales (or clinic procedures) are translated into couple years of protection or whether output is described in some other way. What matters is that objective output criteria be established and published, and that costs, which may sometimes need to be estimated, be cited and compared with output. All

Figure 4.1

Sweden's Black Jack condom helped inspire wry humor in social marketing promotions.

family planning service organizations would benefit greatly from this process.

Get a soul. An important ingredient of publishing output and cost/output information is having convictions about what you want to do specifically and what you want to accomplish in the world. Organizations that do what they do primarily to benefit from government contracts for these services are not, in the long run, as effective as they could be. Having convictions does not mean quarreling with donors (though that may occasionally be appropriate) or failing to carry out a donor's mandate. It does mean believing in what you are doing, not just getting contracts. The major donors generally welcome at least some level of professional conviction on subjects relating to family planning and AIDS prevention, though I confess they have not always welcomed the degree of determination—some would say cantankerousness—that I myself have sometimes brought to the table.

Do not become a proposal factory. Too many organizations that make their living from government contracts consider the winning of the contract to be the end point in defining success. This is a dreadful trap. If you break out the champagne every time you win another grant or contract, rather than when you actually accomplish something useful, your vision and your corporate persona are in grave danger of disfigurement. The success of organizations conducting socially motivated service programs is measured in how successful their programs are, not how much income they can generate.

Measure yourself against the best. If you are in the business of providing family planning services, do not be satisfied with desultory service, small numbers, and high costs per CYP. Standards exist; social marketing statistics are well documented, both in the DKT annual statistical reviews and in annual SOMARC sales reports. DKT's reports contain charts that show total CYPs for all significant (over ten thousand CYPs) programs as well as CYPs as a percentage of target markets (prevalence). If you use Bangladesh, Colombia, and Jamaica as standards for your programs (all three have consistently served 10 percent of their markets for a good many years), you will have set your sights high, and yours will be a better organization for it.

Persist. Both donors and host governments can occasionally be bullies. Host governments in particular often want to make sure you know who is boss. The Bangladesh program was closed down for several months some years ago for little reason other than that the government wanted to make sure social marketing program management knew that the government was still in charge. The Vietnamese government shut down the DKT project for six months in 1994, probably for the same underlying reason. The Egyptian government has imposed its authority rather imperiously on several occasions. So has the Indian government. Donors, too, will sometimes try to impose their will beyond appropriate boundaries. Under these circumstances you must persist and you must stand by your principles. Professionals working together can iron out problems and solve project dilemmas. But do not allow yourself to be bullied. This is sometimes a fine line. When your principles are challenged you may need to be polite but firm, you may need to agree nominally to do some things you hope you won't have to do, or otherwise compromise. But do not compromise to the point where you undermine your own principles, or you will find that you are demeaned as a person and your project is diminished as a result.

Have fun. You get to devote at least half your time to a marketing and selling activity that is essentially enjoyable, and no one is asking you to make a profit! This ought to be very gratifying, and for the best managers it is. So don't forget to enjoy yourself, to celebrate your successes, and to include your donors and your government counterparts in those celebrations.

Competing and Cooperating

A (usually) healthy spirit of competition among PSI, SOMARC, and DKT has kindled a creative tug-of-war for ideas as well as for social marketing territory. While the competition for funding can be intense (and occasionally turns bitter), cooperation is also possible. Both DKT and SO-

MARC operate in the Philippines, for example, without serious problems. Further, the philosophical competition has been a stimulating addition to both the literature and the dialogue on where social marketing should go and what it should accomplish. Indeed, the competition for ideas in contraceptive social marketing has been an important impetus behind this book.

GOVERNMENT FUNDING/PRIVATE MANAGEMENT

The great majority of international funding for family planning has been provided by multilateral organizations and rich-country governments to the governments of developing countries. It is easier politically for governments (and organizations of governments like the United Nations) to send their funds to other governments rather than to convey them to private entities. The UN agencies, including the World Bank, follow this government-to-government practice almost exclusively, and the effectiveness of their programs in the population assistance arena is greatly reduced (and their negative influence on economic development increased) as a result. This practice was reinforced by the Cold War, when governments—particularly the United States and Soviet governments—fell over each other to supply development assistance to LDC government bodies for political purposes. Mobutu's corrupt Zairian government, for example, received generous U.S. "development" aid in exchange for Zaire's assistance with American policy in Angola.

Another liability has been that direct government-to-government assistance, even when the recipient country was relatively free of corruption, often tended to make bloated bureaucracies even bigger and to further socialize economies rather than pushing them toward free-market reforms, thus undermining economic development. And, nearly always, government-to-government aid provides funds to governments to carry out programs that governments simply are not very good at carrying out. President Gerald Ford once remarked that if the U.S. government went into the business of making beer, it would have to charge $90 a six-pack for the product. He was referring to the fact that government operations are inefficient almost by definition, and he was absolutely right.

Social marketing is particularly inimical to government management. Social marketing sales staff, for example, normally get paid a commission based on the number of contraceptives they sell. The commission scale can often be a vital part of a successful social marketing effort, and the best salesmen and women often make very substantial incomes. This very idea is antithetical to government operations; it is considered vaguely immoral to have anyone on the government payroll making a lot of money. Indeed, some government officials have complained to social marketing managers that the employees of the private CSM organizations make too much money relative to the government counterparts with whom they deal.

There are many other reasons why social marketing is better managed by private organizations, but it suffices for the moment to point out that a modus operandi (social marketing) that depends on private-sector techniques and institutions is most effectively managed by private entities.

Very much to its credit, USAID, alone among the major donors, recognized this truth quite early in the development of international family planning assistance. For example, while the United States provided significant funding to the government of India for social marketing there (having lost the argument with the Indian government about GOI management), USAID also supplied funds for the privately managed test market project in Kenya. Similarly, while USAID gave large-scale funding to the government of Bangladesh for its family planning program, it simultaneously provided very substantial funding to PSI to operate social marketing there through entirely private channels. Few other donors were as forthcoming in the direct support of privately managed activities until the mid-1990s. There now seems to be wide and growing recognition that service programs are often better managed by private entities than by governments. The Swedish government, the British government, the European Union, the Dutch, and most notably the German KfW, all began supporting privately managed social marketing in the 1990s. Until then, USAID was virtually alone in supporting any kind of family planning activities through the private sector.

NOTES

1. PROFAMILIA (Colombia), Family of the Future (Egypt), PSI (Bangladesh, Nigeria) all designed their programs and took them to donors for support with no bidding. Country programs that were bid for include: the first Jordan project (now terminated). Nigeria/Sterling (project terminated), and the El Salvador and Nepal projects (limited impact after twenty years).

2. The implementation process in the present (late 1990s) USAID program for the State of Uttar Pradesh calls for approvals by the federal and state governments *and* by District committees (a District is a subunit of the state) "made up of representatives from the Government, voluntary and private sectors [that] will determine project priorities and activities in each district. The District Magistrate will head the Committee, the Society [called 'State Innovations in Family Planning Services Agency'] will work with the District Committees to help them establish their priorities, budgets, and goals" (State Innovations in Family Planning Services Agency [SIFPSA], updated brochure: 7). The mind boggles at the prospect of

getting anything important (or the slightest bit controversial) through this bureaucratic blockade.

3. The SOMARC contract was terminated in 1998 and was replaced by a new program called "Contraception Marketing Strategies," to be conducted by Deloitte Touche Tohmatsu, with PSI acting as a subcontractor.

5

"I'm Up to Here with Experts":
Selling Contraceptives in Sri Lanka

At the height of the famine threat in the Indian state of Bihar in 1968, I was working for the relief organization CARE. We had perhaps twenty Americans in India assisting with famine relief efforts in Bihar, a populous east Indian state. Working with us were perhaps three hundred Indian employees along with one or two Canadians and citizens of other countries. On a particularly frantic afternoon in New Delhi, where a senior government official was attempting to coordinate the relief efforts of his government with those of the many dozens of private organizations working to avert the famine, he said to me, "Thank goodness you chaps come out here and actually do some work. I'm up to here with experts and advisors, there are more than I can use. But I can use all you CARE chaps I can get. You roll up your sleeves and work to get things done."

As we have seen, certain visiting experts in India have worked hard and had a profound and positive impact on the country's welfare. But since that day in New Delhi, I have never apologized for going to another country and actually doing things—managing programs, selling contraceptives, providing nutrition supplements to kids. Yet most foreign family planners in developing countries have always been defensive about being there, and have tended to insist that they are only "advising" or "training" local counterparts, or otherwise behaved as if they have no authority or obligation to accomplish concrete objectives. In family planning particularly, Westerners are supposed to get in and get out, offering "technical assistance," "appropriate technology," and (sometimes) a certain amount of training and education, and then go home. This has always struck me as a far too circumscribed view of the role of foreigners in the world.[1]

The idea, of course, is that a foreigner should not intrude in the internal operations of another country. That is certainly true when it comes to interfering with the functioning of government or the political process, but I think it reveals a short-sighted view of the private sector. Foreigners, including "Westerners," have been managing commercial and humanitarian activities in developing countries for many decades, and it is likely that they will do so increasingly as we move into the twenty-first century.

Similarly, the citizens of developing countries are managing more and more operations in the industrialized countries. Several of the most notably effective officers in private American family planning agencies in the United States have come from India. The doctor in charge of America's largest anti-AIDS effort in 1995, a $160 million international program called AIDSCAP, based in Washington, was a citizen of Ghana.

To those who say it is perfectly all right for developing country citizens to work in family planning in the United States but not the other way around, I can only ask: Why? Is there something particularly gruesome about "Europeans"? Are (LDC) nationals so fragile that they cannot deal and work with outsiders? Even acknowledging the special sensitivities surrounding the "genocide" issue (the now-seldom heard and largely spurious argument that foreign aid for family planning is movivated by the desire to limit the population size, and, therefore, the power and influence of LDCs), I think it inappropriate and discriminatory to ascribe ill motives to all outsiders. And surely it is condescending to assume that the international exchange of managers should only go in one direction; Ghanaians and Indians and Americans and British and Filipinos are all capable of managing family planning programs (as well as countless other enterprises), in each other's countries, and, to suggest that the citizens of some countries should go only to "advise" is to deprive the world of both important managerial talents and the kind of potpourri of cross-fertilized management ideas that lead to ever better ways of accomplishing things.

Another reason I favor the emphasis on managers rather than advisers or consultants is that we seem to have something of a shortage of the former and a plethora of the latter. For reasons that quite baffle me, those persons interested in international development, and international family planning programs particularly, seem to have a bent for research and for, studying problems rather than working to solve them. The pool of available people who take pleasure from designing research protocols, supervising interviews, and analyzing data, seems to be much bigger than the pool of potential family planning managers. There are others who enjoy advising on policy matters and others still who most enjoy training. These are all important functions, but so, surely, is the delivery of services, and it is this latter activity that seems to attract the fewest international participants.

To me, it is vastly more satisfying to get out there and *do* it—that is, manage programs that deliver contraceptives or perform sterilizations or insert IUDs—than to analyze and advise on the many variables that go into understanding demography, epidemiology, and other matters related to fertility control. When DKT sends an American to the Philippines or a Filipino to Brazil, that person is expected to go to work, to manage, not "advise."

The process of getting started with the CSM in Sri Lanka sheds some light on this issue. This venture represented the first privately managed nationwide social marketing project (India's was a government run program; Kenya's was a test market in one region), and the first social marketing of oral contraceptives anywhere.

John Davies, a Canadian pharmacist, was hired for this assignment. John had owned and operated a pharmaceutical business in Canada before moving to the West Indies for two years where he organized the import and distribution of medical supplies for the government of Saint Lucia. Now he had become intrigued by the social marketing idea and the possibility of designing and managing a program that would show how it could work.

When he visited me in my office in 1973 just before departing for Sri Lanka (called Ceylon until only a few months earlier) he took due note of a scribbled message I had stuck on the wall over my desk: "JD—lose your autonomy and you're dead!" I had posted this reminder to both of us because the donor, the IPPF, had expressed some discomfort with making its funds available to us, an international organization, rather than to the family planning association in Sri Lanka, as was its usual practice. IPPF's discomfort had manifested itself in the suggestion that it might take an active role in decision making in the conduct of the project. We knew already that in a program of this kind the manager (or management team) must have full authority to manage the affairs of the project. This means hiring and firing staff, commissioning market research, selecting advertising agencies, designing packaging and communications, contracting with distributors, and doing everything else necessary to implement the enterprise.

If John had gone to Sri Lanka to "advise" the local family planning association, or if he had arrived with a mandate to start a program and the donor had subsequently peered over his shoulder on programmatic decisions, the project would almost certainly have failed. Fortunately, I was wrong to be concerned about donor interference. For two years we were given the necessary autonomy to get the program rolling.

Family planning activity in Sri Lanka was extremely limited in 1973. The Swedish government, through SIDA, had a family planning expert on the scene supervising research and helping make available relatively small numbers of condoms and birth control pills via government health department networks, the condoms being distributed through the somewhat imperious sounding Office of Public Health Inspector. The Family Planning Association's initial efforts at distributing and selling condoms through the private sector had foundered, and a large overstock of Durex condoms had accumulated in the FPA warehouse. No demand-creation for contraceptives had ever been tried. We were about to find out if contraceptives could be advertised in a conservative religious culture. Buddhism and Hinduism were powerful influences in Sri Lanka's daily life.

John landed in Sri Lanka in March 1973. One of his first acts was to hire Terry Louis, an experienced Sri Lankan marketing expert who would contribute enormously to the enterprise and subsequently to social marketing programs in other counties.* Over the next six months John and Terry hired staff, designed and contracted baseline family planning knowledge, attitude, and practice (KAP) surveys, commissioned a local advertising agency, completed pretesting and selecting the brand name for their first contraceptive (Preethi condoms), organized their packaging, contracted for radio and newspaper ads, contracted for the distribution of Preethi (Preethi means "happiness" in Sinhalese and Tamil, Sri Lanka's two main languages), and launched the product. For some years, this record—six months from arrival to marketing a product nationwide—stood as social marketing's "fastest launch" record.

John and Terry turned out to be an exceptionally creative and effective marketing and management team. They rediscovered that printed messages could be powerful even among illiterate people. "A common sight in Sri Lanka is two or more persons grouped around a newspaper with one person reading to the others," John noted (Davies, 1978).[2]

John and Terry were particularly imaginative in promoting oral contraceptives. They took great care to include the medical community in their promotional efforts. These practices in turn led to an ingenious device for promoting oral contraceptives. The birth control pill was legally a prescription-only item in Sri Lanka, and even though the pills were actually easy to buy in pharmacies without a prescription, our political perspective, as well as our relationship with the medical community, demanded that we follow the letter of the law quite carefully. John and Terry devised a newspaper ad for Mithuri ("woman's friend") pills, which contained a prescription form, including the big "Rx" in the corner, and a place for a doctor to sign. After explaining birth control pills, the advantages of Mithuri as a contraceptive, and brief instructions for its use,

---

*When Terry Louis died in 1990 at age 55, social marketing lost an especially skilled and enthusiastic proponent.

the ad invited the reader to take the prescription form to her doctor to be signed. While the system was readily susceptible to abuse, it combined the advantages of complete and accurate information with easy accessibility to a life-saving product. Mithuri pills have continued to be the most popular birth control pills in Sri Lanka to this day.

As the project geared up in 1973 John and Terry were determined to demonstrate that this new approach could provide both a quick and a major supplement to government family planning programs. They were out to create a project that *worked*. Their professional collaboration and common vision were enhanced by a growing personal friendship, and they had the authority they needed. They went about their task with a combination of professionalism and zeal that I have seldom seen before or since. The result was rapid success with Preethi. Sales grew to 3.8 million in 1974 and to 5 million in 1976, a record that eclipsed previous social marketing achievements.

The nationwide launch that put the Preethi condom (and later Mithuri pills) in virtually every city and major town in Sri Lanka, and the project's very early success provided dramatic proof of how quickly and efficiently social marketing could contribute to family planning in a developing country.

The Sri Lanka project, like PSI's first effort in Kenya, included a good deal of research. Pre-launch research data indicated very positive attitudes on the part of retailers toward family planning and toward condoms; pharmacists and other retailers approved of family planning by more than 90 percent. Most were aware of condoms and approved of stocking them; a substantial majority was willing to display them. In 1973 this represented an unusually supportive atmosphere.

Sri Lanka had other advantages as well. Even in the 1970s the society was highly literate by developing-country standards; infrastructure and logistics were in relatively good shape; the country was compact and most of its population could be reached through adequate communications and transportation systems.

All Preethi advertising and marketing was designed to reflect the joy and desirability of having happy, healthy children in the home along with the kind of satisfying life that the adequate spacing of births could enable. The theme throughout the two-year launch period was, "Until you want another child, rely on Preethi."

This became one of the early classic slogans of social marketing. It was used as a headline in newspaper ads that were accompanied by visuals of small families enjoying the benefits of birth spacing. (See Figure 5.1.) What made the campaign politically acceptable to almost everybody was the positioning of the product as a contraceptive for married couples, particularly married couples who either had or expected to have children. As the campaign progressed and the early reservations about advertising

Figure 5.1

An early social marketing classic, this ad was quickly accepted in conservative Sri Lanka in the 1970s. The slogan was adopted by several other programs, with a less exclusive focus on males. Reproduced courtesy of PSI.

contraceptives abated, more controversial details were gradually added. In the later stages of the campaign the use of such phrases as "Preethi is gossamer-fine for marital (sexual) happiness" became quite acceptable.

As we have frequently found in other countries, the only people who objected to the Preethi campaign were "elites" who said they were complaining not on their own behalf, but on the behalf of others. John and Terry report that

Interestingly, the only backlash from overt retailing and advertising of a contraceptive came from the elite. Three complaints were registered by English-speaking city residents, while the executive of a religious organization made a representation to the Ministry of Health. However, several hundred letters from rural residents, most of them written in Sinhala or Tamil praised the product and expressed thanks for making it and the instruction available. (1977:84)

Square metal signs bearing the Preethi name and logo sprouted all over Sri Lanka. On a drive through the Sri Lankan countryside and villages in 1974 or 1975, one could not fail to encounter dozens of such signs.

These shop signs provide a double benefit to a social marketing program because they let the consumer know not only that the product is available in that store, but that the owner or manager of the store approves of the product and is happy to sell it. This minimizes the condom embarrassment factor that seems to exist in nearly every culture.

Because this was one of the social marketing's earliest efforts, John and Terry took great pains to measure and analyze their work. The 3.8 million condoms sold in 1974 translate, by today's conversion tables, to 38 thousand CYPs (couple years of protection) or adequate protection for 2 percent of Sri Lanka's couples in that year—a very promising start.

The cost per CYP, that is the cost to serve one couple for one year, was just over $8. This is in line with later CSM programs and was about half the cost per CYP calculated at that time for government programs.

One interesting lesson that emerged from the Sri Lankan experience—and particularly relevant in light of the slow growth of social marketing in nearby India—was the importance of making quick modifications in the field. For John and Terry, the private-sector nature of the management team, its small size, and its focus on a clear and well-understood objective meant that decisions could be made quickly, and strategies could be swiftly readjusted in response to feedback from the field. They cite two specific examples.

The first was developing the retailers' role. A survey of retailers had indicated a willingness to display the Preethi product but considerable reluctance to recommend it. To counter this resistance to recommending the product, John and Terry designed a "congratulation kit" to be delivered to each retailer carrying Preethi condoms. The kit contained a letter certifying the role of the retailer as a family planner, a preview of upcoming advertising, and leaflets to be distributed to potential customers. This had the immediate effect of giving retailers a sense of participation in the program, of being family planning "experts," and generally encouraging them to more freely recommend Preethi to their customers. Tim Black had found exactly the same thing in Kenya, less than a year before. "Many shop owners appeared to enjoy . . . their role of 'resident expert' " in family planning (Black and Harvey, 1976: 103).

A second example of modifications based on feedback was the fine-tuning of the communications messages. The strongly positive response to the first Preethi newspaper ads, some of which offered information and samples, led to the development of a mini–mail-order business. Ads offering free booklets on family planning were placed in newspapers and were offered over the radio and on bus signs. The newspaper advertising was particularly effective and brought in nearly 22 thousand brochure requests for an ad cost of $1,400, an astonishingly low cost ratio. All respondents were sent literature, as well as a complete "mobilization kit" that contained information about the many advantages of family planning, a Preethi sample, and instructions for use. None of these marketing methods were new to Sri Lanka. On the contrary, the use of traditional marketing techniques, including the use of the postal system, was one of the program's strongest assets, conveying a quick and powerful impact.

PIONEERING THE SOCIAL MARKETING OF ORAL CONTRACEPTIVES

The project took an equally imaginative, but somewhat more careful approach to the social marketing of birth control pills. After all, this would be the first time ever that an oral contraceptive would be marketed as part of a national family planning program. After John and Terry conducted some informal market research, the word Mithuri, meaning "(woman's) friend" was chosen as the brand name for the pill. A test market experiment was set up in the Galle district in Sri Lanka's southwest, chosen because its socioeconomic characteristics were fairly typical of the Sri Lankan population—if anything a bit more challenging than average. Family income there was low, frequently less than US$150 per year. The doctor/patient ratio was about 1/5,000, also low by Asian standards. Informal surveys indicated that most private doctors supported the use of reliable contraception and, importantly, that "they did not have the time to educate and motivate their patients toward contraception and hoped that the program would help by promoting contraceptives and lowering prices" (Davies and Louis, 1975:1).

An instruction leaflet was prepared for each Mithuri package in the three principal languages of Sri Lanka (Sinhala, Tamil, and English). Each Mithuri package contained two cycles of pills and was sold to the consumer for US29 cents. Before Mithuri was launched, an introductory letter was sent to each of the private and government doctors in Galle district. The letter explained that the program would help to educate their patients about the nature and correct use of the pill. A few days after the letter was distributed, a personal call was made to each doctor by a PSI medical representative (a trained salesman with a background in pharmaceutical sales). The doctor was shown PSI's preprinted Mithuri prescription, the patient instruction leaflet that came in each pack, and *The Woman's Friend*, an information booklet that would be sent to prospective users and promoted in the media. It was explained that all of these were designed to save the doctor's time while assisting him or her to help patients and the nation.

Two months later, after the program had been launched, a second letter was posted to each doctor, offering a selection of journal articles concerning oral contraception. In the same letter, the doctors were asked to forward their comments and suggestions about the program.

This policy of including the medical profession as part of social marketing of oral contraceptives paid off handsomely.[3]

A few of the doctors' comments were:

"I wish you all success, since with proper availability of contraceptives we might see fewer butchered abortion cases arriving in the hospital."

"We are overworked, and can't spend time promoting family planning. With this programme you prepare the patient and give her follow-up reassurance for which we don't have the time."

"I'll gladly sign the prescriptions, but you should take the pill off prescription since none of us has time to examine the women anyway. Why don't you let the indigenous physicians [Ayurvedics] dispense the pill also? They are even closer to the masses than we are and have greater influence."

"Your . . . reprint mentioned the anti-anemia properties of the pill. My patients could use the Pill for that purpose alone, I think."

The result of this work led John and Terry to the following early conclusions:

Doctors will support and participate in a non-clinical approach to contraceptive distribution. All the doctors in the area cooperated fully in supporting the programme. They signed preprinted prescriptions, some of which were offered to the patient by the doctor, and some of which were brought to the doctor by the patient. The doctors' comments illustrate that they were quick to regard oral contraceptives not so much as a prescription-only "medicine," but as one method of helping to solve a pressing social problem which impinges upon the field of preventive medicine; that is, they saw that effective contraception lightened the load of such cases as infant malnutrition, pregnancy complications, referred septic abortions, etc. Rather than resenting overt promotion of the Pill, the doctors welcomed it.

Incentives by post can enhance continuity rates for oral contraceptives. The Mithuri programme has attempted to increase continuity rates in several ways. On registration, the new user was sent a copy of *The Women's Friend* booklet, free of charge. The booklet was accompanied by a covering letter which congratulated the woman for choosing this reliable method of contraception and informed her about side effects, getting pregnant when desired, etc.

Six weeks after registration a second letter was sent to remind her that she was well protected by a good method which she should continue; and that an attractive, little plastic purse was available only to Mithuri users, on the receipt of two empty Mithuri packs (which represented the purchase of a four-month supply). This strategy was intended to address specifically the problem of early drop-outs by reinforcing the OC habit during the first few months (Davies and Louis, 1975: 2–3).

Meanwhile, Preethi sales were approaching 0.4 per capita, or 1.5 percent prevalence. On a per-capita basis this was about double the rates of Nirodh in neighboring India. Despite this and despite our strong objections, the IPPF decided to take over the management of the project from its London office in mid-1975. The use of an international intermediary like PSI was just too alien to IPPF's normal way of doing business. London management would be an interim measure before handing the project over to the Sri Lanka Family Planning Association, which would fit IPPF's normal structure.

Since 1976, sales have grown slowly, reaching 7.2 million condoms in 1996, holding their own at 0.4 per capita, as Sri Lanka's population grew to 18 million. Pill sales increased to 750 thousand.

The brief Sri Lankan experience provided a rich lode of experience, conclusions, fresh hypotheses and, most of all, proof positive that a national, privately managed social marketing program could be quickly and effectively launched with a dramatic increase in national contraceptive use as the result. It reinforced our belief in the value of using a foreigner to get things started, and in the importance of managerial autonomy. It also demonstrated the importance of involving the medical profession in promoting the use of the Pill. And, of special consequence in the early years, the Sri Lankan experience demonstrated that the mass media advertising of contraceptives was possible even in a very conservative religious culture.

NOTES

1. Describing the contemporary tendency to send experts rather than workers, Anders Aslund observed that Ukraine, in 1996, was "flooded with [foreign consultants], more than can be used" (*New York Times*, Aug. 8, 1996, p. A27).

2. The effectiveness of written communication among illiterate populations had been documented before but had been largely ignored by family planners until John and Terry learned to take advantage of the fact that, if people are interested in a written message—a letter, newspaper, or brochure—they will find someone to read it to them. Today, as primary education becomes more universal, "someone" is often the child of a parent who needs help with reading. (See Cernada (1970) and Schramm (1971).)

3. The Sri Lanka policy was also an ironic precursor of difficulties encountered in the social marketing of pills in Bangladesh, where marketing and promotion were done somewhat more casually and with problematic results (see Chapter 6).

6

Social Marketing in Bangladesh

Establishing a social marketing program in Bangladesh in 1975 presented a huge challenge: the country had been devastated by war, was desperately poor, and was further burdened by very low literacy and the most tenuous infrastructure. By 1995, serving 2.5 million couples, the Bangladesh project had become the largest social marketing project in the world, surpassing the older Indian CSM project that operates in a market almost ten times bigger than Bangladesh's.

The Bangladesh project represents the epitome of the "traditional" approach to social marketing, employing imported, subsidized contraceptives that are made available at a price to the consumer that is below the cost of manufacture. It has been operated by two organizations, both of which are dedicated exclusively to furthering and maintaining the project and its family planning goals. The local organization, Social Marketing Company (SMC), acted as managing partner with PSI for many years, and took over complete management responsibilities in 1997, when PSI withdrew. PSI started the project and managed it for two decades before arranging the turnover to SMC.

The project is an unquestioned success. It has operated for twenty-five years, in tandem with a massive government program, and these efforts together have pushed contraceptive prevalence from less than 5 percent in 1975 to over 40 percent by the end of the 1980s, a performance Population Action International calls "remarkable . . . given the country's extreme poverty, high levels of illiteracy, and low status of women" (Population Action International, 1993:1). The project is also expensive.

Despite being highly cost efficient, with the cost per couple year of protection in the late 1990s at around $3.75, it is expensive for the simple reason that it is big—$3.75 per CYP multiplied by 2.5 million CYPs comes to nearly $10 million per year, a significant investment in the landscape of international family planning budgets. (These costs, like all project costs and CYP costs in this book, represent net total costs to the donor(s) including the cost of contraceptives.)

The project has been carefully evaluated and written about. It is the only social marketing program to be widely studied in American business schools, by way of a Harvard Business School case study (Rangan, 1985). It was the first project to make substantial use of mobile film units, a particularly effective and dramatic medium in a country of very low literacy. It was the first social marketing project to reach the "Holy Grail" of social marketing—the annual sale of one condom per capita, which it achieved nine times in the period 1984–1997. It is the only social marketing project besides India to have sold more than a billion condoms. It is one of very few projects to have employed a substantial generic, nationwide mass media campaign for family planning, and one of very few whose impact has been rigorously assessed through surveys and interviews. And it was the first project to carry contraceptive logos on boat sails (Figure 6.1).

For more than two decades, the Bangladesh project has exerted a substantial cultural influence on the people of Bangladesh. An entire generation of Bangladeshis has grown up accustomed to hearing and seeing daily advertisements for contraceptives, and to seeing contraceptives available in conspicuous eye-catching containers at a great variety of small and large stores. They have seen entertainment troupes promoting contraceptive products, and radio, television, cinema, and mobile film messages about birth control, reproduction, and contraception. Most Bangladeshi children have been regularly exposed to these messages while they were growing up, and all this to a degree that would not have been possible in most other countries, including the industrialized countries where children are "protected" from such information. But because the Bangladesh government was so committed to the importance of fertility control, and because the government (unfortunately) is such a powerful actor in the daily lives of Bangladeshis, the project was able to air contraceptive messages that would have been prohibitively controversial in many other settings. The contraceptive message has been spread well into the countryside by mobile film units—trucks equipped with screens and projectors that travel the Bangladesh countryside drawing thousands of people of all ages. These early evening entertainment events feature popular Bengali musical scenes interspersed with condom and oral contraceptive ads and information films about family planning and reproduction. The first five or six rows of the audiences, seated on the ground

Figure 6.1

The Raja condom sail has come to symbolize the use of nontraditional advertising media in countries of low literacy. Reproduced courtesy of PSI.

in front of the screen as the sun goes down, are invariably young children who have come to delight in all facets of this now very popular entertainment form in Bangladesh.

For more than three years, brand advertising for contraceptives was accompanied by a massive generic campaign designed to address people's concerns about contraception, to persuade them of the efficacy of birth control, and inform them about contraception and reproduction. Indeed, it is likely that a typical young Bangladeshi at the normal threshold of marriage (around age 15 or 16) is better informed today about birth control than his or her counterparts in the United States or most industrialized countries, with the possible exceptions of only Scandinavia and Holland. Discussion of family planning is routine: messages on the subject are everywhere; nobody thinks much about it anymore. And 45 percent of adult Bangladeshis now use some method of birth control.

It began in 1974, when PSI's: Bob Ciszewski and his wife Suni arrived in Dhaka (then spelled Dacca). The following is Bob's substantive and marvelous description of those tumultuous early years:

Bangladesh, in June 1974 when we arrived, did not appear to be a viable country. The war of liberation from Pakistan in 1971 had cost more than a million lives, while earlier murderous oppression by the Pakistani occupiers had resulted in the near elimination of the country's educated elite. Some 10 million Bangladeshis had fled to India, many of the most capable never to return. Nature added to the brutish beginnings of the country by providing a cyclone (hurricane) in 1972 which may have killed another two million people, and devastating floods in 1974 which fostered a famine in which several hundred thousand more died. It was a country with a shattered political infrastructure, and one with its agricultural base in shambles. Nothing worked. Poverty ruled. Hunger was everywhere. There were few essential services, and people were dying in the streets of Dhaka as well as in the villages.

Despite the heavy population losses of the early 1970's, Bangladesh was still the most densely populated country in the world (other than "city-states" such as Singapore and Monaco), with some 1800 inhabitants per square mile; if at that time all the people in the world had been put into the United States that density would not have been reached.

Few people believed that success was possible for a program which had to rely on mass media to cause behavior change in a population which mostly could not read, which did not have radios and for which television was a rumor. Why should they have fewer children? Children were not only a source of joy—rare enough any time and especially during those years—but also a kind of social security; sons were needed to care for the parents in their old age.

But we too often ignore the practical side of things. A mother or father doesn't need to be educated or very sophisticated to see that the difficulty of providing for a few is exaggerated by having more. People generally want a better life for their children than they themselves have had, and clearly that was out of the question for the average Bangladeshi mother, who was producing 6 or 7 children.

We felt the audience was persuadable, if not easily to be reached. Still, most of the involved people—donors and Bangladesh government—predicted early and expensive failure. (It was also predicted that religious leaders would not allow promotion and use of contraceptives. In the years that followed, essentially no resistance came from the clergy.)

From our temporary offices in the Intercontinental Hotel, I hired staff and tried to make the connections which would be necessary. We were required by the donor, USAID, to begin with rather extensive market research.

With the exception of carefully-managed and culturally sensitive focus groups or other in-depth studies, I have always been doubtful about making important decisions based on research alone, especially in third world economies. My reasons for this are pragmatic ones: I have seen a lot of misinformation generated by research developed and carried out by academics and persons who have little or no real connection with the people being surveyed. Answers are more often than not given to satisfy the subjects' perception of what the questioner wants to hear. There was a case many years ago in rural India, where researchers in one area noted over a period of years a consistent and surprising increase in acceptance of family planning and usage of contraceptives. Family planners finally fielded an effort to find out why this was so, to determine how the secret of this success could be applied to other areas of India. What the more careful follow-up survey revealed was that the villagers had reported that they were using contraceptives (which in nearly all cases they were not) because the young surveyors—college students from the "city"—seemed pleased with a positive response. Some villagers suspected, as I recall, that the researchers were paid more for a positive response, and it was considered polite and quite correct to help them with positive, if misleading, answers.

Sincere but naive researchers in other fields as well are often misled, sometimes by their own eagerness. An American anthropologist we knew in Bangladesh in 1977 was studying sexual and marital habits of local people and was having little or no success in getting them to talk. At a dinner party in the home of a prominent Bangladeshi couple he, always working, decided to come to the point, and asked the hostess if Bangladeshi women "liked" sex. She was taken aback by the question, as the subject was not one normally discussed at dinner parties. But knowing that foreigners were strange in habit, she considered the appropriate reply and, since she wasn't sure what impression a positive response might create, answered in the negative. When the consultant's report was issued some months later we were not surprised that a key finding in his research was that Bangladeshi women do not like sex.

In 1974 Bangladesh the issue of research was almost moot in any case, as no rural market research, as far as we could determine, had ever been done. Why? Simply put, because rural people had little money, and weren't considered important enough economically to bother with. Commodities sold to rural people were most often unbranded ones: sugar, salt, bulk tea, kerosene, cloth. The one big exception, cigarettes, were supplied by a monopoly which put the product in what was felt to be acceptable packaging and sold them at a "rural" price. Smokers bought. Classic questionnaire-based market research would have been of no practical value.

We compromised by designing small and fast tests, often based on participation by the subject. And we were always wary of survey results. For example, we tested a variety of brand names via traditional means, showing graphically a variety of possible names, speaking those names to the subject and letting him or her choose the most appealing. For condoms the clear winner was the name "Tripti," meaning something close to "satisfaction." It was not a word of very common usage by the man on the street, however, and I was uneasy about the word. Finally we decided to do a practical test by putting Tripti and the runner up (and very common) name, Raja, side by side in a limited number of rural outlets, at the same price and with equal display emphasis, to see which brand consumers would choose. This not very scientific but very functional test resulted in our selection of the name "Raja," which outsold the "research" winner five to one. I still believe the respondents originally chose Tripti because they felt the questioners—again, more educated "city" people—would prefer such a name; when an actual purchase transaction was made, however, they chose the one they felt more comfortable with. And indeed, to date people have bought more than 1.7 billion Raja condoms.

These kinds of pragmatic tests, combined with more traditional but carefully watched research, kept us busy until the official launch of Raja condoms and Maya oral pills in late 1975. The experiment to determine whether even in Bangladesh people could be persuaded to buy and use "popular" contraceptives was underway. We very often heard the words "if you can do it here, it can be done anywhere."

Bill Schellstede, a good friend and for some years director of the Bangladesh project, once said "Selling the rubbers is the easy part." He meant that in social marketing of family planning products the marketing obstacles, ponderous as they may be, are insignificant compared to the bureaucratic and political ones. Marketing experts galore were being created in the several bureaucracies, and it seemed that everyone who had anything at all to do with the program knew how to sell the products better than we did. Unfortunately, many of those with newly-found marketing skills were in positions of authority, and greatly added to our burdens by directing us to carry out this or that proposition based on personal whimsy.

We listened, as prudently one must, to notions about graphics and advertising. Why had we developed a logo showing a woman with her hair down? Didn't we know that having hair down implied that she was reckless and wicked? Did we want our product identified with the reckless and the wicked? And why use print advertising with a largely illiterate populace? (One answer: traders and shopkeepers do read and must be informed.) We listened to cultural "wisdom" about distribution. (Shopkeepers are greedy; we should distribute only door-to-door, or through post offices and/or police stations, where trained public servants would explain the use of the products and would never overcharge.)

Some ideas, those, say, of high government officials or of donors, we were forced to try. One such was the sale of products through post offices, a dismal failure which perhaps demonstrated that people want stamps and mail service from the postman, not family planning advice and contraceptives. Another was the belief that poor people would easily pay more than we were charging for contraceptives, and that we could triple our revenues by tripling our prices. After all, the reasoning went, there is very little difference between one penny and three. The result was an abrupt and dangerous decline in sales, and the prices had to be lowered again a year or so later. A complete explanation of this important price experiment has been published separately. [See chapter 8 and Ciszewski and Harvey, 1995.]

Perhaps the hardest thing to deal with was the widely-held opinion that there was something vaguely immoral about selling things to the poor. Particularly among the voluntary and international relief communities there was much talk about social marketing competing for the consumers' scarce money, and the possible diversion of resources from more basic needs such as health and nutrition to contraceptives. The poor had a hard enough time; to *sell* them products—for their own benefit or that of the nation was, if not criminal, certainly a demonstration of notable lack of humanity.

The combined effect of the variety of bureaucratic objections and obstacles was to slow the process of decision-making and the building of the network which finally emerged. It was frustrating, and in some instances near-disastrous, but since marketing progress could be seen, the objections eventually faded. Perhaps, we heard, it was not after all a totally bad thing to expect the user of the product to pay at least part of the cost of getting it to him, especially since he did it voluntarily and with a positive purpose.

SUNI'S "CLINIC"

My wife, Suni, at one time operated an informal family planning clinic out of our home in Dhaka. She was drawn to this effort by the terrible conditions of poor street women, and began to offer those in our neighborhood counseling, advice, and free contraceptives, which were supplied to us by the government. It was never a big operation, serving a maximum of perhaps 250 women at any given time, but was very important in the lives of the clients. It was also an excellent sounding board for our marketing efforts.

Nobody had ever bothered to learn what impressed or irritated the poor, who as a group were to be our major target. Having little money and hence no commercial importance, these people were ignored by commercial interests, and it was a challenge to try to decide what kind of advertising and promotional messages, or even what kinds of products might be interesting, useful, and in the case of promotion, not offensive. Suni's clinic provided a microcosmic look into the lives of these poor women.

We asked them about brand names. We asked them about packaging. We presented product ideas and educational concepts. One case I remember vividly happened when PSI was asked by government to consider including a spermicidal foam in our product line. A Western donor had given several thousand cases of Emko foam to the government's family planning department. We were intrigued by the idea, and decided to do a trial consumer evaluation with Suni's women. Government quickly delivered a few cases to the house.

The product was of high quality and was popular in America. Packed under pressure in a tin, it was a rather sophisticated concept and turned out to be quite astonishing to the women. One had to hold a plastic tube (supplied with the product) to the mouth of the tin, press a button and fill this tube with foam. The contents of the tube were then transferred, via a plunger kind of thing, into the vagina of the user. This process could be done—in a modern Western bath-room—in less than a minute. But the idea of having to go through such a rig-marole in the darkness of a one-room hut with husband waiting impatiently was so amusing that the women literally rolled on the ground laughing. A typical comment about that product was that it produced a quite pretty foam but that by the time the preparatory process was completed, their husbands would be finished and asleep. We refused to handle it, and it later turned up on the open market for sale as a shaving cream!

We were able, and history indicates that we weren't very wrong, to change and sharpen many advertising and other concepts as a result of Suni's back-door clinic. The poor women we dealt with were honest and direct: if they thought an idea or concept was too strange or radical they let us know, and we listened. We very often concluded that we had better give the topic at hand a bit more thought.

I suspect the donors would not have been impressed with these modest and basic methods of market research. We never told them. Yet, given the times, the lessons learned from "Suni's women" were invaluable.

ADVERTISING AND PROMOTION

Social marketing uses advertising to a quite different end than does regular com-mercial advertising. Normally, an advertiser wants his product to capture a share of an existing market. Suppose you are in the food business and believe there is room for more competition in the canned tuna market. Your first task is to use market research to determine the size and demographics of the market—that is, how much tuna is sold, who buys it, etc. From that information you will estimate how much of this existing market you can capture. You design packages to attract the buyer to your tuna rather than the others on the shelf. You have your agency design ads to point out the advantages of your tuna over that of the competition. In short, you try to persuade people to choose yours over the others, and if you are very successful and capture a small fraction of the total market, you have done well. Social marketing has different ends, and that makes it considerably more complicated.

First, and most basic of all, social marketing does not seek simply to capture part of an existing market. Whatever the size of the market is, and whoever is serving it, we arrive on the scene with a mandate to expand it.

So the challenge of our first years in Bangladesh was to use our advertising budget in a way which would sell product and, just as important, persuade people to adopt and stick with family planning.

Because we were generously funded, we were able to use the available media lavishly. We knew considerably less than we would have liked about our target audience and about the reach of media in the country, so the freedom to use all media turned out to be very valuable indeed.

In our enthusiasm we strayed into promotional areas which at times attracted the wrong kind of attention. It was after midnight not long after we had the full campaign going that my phone rang, and kept ringing until I answered it. The voice informed me that the private secretary to the President wished to speak with me. He came on the line and rather quickly convinced me that it would be in the program's interests, as well as my own, if the President, who passed through one particular intersection every morning on his way to his office, did not have to see the several small but rather boldly illustrated contraceptive billboards surrounding that intersection. He would be ever so grateful if I would assure him that the offending boards would not be there at 6 A.M., when His Excellency was due at that crossing.

I was able to round up enough of the staff, and some few tools, to have the boards down well before the deadline. We assume the President was pleased. At least we found out that our ads were being noticed.

In another instance, we managed to convince the owner and pilot of Bangladesh's only small private airplane to drop leaflets touting family planning and our products. This was the first time such a thing had been done in the country, and it caused a sensation. Even the press, which had been alerted, was on hand to take pictures of the leaflets coming down and people scrambling for them. Unfortunately, many fell on a mosque and a nearby girls' primary school, and once again we were admonished not to continue this facet of promotion.

Still, for the first several years, we carried out a media blitz such as had never been seen in Bangladesh, and even those who complained about its lack of market segmentation and media discrimination have admitted that it worked.*

A year or so after the products were introduced, it was apparent to us that, left alone to plan and market, we could succeed. An assessment team from AID in Washington arrived to examine progress and recommend whether or not to continue. Their report was positive, and our contract was renewed. Years later one of the assessment team admitted to me that they had a mandate from the Population Office in Washington to try to find cause to shut the program down, as it was felt to be too controversial as well as overlapping other AID efforts and interfering with the implementation of the contraceptive "inundation" concept. In the event, the team could find nothing on which to base a negative recommendation.

As this is written, the social marketing program has been going on in Bangladesh for more than 20 years. It succeeded against almost universal anticipation and has prevented an estimated 2 million unwanted pregnancies.

And the country has survived; people are better fed and housed and educated than anyone would have predicted during the hard early years. Almost certainly social marketing has contributed to that most satisfying process.

MOBILE FILM UNITS

As noted, a special characteristic of the Bangladesh project has been the mobile film units employed to communicate the family planning message and to promote the project's brands. In 1996 there were at least fifteen such units traveling around this Wisconsin-sized country of 115 million people, each performing an average twenty times per month before audiences averaging three to four thousand people. Even allowing for some overlap, this means that the family planning message is reaching

*Market segmentation is the identification of specific "segments" of a market by (usually) demographic characteristics, such as rural married women, 18–30-year-old males, etc.

from 8 to 10 million Bangladeshis every year by way of this unusually popular medium.

Mobile film units are particularly effective in Bangladesh because the reach of other mass media is limited. Rural areas still had few television sets in the late 1990s. Radio reaches far more but its impact is limited; few things have the impact of moving pictures combined with sound. Bangladeshis can also be reached with advertising at movie theaters, called cinemas in most of Asia. Showing ads before the films is a common practice, and the CSM project has run both television-type spots and slide advertisements at hundreds of Bangladesh cinemas. (This is just what Nirodh program designers and proponents wanted to do in India in 1968–1969. Sadly, they were never allocated the necessary funds.) But nothing has compared with the success of the mobile film units.

The first time I saw one of these units in action we had driven at dusk into a market town to an open field that was used for sports during the day. The screen had been set up and loudspeaker announcements had been made about the coming entertainment for the evening. People of all ages began drifting in and seating themselves on the ground in front of the screen or standing in ranks behind those seated—mothers with babies, children of all ages, and men in groups, smoking and making jokes about the sexual content of the movies and advertisements that were to follow. Clearly many people had seen the program before, yet they were looking forward to seeing it again.

The showing began, and during one of the five-minute "educational" spots about how to take the Pill and how to coordinate the first use of oral contraceptives with the menstrual cycle, there was a short discussion of menstruation that included a glimpse of a woman's sari that had been stained with menstrual blood. This moment had obviously become an icon in sex education in Bangladesh. Practically everyone seemed to recognize it and men were nudging each other with their elbows during the moments leading up to the "bloody sari" incident in the film, making what I was told were very crude remarks on the matter. But the point is that everybody understood what was going on; everybody had already learned something about the reproductive cycle; and nobody was the least bit embarrassed, despite the fact that there were hundreds of children present at a performance that would include the open discussion of contraceptives and reproduction.

SELLING ON STAFF

Another unusual feature of the Bangladesh project is that it has relied for most of its life on distribution through salesmen and other sales professionals who are employees of the project, rather than on an independent distribution company. (For more on this, see Chapter 10.) When the project first got under way in 1974, Bob Ciszewski selected Fisons, a distribution firm in Bangladesh that handled a variety of pharmaceutical and nutritional products. Its salesmen called on tens of thousands of pharmacies and other consumer goods outlets, and it seemed well equipped to distribute Raja condoms and Maya oral contraceptives. Bob entered into an agreement with Fisons to handle the packaging and sales of these products, and Raja and Maya were made available to them in case lots; an agreed-upon margin was provided and the arrangement appeared satisfactory to all concerned. Sales in the first year appeared to be adequate, and all of us hoped that the relationship with Fisons would be a continuing and mutually profitable one. By the end of 1976, however, the sales picture was beginning to deteriorate, and Bob felt this signaled trouble ahead. It was becoming clear that Fisons was simply not giving adequate attention to Raja and Maya and that, despite the fact that their margins on both products were generous in percentage terms compared to those on their own products, the absolute amount of money they earned on the sale of the contraceptives was just not enough to hold their attention and to motivate them adequately. Besides, transportation and delivery were expensive, and condoms (compared with Fisons' other products) were bulky. In 1977 Bob determined that the relationship with Fisons would have to end, and that we should take over the distribution function through our own project employees. We accordingly ended our agreement with Fisons and began hiring the additional sales staff necessary to handle this part of the project.

To Bob's surprise and to my astonishment, when word of the decision to switch from the local distribution company to handling distribution through project staff got back to Washington, all hell broke loose! The ensuing brouhaha taught me a great deal about governmental decision making. I immediately got a call from Hal Pedersen, a family planning official at USAID and a major player in the contraception revolution being carried out by Rei Ravenholt and his team at USAID's Office of Population at the time. Hal was a man I deeply admired.[1] He had been one of Ravenholt's key lieutenants in persuading people in other parts of the U.S. governmental structure that the shipment of massive amounts of contraceptives to developing countries could and should be the cornerstone of the U.S. government's population/family planning program in the 1970s. This was a revolutionary approach at the time and revolutions are resisted by bureaucracies with some ferocity; government servants protect the status quo as a lioness protects her cubs. In justifying the policy of massive contraceptive distribution, Rei and Hal and a good many others had done proud battle within the U.S. Agency for International Development, the U.S. State Department, and before the U.S. Congress.

Social marketing was even more controversial. Despite the brief fling with social marketing in Kenya in 1974 (which had petered out before it went national), this approach was still very new to USAID. It involved not only the large-scale distribution of contraceptives in developing countries, but also high-profile, mass-media communications campaigns, including the advertisement of branded contraceptives, something that created many legal and political problems when it came to using U.S. taxpayers' funds. The atmosphere was tense, to say the least. One senior staffer at USAID went on record at the time stating that "the social marketing project in Bangladesh cannot succeed; and if it does succeed it will be in spite of and not because of PSI."

Throughout this process dozens of deals had been struck inside the USAID and State Department bureaucracies, chits had been called in, justifications had been created by the ream, and cover-your-behind memos papered the files of the agency, all to justify the modus operandi in Bangladesh.

When Hal reached me on the phone, he was livid. How could we pretend to have a social marketing project if we were not using a local distribution company? Without a local distribution company, the project could not possibly succeed! Without the involvement of the local distribution company, it would not even be social marketing!

Hal had virtually limitless leverage with me. He was a pioneer, a tough-minded revolutionary of the kind you seldom find in government service. And, of course, USAID was paying for this whole show and that gave me little room to maneuver. Among the many justifications that papered the files in USAID on the Bangladesh social marketing project was, I am now sure, a strong reliance on the argument that these programs would use a local distribution company that could eventually take over the operational responsibility for the project, and thus, at some point in the future, phase out the need for additional donor inputs. In other words, an exit strategy had been built into the justification for funding the project, and what we were doing was ripping to shreds a central component of that strategy.

Managing a project a long way from home has some great advantages. If Bob and I had been in charge of social marketing in western Pennsylvania, Hal would have told us to change the decision and we would have had no choice but to comply. But Bob and, most importantly, USAID personnel in Dhaka, were fifteen thousand miles away and were not so concerned with documenting justifications for the files; their focus was on making the project work. Bob was able to convince his counterparts at USAID in Bangladesh that this move was essential if the project was going to succeed, and we proceeded to take on the distribution function despite the dismay in Washington.

Subsequently, the project's own sales and distribution structure in Bangladesh grew quite strong. We were able to hire some of the best salesmen in the country, and a number of them have performed astonishing feats. Their focus, unlike Fisons', is exclusively on contraceptives.[2]

In 1982, for example, a particularly effective salesman named Mohiuddin Chowdhury hatched a scheme for expanding his sales reach by working with the peripatetic sellers of used bottles and clothing, as well as the "choorhi-wallahs," who move through rural villages selling glass bangles. These wrist bangles are considered an essential cosmetic by South Asian women, and bangle sellers travel in even the remotest areas. Chowdhury was able to persuade the Arats, or big men, of these mobile business chains to carry Raja condoms, and sell them in thousands of villages in Sylhet Province. This arrangement helped Chowdhury sell a record 5,285,800 condoms in his territory in 1983.

THE MAYA DILEMMA

One early problem concerned sluggish sales of the oral contraceptive Maya. The situation typifies the kind of mistake that can take place when decisions are made that fail to take local traditions into account. Bob Ciszewski tells what happened:

Maya was to be the popular pill, selling at a price anyone with disposable income could afford (about 3¢ per cycle). As the pill was an "ethical," or prescription, product, it would normally have been promoted to doctors and sold only through pharmacies. But doctors and pharmacies were few, and we were in a hurry. With some misgivings, I decided to more or less ignore the medical profession. In addition to being scarce, doctors were mostly urban, and something like 70% of Bangladeshi women never in their lives would see a real doctor.

So we did a minimal amount of promotion to physicians, directing our advertising and promotion primarily towards shopkeepers and consumers. We introduced a radio jingle which to everyone's surprise became extremely popular, with just about everybody in the country humming along. We sold pills into general and grocery stores as well as pharmacies, and placed ads telling consumers how to use the pill and asking literate people to pass along the information to those who couldn't read. It was well-done and comprehensive, possibly the best consumer campaign ever done to that time in Bangladesh.

Before Maya was introduced, pills were present only in urban pharmacies, which numbered only a few thousand. Now, with sales to shops booming, we had pills in tens of thousands of outlets nationwide and hundreds of daily messages going out via radio and other media pointing out the advantages of pills in general and Maya in particular. We were set to revolutionize the oral contraceptive business.

More than a year later, sales were acceptable, but clearly there was less consumer demand than we had expected. Shopkeepers reported that sales were waning.

We redoubled our advertising efforts, redesigned campaigns, questioned consumers, did all the classical things to try to find out what was wrong.

While we had not completely ignored the urban physicians, we had not included them to the degree which an "ethical" product like the oral contraceptive was felt to demand. And they were suspicious. What kind of pill sells for such a low price? Was this some kind of hoax? Could they risk their reputation by recommending such a thing?

While they were not enthusiastic, we had anticipated this. After all, our pill was not for the urban rich but rather the rural and urban poor, the women who would never see a real doctor.

Then we looked at the rural situation very deeply, something which we should have done much earlier.

The rural medical practitioner (RMP) or, as they are known non-pejoratively in Bangladesh, "quacks," are a formidable group. Informally trained, sometimes as doctors' assistants, military medics, or by their own fathers who themselves are RMPs, they are the *de facto* medical establishment in rural areas. By completely ignoring them in our introduction and subsequent promotion of Maya, we had turned them resentfully against us, and they were reacting. We learned of cases in which they blamed everything from menstrual cramps to sprained muscles on Maya; they were advising women to stop taking the pill, and much of the reason for the slow start of the product was that a lot of women dropped out after taking just one or two cycles. And since what the "quack" told one person was more often than not repeated to dozens of others, we were faced with a serious rural consumer revolt. We decided to act to bring the RMPs into our camp.

It wasn't really very difficult. A series of training classes complete with certificates of completion was planned, and over the next few months hundreds of RMPs were invited to the nearest town or city as our guests to learn more about family planning, Maya, and our program. The reaction was quick and positive. They were an important and influential part of rural society, and should have been included from the beginning. Since that time (and the training and orientation classes continue today) they have never wavered in their support of us, and have been a potent factor in the success of our rural marketing efforts.[3]

MULTI-MEDIA

The Bangladesh project is also notable for using virtually every advertising medium used anywhere in the modern world. In addition to radio, television, and print media, there was advertising on billboards, sides of buildings, and, notably, on the sails of waterborne vessels plying Bangladesh's rivers where much of the freight in the country moves (Figure 6.1). There were also traveling entertainment troupes, banners and buntings in stores and shops, advertising on scoreboards at athletic events, advertising on rickshaws, in schoolbooks, and on shopping bags (Figure 6.2), and, of course, there were the mobile film units.

THE GENERIC CAMPAIGN

Another important ingredient in the Bangladesh social marketing project was a three-year generic campaign that got under way in 1982.[4] The purpose was to motivate people to practice family planning. The message

Figure 6.2

The Raja logo is everywhere in Bangladesh. Over 1.7 billion
Raja condoms have been sold. Reproduced courtesy of PSI.

content of the campaign was carefully researched, the messages were
designed to address specific issues revealed by the research, and the results were carefully measured by before-and-after surveys. Manoff International, a small health communications firm whose president had a
background of advertising success on Madison Avenue, was hired to conduct the research and design the messages. The bulk of this effort fell to
Daniel M. Lissance, an experienced advertising researcher, who remained
resident in Bangladesh to take charge of this part of the project.

The first step involved research among urban and rural men and women, non-users as well as users, of family planning methods. Individual in-depth interviews were employed. A particularly productive technique was the photo sort, in which respondents were asked to sort photographs of local men and women representing a wide range of age, social, occupational, and economic types, into two groups, those who they thought were likely to practice family planning and those who they thought would be unlikely to do so. Respondents were asked to give their reasons for assigning the photographs to one or the other group and also to select the photograph of the one person they would most like to have as a friend and to explain why. This approach yielded significant insights into the reasons underlying expressed attitudes, and the interviews taped at the time provided some of the language later employed in the development of specific messages. As reported by Lissance and Schellstede, the research findings confirmed that previous information education and communications programs, primarily those conducted by the government, were able to generate almost universal awareness of the concept of family planning and relatively widespread awareness of the benefits of limiting family size. Yet the research also clearly indicated that these benefits had not been internalized by the target audience, and this lack of internalization was due to a number of blockages or "resistance points" that worked against the adoption of family planning even among those not desiring any more children. Chief among these resistance points were:

• The religious factors. The number of children a couple will have was thought to be determined by Allah and Allah provides sustenance for every child he sends. For a devout Muslim to make his or her own decision about how many children to have is, in effect, to enter into competition with God.
• Lack of communication between spouses. It was revealed that most couples thought that the number of children they should have and when to have them was not a proper subject for couples to discuss with each other. For a wife to initiate such a discussion would be unseemly in rural society particularly.
• Fear of health problems. The research revealed that many people thought that birth control measures of any kind were potentially dangerous to health and might ultimately lead to death.
• Ignorance about contraceptive options. Despite a high level of awareness of the existence and purpose of family planning there appeared to be massive ignorance and confusion about specific means of birth control.

Message Strategy

The strategy finally settled on was specifically designed to minimize these resistance points, except for the religious issue, which the government did not wish to be addressed. The communication strategy identified rural men as the primary target audience, rural women and urban

men as secondary target audiences, and opinion leaders and other influential persons as the tertiary audience. This strategy positioned modern
contraceptives as safe to use; it encouraged husbands to discuss the subject of family planning with their wives and to choose the method most
suitable to them both; and it stressed the personal and economic and
health benefits of family planning.

Further the message strategy encouraged information-seeking behavior
and directed those desiring additional information to an easily accessible
source, particularly three project-sponsored radio programs where listen-
ers' questions about family planning methods were answered over the
air by an authoritative figure. The strategy also positioned the adoption
of family planning as "the right thing to do" and as "the wise man's
decision."

An all-media campaign was developed to implement the strategy, consisting of a barrage of radio spots and films shown on television and in
cinema halls and on the project fleet of [then] eight mobile film vans. An
important component of the campaign was the creation of the radio serial
drama—a soap opera—in which the principal character was Laily, the
government family planning worker, a device which enabled the writers
to integrate family planning materials smoothly into the dramatic fabric.

In a personal communication, Dan Lissance continues the narrative:

A total of fourteen one to one-and-a-half-minute film messages were produced
over the three-year period. While all of the messages focused on the strategic
objectives of the campaign, they covered a wide range of issues and concerns
characteristic of Bangladeshi rural society, and did so in an often provocative
manner by, for example, questioning the hallowed husband-knows-best attitude
prevalent in this society, and demonstrating that ignorance of the importance of
family planning was not confined to the uneducated segment of society, but could
be found in high places as well. Thus, one spot deals with a teacher (a highly
respected member of rural society) who advises a poor rice farmer to adopt family
planning to better his lot in life. When asked by the farmer which method of
family planning he himself uses, the teacher replies "condoms." After the farmer
leaves, the teacher confesses to the audience that he lied, that he and his wife
had not practiced birth control in the past, but would do so in the future. The
spot ends (as all spots in the series do) with the line "I used to be a fool, but
now I am a wise man." In another spot, the village headman who doles out sage
advice to the villagers who consult him on a variety of important issues is challenged by his wife about his inability to control the size of his own family. Rue-
fully, he confesses that he heard the family planning messages on the radio, but
did not think that they applied to him.

A number of spots in the series took cognizance of emerging positive developments in the rural economy, such as the gradual electrification of villages, the
building of roads and bridges, women's income-generating activities, and coupled
the material benefits of these developments with the similar benefits that would
be derived from family planning. The minidrama format of the spots permitted

us to present the analogies in a very human, down-to-earth, non-preaching manner.

Because of the provocative nature of the spots, all were carefully pretested among samples of the rural audience to ensure that they would not be considered offensive (impolite perhaps, but not offensive). After all, respected personages in a community are not normally criticized, let alone referred to as fools. Another line in the spots admonished viewers not to pay heed to "ignorant tales spread by ignorant people." Who were these "ignorant people"? Community leaders? Religious leaders? The spots didn't say; the audience drew its own conclusion. While the impolite phrases used in the spots came in for some criticism, that criticism came, as is usually the case, from government officials, some of whom charged that "a bunch of foreigners are calling our people fools." And there was even an objection voiced by a member of the donor community that our portrayal of rural wives as obedient creatures who depended on their husbands for their wisdom in all matters, was counter-productive to a policy objective to uplift the status of women in Bangladeshi society. Nevertheless, these criticisms were not severe enough to cause us to change campaign strategy, and the slogans "I used to be a fool, but now I am a wise man" and "Don't listen to ignorant tales spread by ignorant people" quickly became part of the rural vernacular. (1996)

WHAT DID IT ALL MEAN?

The combination of generic advertising, brand advertising, brand promotion, and wide-scale availability of truly affordable, high-quality contraceptives throughout the country, in tandem with a strong government family planning program, has turned Bangladesh into a modern society with respect to the practice of birth control, even as it has remained well behind the rest of the developing world economically and in terms of health, education, and the status of women. Figure 6.3 shows the growth of CYPs in the Bangladesh program from the beginning through 1996. As can be seen, the Bangladesh project broke through the 5 percent "Success Line" back in the mid-1980s and has reached double that level, meaning it has reached a standard of success twice that which is considered successful in most other programs. Only Colombia and Jamaica, which are considerably wealthier (and smaller) than Bangladesh, have programs that compare with this record.

Note the sharp sales decreases in 1985–1986 and again in 1990–1991. The dip in 1985 was the result of overstocking at all levels of the distribution chain in 1984, a common phenomenon in CSM programs. In 1990–1991, the drop was the result of price increases, an "experiment" described in Chapter 8. The decrease in 1996 is the result of phasing out Maya and Ovacon pills, which had been supplied by USAID from the Syntex Company, and phasing in two new oral contraceptive brands supplied by Wyeth, the winner of the new USAID pill contract. Even in the best programs, such vagaries are common.

The project saves at least forty thousand lives every year in Bangladesh

Figure 6.3
Bangladesh Social Marketing Project, Couple Years of Protection (CYPs)

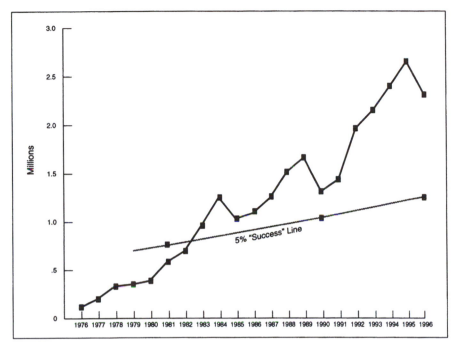

(see Appendix 4). It promotes economic development by giving families the wherewithal to plan their futures and their children's futures. It facilitates education by permitting families to space pregnancies and births in a way that will maximize the educational opportunities for each of their offspring. It has enormous beneficial impact on maternal and infant health, and it costs less than $4 per family per year. Continued support of this project would seem to be an enormous bargain.

NOTES

1. There have been sad moments in the writing of this book. I learned, while researching this and other chapters, that Hal had died in December of 1990. Another staunch early proponent of contraceptive social marketing, Moye Freymann, died in 1996.

2. Oral rehydration salts, a lifesaving formulation for infants and young children suffering from dehydration due to diarrhea, were introduced into the project in 1986. Small packets of this sugar/salt combination are sold by the same sales staff that sell the contraceptives. This appears to be a very synergistic relationship. It enables the contraceptive salesmen to include a lifesaving and relatively fast-

moving product in their arsenal, and it is a product that logically sells in the same outlets that sell oral contraceptives—pharmacies.

3. The Maya story is featured in the Harvard Business School Case Study (Rangan, 1985); thousands of students at U.S. business schools have examined and recommended solutions to the dilemmas here described on their way to an MBA degree.

4. This section is drawn largely from D. M. Lissance and W. P. Schellstede, "Evaluating the Effectiveness of a Family Planning IE&C Program in Bangladesh," Population Services International, 1993.

7

Why Brand Names?

A great deal of social marketing is done without reference to brands. Campaigns to convince people to stop smoking, or buckle up, or stay off drugs, have become commonplace in many countries, and this type of social marketing will no doubt expand as health and safety problems are increasingly recognized and understood.

But contraceptive social marketing is *about* promoting branded products, and there are many advantages to social marketing with a brand. Measuring results through sales is one crucial advantage (see Chapter 9). Here are a few more:

- Brands convey quality and build consumer confidence.
- Brands invite (useful) comparative claims.
- Brand names, especially for condoms, can become generic and facilitate purchase.
- Promoting branded products never seems patronizing.
- Branding permits market segmentation and image building.
- Branded products are easier to keep stocked at retail locations, making them more convenient.
- Brand advertising takes on the advantages (benefits) of the entire category.
- Brands help define and focus a campaign.
- Brands offer opportunities to play on words.

These advantages actually describe how much people of diverse cultures have in common, at least when it comes to consumer habits.

Brand advertising conveys quality. While many of us know intellectually that generic brands of some products are likely to be just as good as advertised brands, we still tend to believe that an advertised brand is a product of higher quality. In the case of condoms, for example, we are likely to think that Trojans—or in Bangladesh, Raja—condoms are significantly superior to just plain condoms, particularly if the condoms are supplied by the government or another social agency.

Brand advertising also lends itself to comparative descriptions, which further impute quality: "Use Trust, the Strong Reliable Condom" sets Trust apart from run-of-the-mill products in the same category and creates a good lead-off for a campaign.

In the case of condoms particularly, a heavily advertised brand can become generic, especially in underdeveloped economies like Vietnam and Ethiopia, with the result that embarrassment at point-of-purchase can be lessened. The Trust campaign in the Philippines, for example, was built around the slogan, "Don't Say Condoms, Just Say Trust." This campaign included a number of ads that conveyed the idea that asking for Trust was an everyday event that should simply be taken for granted (see Figure 3.2). Similarly, the Nirodh condom in India, Raja in Bangladesh, and Hiwot in Ethiopia all have reached the level of generic status, which provides definite point-of-purchase advantages. It is less embarrassing to ask for "Trust" or "Hiwot" than for "condoms," in part precisely because these brands are heavily advertised.

Brand promotions don't patronize. An often overlooked point about brand advertising is that it positions contraceptives in the marketplace as normal consumer products, rather than something the government or another agency is promoting as socially useful. Most governments tend to be patronizing by nature, and when they advocate family planning (or, of even less interest to the buying public, population control) their entreaties and campaigns are often considered by consumers to be a boring imposition rather than a benefit. For example, for many years the Indian government campaign relied on the slogan, "Two or Three Children Are Enough." This struck many ordinary Indian citizens as being quite beside the point when it came to their own lives and reproductive habits. Far more appealing is "Until You Want Another Child, Rely on Preethi," the slogan for branded condoms in Sri Lanka. The Preethi slogan conveys a substantial benefit to the consumer, while the Indian government slogan is preachy.

Branding promotes market segmentation and image building. In the Bangladesh project, the Raja condom was well established as Bangladesh's "mainstream" condom brand, and then the Sensation brand was introduced at a higher price to appeal to a more upscale market. (As is frequently the case, the "upscale" characteristics also appealed to low-income markets in Bangladesh.) In terms of image making, if the Sensation condom is associated with the good life in an urban setting (television ads featured a well-to-do Bangladeshi man getting into a Mercedes), this not only imparts quality to the product (like the brand Mercedes in this sentence) but simultaneously contains the important message that even the wealthiest and best-educated people in society use condoms, and their lives are the better for it. Similarly, some condoms may be associated with sex and sensuality (the Panther brand in the Philippines; the Kama Sutra brand in India). (See Figures 3.2 and 3.4.) This, too, expands the market.

It is much easier to keep branded (as opposed to generic) products stocked in retail outlets. One of the great advantages of social marketing as a way of promoting family planning is that it makes the product *conveniently* available. In Bangladesh, the Raja condom is available in more than 120 thousand retail outlets—from major pharmacies to tiny stalls and even crate-top "stores," consisting of a boy sitting behind a box on the sidewalk. These young retailers often sell just two products (neither of which they themselves are supposed to use): cigarettes and condoms. Retailers pay attention to mass media advertising, and they are inclined to stock advertised brands.

Brand advertising takes on the benefits of the entire category. When promoting a categorical benefit ("Use condoms to space your children"), copywriters do not have the luxury of particularized brand advantages. ("Use Zaroor condoms to space your children; Zaroor is manufactured to ISO 4074 standards.") But brand promotion does not prevent an advertiser's taking full advantage of the generic benefit—that is, if using condoms conveys a benefit, then using a particularly good condom conveys an even greater benefit.

Brand names generate their own ideas and identities and also facilitate the creative process. An oral contraceptive called Choice (India, Vietnam) means you, the female client, have a choice not to become pregnant. A condom called Protector (several African countries) protects you from pregnancy as well as from sexually transmitted diseases.

Brand names can also describe desired qualities or attributes, which may include plays on words. The Prudence brand in Brazil, for example, uses the slogan: "Use Prudence, it may save your life." In Francophone, West Africa, Prudence [Pru-DAWNCE] seems to have been particularly memorable. Steve Chapman relates this story:

Whenever I was asked about my occupation while traveling in West and Central Africa, I would say that I was a seller—"un vendeur." "Of what?" I was always asked; to which I would simply respond "Prudence." Of the hundreds of times I have said that, I can only remember one time when the person did not respond knowingly, and that is when I said it to a Catholic nun in Rwanda just a month or so after we started our project there.

Another example of the resonance of Prudence came in an advertising campaign using the slogan "Confiance d'accord, mais Prudence d'abord." [Roughly: "Confidence, of course, but Prudence first."] I was in Senegal—far from the Ivory Coast where that slogan was used—and was trying to buy something in the market there. Despite years of trying, we had not started a project in Senegal and thus Prudence had never been marketed there, though there is a fair amount of movement between Senegal and the Ivory Coast. I was bartering for something and the question whether I trusted the seller's claims arose—"Confiance?" I said "d'accord"—since that is a common phrase. But, then the seller said "Mais Prudence d'abord!" I asked why he responded that way, since that came from an advertisement for a condom in the Ivory Coast. He said simply that he knew that it came from a condom advertisement, that he had never seen it, but that it was a popular slogan in that market—1000 tough miles or so from the Ivory Coast. As an aside, that advertising campaign in the Ivory Coast won a "golden palm" or similar award as the best advertising campaign in Africa in 1993.

Indeed, I have said to African taxi drivers in Washington that I sell things in Africa, and, inevitably, the Francophones know Prudence, while Gold Circle, Protektor, and other brands from English speaking Africa are not known (Chapman, 1996).

Another brand name selected deliberately for its meaning is Jeito (Jaytoo) in Mozambique, the Portuguese-speaking country in southeast Africa. Jeito means know-how, or skill, with implications of fun. By extension the term is often used to mean a good lover.

This name created an "automatic" slogan: "So com Jeito," or "only with Jeito." The slogan has the felicitous double meaning of "[do things] only with skill/style," and "[make love] only with Jeito condoms." The slogan was easily turned into a memorable jingle.

DE-BRANDING

What if we couldn't use brand names? An interesting analysis of this issue was undertaken by a panel on behalf of the Canadian government. Seeking ways to decrease incentives for people to take up smoking, the Health Department commissioned a group of studies on what might happen if cigarette makers were forced to go generic, removing brand names and distinctive logos from their packets and advertising. The studies were summarized in a report, "When Packages Can't Speak: Possible Impacts of Plain and Generic Packaging of Tobacco Products," submitted to the Canadian Health Ministry in 1995. The study began by noting some previous work underlining the importance of packaging and branding. "For first-time purchasers, packaging is almost as important as the product itself" (Government of Canada, 1995:32, citing Opatow, 1984). "No single factor is as important at the point of sale as the package . . . [it] is the manufacturer's last chance at a customer" (Government of Canada, 1995: 2, citing Gershman, 1987).

The studies tended quite strongly to the conclusion that "de-branding" of cigarettes would have a depressing effect on cigarette use, particularly on the initiation of smoking by teenagers: "Plain and generic packaging of tobacco products (all other things being equal), through its impact on image formation and retention, recall and recognition, knowledge, and consumer attitudes and perceived utilities, would likely depress the incidence of uptake by non-smoking teens, and increase the incidence of smoking cessation by teen and adult smokers" (Government of Canada, 1995:14).

These findings serve as a good reminder of just how powerful branding, brand images, and packaging of products can be. While the choice of any particular brand name seldom affects the outcome of a social marketing program, the exploitation of brand names through advertising, promotion, and packaging is an important and powerful component of the social marketing process. Brands have power. As social marketers of branded products we should recognize that we work with potent tools that must be treated with respect.

WHAT'S IN A NAME?

Much heat and many research dollars have gone into the selection of brand names for social marketing products, especially condoms. Donors, implementing agencies, and government officials have argued at some length the relative merits of a condom brand name that means "shield" in the local language, as against something a little more macho like "panther." Focus groups and other research on customer preferences for brand names have been part of social marketing projects' start-up activities for decades. The early 1990s saw an especially heated controversy about brand names for condoms intended primarily for AIDS prevention, as opposed to those positioned as family-planning products.

In the early days of social marketing, brand names were selected with some care. Social marketing's first product, Nirodh, means "shield" or "protection" in Hindi, India's most widely spoken language. The carefully considered Sathi in Pakistan ("companion"), Preethi in Sri Lanka ("happiness"), Dhaal in Nepal ("shield"), and Raja in Bangladesh ("king" or "prince") are all respected major condom brands in the social marketing panoply, and all have meanings related, at least tangentially, to their purpose. So do Protector (Niger, Togo, Uganda, Zimbabwe), and Protektor (Bolivia, Mexico).

Branding focused on desirable human attributes has also gained popularity. Prudence is sold in Côte d'Ivorie, Zaire, Burkina Faso, Cameroon, and Brazil. Trust is sold in the Philippines, Vietnam, and Kenya.

Animals have also been popular in condom branding, especially big cats.[1] Panther in Jamaica, Ghana, Sri Lanka, and the Philippines; Pantè (panther) in Haiti; and Mithun (bull) in India. One animal-related attempt that might have caused problems turned out to have a happy (or at least neutral) ending. Dan Lissance recalls the evolution of the Prudence logo in Zaire:

In Zaire, when we designed the Panther condom pack for Prudence we wanted to get away from the ferocious beast used in other countries and more in the direction of a nonthreatening, amicable pussycat. In the process we ended up with something that resembled a jungle cat only slightly different from a leopard, whose skin always draped the head and body of Zaire's omni-present dictator, Mobuto Seseseku. Some people had misgivings about that, but who knows, it may have helped more than it hurt. (Lissance, 1996)

Other important condom brands include Masti ("pleasure") in India, Piel ("skin") in Peru, and Salama ("health, safety, peace") in Tanzania.

Many of these are wonderful, imaginative names. But at the end of the day, it is what the campaign makes of a brand, rather than the choice of a particular name that seems to matter. The best-known brand of commercial condoms in the world today is probably Durex, a word that doesn't mean much of anything to anyone, except what the Durex folks have made it mean. Similarly, while the word Trojans (the leading U.S. brand) has meaning, it doesn't say anything about the attributes of the product. And it is hard to think that the English terms "Sweet Harmony" and "Wrinkle Zero" connote much of anything to Japanese consumers who, nonetheless, buy those as well as many other brands.

The controversy over AIDS prevention versus family planning helps illustrate the nonimportance of the actual brand name. Family planners had valid historical reasons for being concerned with this issue. In the industrialized countries during the first half of the twentieth century and beyond, condoms had come to be associated with venereal disease. Family planning campaigns around the world had invested millions of dollars making the condom a "respectable" family-planning product to be used by married couples. Family planners were, therefore, reluctant to begin promoting the traditional family planning brands for the purpose of preventing the transmission of HIV. Many experts believed that social marketers should introduce a second or third brand of condom to be specifically positioned as an AIDS prevention product, thus leaving the "family planning" condom unsullied by any association with disease.

As it turned out, these concerns were unfounded. People the world over use condoms to prevent things—whether it be pregnancy or disease—and they seem to have little difficulty using the same product for both purposes. Two surveys in Africa in the early 1990s (Kodjo et al., 1991; Harvey, 1991b), for example, revealed that a great many users of Prudence condoms used them for both family planning, presumably with their wives, and for STD prevention, including AIDS prevention, most often with prostitutes or other extramarital partners.

The dual, general purpose for condoms also has been widely reflected in condom advertising in the United States. A 1986 Trojan ad, for example, underlines both benefits: Trojans "can help reduce the risk of spreading many sexually transmitted diseases," and "the condom is the most effective method of birth control available without a prescription."

Another creative approach to the multi-purpose functions of condoms is seen in Figure 3.5 in Chapter 3. This social marketing Durex condom ad, part of a "manufacturer's model" (see Appendix 1) social marketing project from Kenya manages to convey the multi-purpose usefulness of condoms without specifically referring to either pregnancy *or* the prevention of sexually transmitted diseases. ("Feel secure . . . each condom is individually electronically tested to give you reassurance of maximum protection and safety.") This is a particularly common approach in markets where condom advertising is controversial, and especially in those markets (and there are several) where advertising condoms for the purpose of contraception is more controversial than advertising them as "health products." (This distinction is made, somewhat startlingly, by the *New York Times*, as noted in Chapter 3.)

So in the case of condoms the answer to the question, "What's in a name?" is "not much," as long as you *have* a name. Understanding of this point has been reflected in the process by which names for condoms are chosen in social marketing programs in more recent years. In Vietnam, for example, the first social marketing brands introduced by DKT were Trust condoms and Choice oral contraceptives. Both these names were borrowed from other programs (the Philippines and India). They were pre-tested in Vietnam against a few other names, but this process was fairly informal and not prolonged. Similarly, when it was time to introduce a second brand of condom in Vietnam the brand OK was chosen, for more than any other reason because it is one of the best-known and understood terms in the world today. (A variation, Okey, is used in Turkey.) Again, some pretesting was done, but not much. In neighboring Cambodia a new condom brand is simply called Number 1. Simplex is a new condom in Indonesia. From these names and other evidence, one gets the feeling that managers just aren't agonizing over the choice of condom brand names anymore. A few have been picked almost whimsically, and they're doing fine.

"POLITICAL" NAMES

Brand name selection in social marketing can also be influenced by political and managerial processes that are just as unscientific as choosing by whim. Sometimes donors have simply rejected carefully pretested, first-choice names because they did not like the name the research panels preferred, and some program managers have refused to accept the decision of a focus group or a pre-testing panel. Again, these unscientific overrides don't seem to have mattered very much and may, on occasion, have helped. (See, for example, Tripti vs. Raja, in Chapter 6.)

This is not surprising. Most of the best-known brand names in the world today don't have any particular meaning, nor are they necessarily easy to pronounce or mellifluous on the ear. The coca that was an original ingredient of Coca-Cola is now held to be dangerous; Pepsi sounds like it was made up out of thin air; Marlboro was a duke, I presume, whose name became the world's best-known brand of cigarettes. Johnny Walker, Guinness, and McLean's were just people's names until the advertising began. So were Gillette and Ford.

There are certain things to avoid, however. It would be foolish to pick a name that has negative connotations, such as one that sounds too much like an obscene or profane word, or which might be otherwise offensive. The first choice for the condom brand in Sri Lanka was rejected because of its similarity to the prime minister's name, for example.

Informal surveys can eliminate some potential problems. An important part of the screening process for brand names in Bangladesh for many years has been the "Pius test." Pius has been a longtime and faithful employee of the social marketing project there, an office messenger who in the early days was frequently questioned about Bengali words as he made his rounds with hot cups of tea. Various brand names were tried out on Pius and his ear for eliminating words in Bengali that just "don't sound right" turned out to be very accurate.

I don't mean to devalue the market research that addresses these issues. Market research is extremely important in deciding how to *position* a brand (for example, as a high-quality import versus a low-cost, user-friendly, easily available local brand) as well as helping determine which product attributes are the most important to focus on. But with the exception of the caveats above, the selection of the brand name seems to be pretty unimportant.

ORAL CONTRACEPTIVE BRANDS

The brand name of an oral contraceptive is probably more important than the brand name for condoms, and greater care is called for. Indeed, the brand name was a central component of the controversy over lagging oral contraceptive sales in the Bangladesh CSM project in the early 1980s, a central theme of the Harvard Business School case study. The original oral contraceptive brand was Maya. Maya is a pleasant-sounding girl's name in the language of Bangladesh. It was chosen with the understanding that the pill would be promoted there as an over-the-counter product, available without prescription in a user-friendly and easily accessible manner. (The *medical* rationale for making oral contraceptives available without prescription in developing countries is virtually incontestable. Since the market for oral contraceptives in such countries consists overwhelmingly of young women who do not smoke, the risks from taking oral contraceptives are exceedingly small. On the other hand, the risks to women from pregnancy, childbirth, and problems relating thereto are, in comparison, extremely high.)

When sales stalled, as described in Chapter 6, part of the solution was to introduce a new brand of pill. The name selected was Ovacon, an English-sounding word that underlined the product's quality (U.S.-made, imported) and gave it a medical/pharmaceutical connotation. Ovacon and Maya were both marketed to the medical profession as well as to the public, and both have notched up impressive and increasing sales over the years. A third brand, Norquest, was introduced in 1991, and it is also doing well. Norquest is the unchanged U.S. brand name, for which no "localization" was deemed necessary.

Even though the brand name needs to be seriously considered in such circumstances, it is unlikely, even with pills, that the name itself will be pivotal in a marketing campaign. For example, the Maya brand in Bangladesh, though trouble-plagued in the early days, was no deterrent to its sales after Maya was linked to Ovacon and the medical and paramedical professions were included in the program. Both the "correct" name (Ovacon) and the "problem" name (Maya) subsequently have done about equally well.

Brand names for pills, like condoms, can evoke an attribute that may be useful as part of a marketing campaign. Choice was selected in Bombay (and replicated in Vietnam) partly for this reason. The marketing strategy for pills in those two programs focused on a woman's choice in deciding to get pregnant or not to get pregnant ("Your Choice provides you freedom to have the next baby when you really want it"), and this has proven to be a powerful theme. Similarly, Perle in Jamaica and Pearl in north India were chosen in part to suggest that each tablet is valuable.

But equally effective have been campaigns promoting unchanged foreign corporate brand names like Microgynon (Schering: Indonesia and the Dominican Republic) and Ovral (Wyeth: the Philippines and Turkey). Such names have meaning only to the experts until they gain meaning as a result of social marketing or other advertising/promotional campaigns.

So esoteric medical-sounding names do not seem to be an impediment to the social marketing of pills, at least in the countries where they have been tried so far. A "local" name does not seem to be necessary and it is even possible that the scientific-sounding names may be useful, particularly for those aspects of the marketing campaign directed at medical professionals and pharmacists.

A MAJOR CAVEAT: "COMPETITIVE" BRANDS

While the choice of a particular brand name will seldom affect the success of a program, it is extremely important that a brand be unique in a particular market. The most likely conflict here is with brands of products that are given away free in a government program. It is vital in such cases to differentiate inner as well as outer packaging, partly because government contraceptives, given away free through public health system networks nearly always find their way into commercial trading networks. If the inner foil package is different from the inner packaging on the social marketing brand, this causes no particular problem, other than representing (sometimes) lower-cost competition. But if the inside packaging (foil for condoms; blister pack for pills) is the same, the trade will become highly suspicious of the socially marketed brand: Why is the same product available, without the outer cardboard package, from other sources? Are wholesalers and retailers perhaps paying too much for the branded version? Enterprising pirates may imitate CSM brand packaging in order to sell the "leaked" government contraceptives. All this wreaks havoc with the trade, and social marketers will lose sales and long-term viability for their brands.

Social marketers who want to build real equity in a brand—the only way to maintain increasing sales levels over the long haul—must be sure their product is unique, or at the very least appears, convincingly, to be unique.

OTHER CONTRACEPTIVES

Injectable contraceptives are usually marketed under their original trademarked brand names. The only injectable marketed on a large scale has been Upjohn's Depo-Provera. Schering's Norminest (sometimes Norigest) was also getting started in some CSM programs in the late 1990s. The use of these names is usually a trademark and product registration requirement (though overbranding or "umbrella" branding may be suitable). Depo-Provera has been successfully marketed in Indonesia and the name has apparently presented no problems. It has also been marketed by name in Colombia, Sri Lanka, Nigeria, Nepal, and one or two other countries.

The IUD most commonly promoted in social marketing programs is one or another version of the Copper T-380 or CuT-380 made by several manufacturers. (There are several variations, designated TCu-380A, TCu-380S, TCu-200, TCu-220C.) The IUD is shaped like a "T" and is wound with fine copper wire. It is "overbranded" as either the "Blue Circle Copper T" or "Gold Circle Copper T" in Indonesia, and this combination appears to be quite satisfactory. The TCu-380A is marketed under that name in Nigeria. This IUD has also been the mainstay of the program in Egypt, marketed under original trademark designations. Organon's Multiload IUD is being marketed by CSM programs in Pakistan and China.

So my advice is this: don't agonize over brand names. Pick a name, get the product on the market, and then make refinements as needed. Avoid names with negative or troublesome connotations and do enough quick and inexpensive research to be sure that the name you choose does not interfere with or inhibit the position you have in mind for the product. Otherwise, don't worry. There are lots of things that go terribly wrong with social marketing programs, from the nightmare of a stock-out (running out of supplies after you have worked night and day to build up demand), to political roadblocks, to funding cut-offs. But the choice of brand names does not seem to be one of them.

NOTE

1. Part of the reason for the abundance of "cat" names is that USAID has for years supplied condoms with a stylized panther on the inner foil.

8

Pricing: The Cornerstone of Social Marketing and the Controversies that Surround It

THE POWER OF THE MARKETPLACE

Social marketing relies on the skills and energies of free-enterprise market capitalism. Making contraceptives easily, inexpensively, and ubiquitously available like dozens of other branded consumer goods gets them to the vast majority of the world's people with a speed unrivaled by any other approach. It is difficult to overestimate the intricacy and potency of the free-market system.

When I first visited Hanoi, Vietnam's capital, in 1993, I expected a drab communist city whose tightly controlled market would be confined to "necessities." Hanoi is no gleaming metropolis, but I was astonished to see—not just occasionally in a specialized shop but in great triangular mountains on street corner after street corner—stacks of consumer goods from all over the world: Cadbury chocolate, Lux bath soap, tinned butter from Israel, cooking oil from Argentina, Cuban cigars, Russian caviar, French wines, Coca-Cola, even Hewlett-Packard printers. These cornucopias were typically topped off with a bottle or two of Johnny Walker Black Label, perhaps the world's best-known scotch and certainly one of its more expensive ones.

The zeal to trade—to do business, to buy and sell goods—was palpable. Indeed, the energy with which people of all cultures trade with each other, buying and selling merchandise in transactions of benefit to both parties, is quite astonishing and utterly universal.

Governments interfere in this process at their peril. The result of such interference is likely to look like the former Soviet Union or today's North Korea. But left to their own devices within a framework of reasonable laws, people will trade their way to prosperity with extraordinary consistency.

Consider how complex this process is. An American supermarket provides an excellent example. Not only are there dozens of brands of commonly used products like Crest and Tide, Colgate and Ivory, there are also soy sauces from Japan, garbanzo beans from California, hummus from Lebanon, fresh produce not only from California and Florida but also from Chile, Mexico, and Haiti; French coffees, Australian wines, Italian pasta sauces, Norwegian kelp, sliced water chestnuts from China, Dutch beer, and tens of thousands of other products from every corner of the globe.

Consider the number of people and the ingenuity required to put just one of these products on an American store shelf: the Australian bottle of wine. Farmers and farmworkers must grow the grapes. Vintners must collect, assemble, and crush the grapes and put the juice in casks. Cask makers must make huge vats from wood and bands of iron. Timber and lumber workers must supply the vat makers with the wood to make the vats. Iron miners and workers and refiners produce the metal hoops that are used to make the vats in which the wine is stored. Other workers and producers provide the vintners with the additional products and services used in the wine-making process: bottle makers; cork makers; label makers; ink makers who produce the ink to make the labels; glue makers who make the glue to stick the labels onto the bottles; box makers; paper makers to make the cardboard for the box makers; transport workers; truckers to haul the cases of wine to the ports; stevedores to load them on the ships; captains and crews to move the wine halfway around the globe, loading, reloading, warehousing, storing, hauling, unloading, unboxing, sorting, and placing the wine on the shelf. All this for the customer, at a price of $7.

Now imagine if you will a "plan" for wine making, overseen by a central and wise authority, producing and bringing an excellent wine from Australia to your neighborhood in the United States for $7. It hardly bears thinking about. And it follows that the resulting wine would not be very good either.

PRICING CONTRACEPTIVES FOR SOCIAL MARKETING

Social marketing is designed to take full advantage of the free-market system. The distribution networks are there; the shopkeepers are there. Virtually every adult on earth is accustomed to routinely making small consumer goods purchases at a nearby shop or store or stall or stand. People are also accustomed to paying certain prices for certain kinds of goods and, in poor countries especially, are greatly constrained in the prices they can afford to pay. Setting consumer prices at the correct level is therefore a key to successful social marketing programs. Margins to the trade, the amount of money and the percentage of the selling price that the shopkeeper may retain as profit, and what wholesalers and distributors retain as profit are also of great importance, but if we do not charge the right price to the consumer, little else will matter. The purpose of CSM is to make contraceptives truly available—convenient and afford-able—to the great mass of the world's low-income citizens, and the right consumer price is therefore a linchpin of successful programming.

Despite the importance of this matter, and despite the fact that the issue of pricing contraceptives in CSM and other family planning programs has been well researched, the setting of prices has often been capricious and arbitrary. The research, and the results of natural pricing "experiments" have, as often as not, been ignored.

What has the research revealed about the pricing of contraception? Two reviews, one by Maureen Lewis (Lewis, 1986) and another by the Johns Hopkins Communication Program (1991), have surveyed the results of the research that was then available. Lewis reviewed fifteen programs and concluded that charging a modest fee for contraceptives (rather than providing them free) did not have a negative impact on demand. But she also concluded that price reductions consistently led to increases in demand and that efforts at "full-cost recovery" reduced the access to needed contraceptive services particularly for low-income couples. The Johns Hopkins review reached similar conclusions: lowering or eliminating fees attracts new users, price increases have mixed results, and large increases generally dampen demand.

Since then even more conclusive experimental work has been done. Experiments in Haiti (Donald and Harvey, 1992), Pakistan (Davies, 1992), and a review of twenty-four condom social marketing programs in 1991 (Harvey, 1994b) pointed strongly to the conclusion that overpricing of condoms, particularly, had a detrimental impact on the sale of condoms in social marketing programs.

A massive national pricing "experiment" in Bangladesh between 1990 and 1994 confirms and broadens these conclusions. In this pricing experiment, prices of condoms and pills were raised in 1990. The price increase had an immediate deleterious impact on sales and on the overall family planning program in Bangladesh. In 1992 the depressed sales levels persuaded program managers to roll back prices to their former levels. Sales immediately and dramatically rebounded and resumed their previous upward course.

The 1991 review of twenty-four CSM programs examined prices and sales per capita for all of the condom social marketing programs that had been in business for more than two years. Prices were assessed on the basis of the wealth of the countries in which the programs were operating, measured by per-capita gross national product (GNP). Per-capita GNP is a crude but consistent and generally accurate measure of the wealth available to the people in a given economy. There are huge disparities between low-income and higher-income countries; in 1991, for example, the per-capita GNP in Ethiopia was barely $100, versus a figure four times that in the West African country of Ghana and twenty times that in Central American Costa Rica. This means that contraceptive prices can be set much higher in Costa Rica than in Ethiopia and still be affordable to low-income people in that country.

Though the remainder of this brief section is technical, it is important and relatively painless. Each program in the review was assessed using per-capita GNP and the price charged for one condom multiplied by one hundred to represent a one-year supply. Thus, in Egypt the price of a single condom was U.S.2.2 cents; a year's supply of one hundred condoms cost U.S.$2.20 and per-capita GNP was U.S.$590. The cost of a year's supply in Egypt therefore came to 0.4 percent (that is, less than half of 1 percent) of per-capita GNP.

The relative price of condoms was plotted on the horizontal axis and the vertical axis plotted condom sales per capita in each of the twenty-four countries (see Figure 8.1). Per-capita sales represent a good proxy for program success—a rough equivalent of contraceptive prevalence indices, as detailed in Chapter 9. On the assumption that we wish to reach the highest possible percentage of couples in our target countries with family planning, the definition of success will normally focus on maximizing the percentage of consumers reached, thus maximizing contraceptive sales per capita. Figure 8.1 shows the relationship between the prices charged to consumers in these twenty-four programs (horizontal axis) and the relative success of these programs based on sales per capita (vertical axis).

The review shows four conspicuously successful programs: Costa Rica, Jamaica, Bangladesh, and Pakistan. All four programs had very low consumer prices, selling condoms at a price below 0.7 percent of GNP per capita for a year's supply.

There were eight moderately successful programs, with sales between 0.2 and 0.5 condoms per capita. All these programs, with the exception of Ghana, priced their condoms below 1 percent of per capita GNP, and Ghana's was just over that level.

At the other end of the spectrum, a number of programs with conspicuously low per-capita sales (for example, the least successful programs—Nigeria, Haiti, Kenya, Indonesia, and Morocco) all had condom prices in excess of 2 percent of per-capita GNP, more than double the moderately successful programs, and three times higher than the very successful programs. While a few programs reported both low sales and

Figure 8.1
Condom Sales per Capita and Consumer Price Index for Condoms in Twenty-Four Social Marketing Programs, 1991

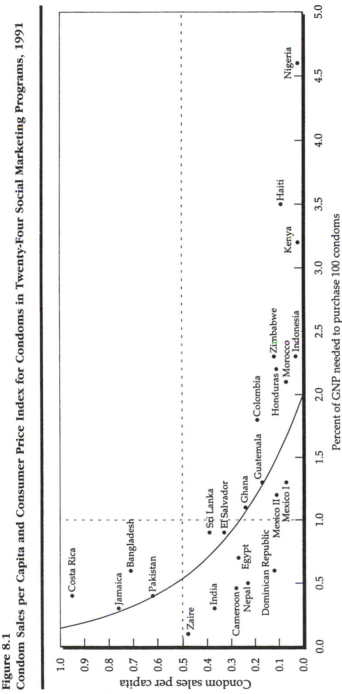

Source: Reproduced with the permission of the Population Council, from Philip D. Harvey, "The Impact of Condom Prices on Sales in Social Marketing Programs," *Studies in Family Planning* 25, no. 1 (January/February 1994): 54.

low prices, the evidence indicated very strongly that low prices are a necessary condition for satisfactory sales levels.

To an economist, of course, this is elementary; it should hardly be necessary to provide massive documentation for the general wisdom that if you charge less for something you will sell more of it, and if you charge more for it you will sell less. However, the persistence of the arguments supporting the self-sufficiency concept has been so intense, and the politics that support the position so persistent, that it has been necessary to demonstrate repeatedly that, in order to achieve higher (and increasing) sales for maximum contraceptive prevalence, contraceptive prices must be set low and maintained there.[1]

THE BANGLADESH EXPERIMENT

By far the most conclusive empirical evidence of this fact in a social marketing program was provided in Bangladesh. Two sets of price changes for the contraceptives in that social marketing program were made, in 1990 and again in 1993. Here was a classic case of a donor, USAID, justifiably concerned about the continuing heavy expense of providing contraceptives to a hugely successful (and therefore expensive) program, determined to find a way of reducing donor costs. The method chosen would attempt to recover a higher percentage of program costs from consumers—that is, by raising prices. Accordingly, in March 1990 the prices on two brands of condoms and two brands of oral contraceptives, representing virtually all of the products available in Bangladesh's social marketing project at that time, were raised an average of 60 percent.

In absolute terms, these increases did not appear very great to USAID or to program managers. After all, the new higher price of the Raja condom was only U.S. 1.3 cents, still very cheap by international standards. Yet the impact on sales was immediate and dramatic. In the twelve-month period following the price increase, Raja sales dropped precipitously, falling from an average of 9.3 million condoms per month to just 5.9 million condoms per month. Sales of birth control pills were less dramatically affected, falling 12 percent in the year following the price increase.

Massive efforts were made to overcome consumer and retailer resistance to the higher prices. The project's medical representatives emphasized to doctors the high quality of Maya pills, as well as their low cost relative to that of other pills; sales personnel reminded traders of the enduring popularity of Raja condoms and of Maya pills (the market leaders), and promised that demand would return. Nothing helped, even a redesigned and expanded mass media campaign devised to upgrade the products' image to more closely conform with their new prices.

As sales plummeted, the number of project beneficiaries (as measured by couple years of protection) dropped from 1.8 million in 1989 to 1.4 million in 1991, and this, despite a strongly established pattern of rising sales that would almost certainly have meant beneficiary levels of 1.9 million by 1991 had the price hike not taken place.

Compounding this tragic decrease in the number of project beneficiaries is the fact that the beneficiaries lost were, almost by definition, the ones most important to the program. The lowest-income beneficiaries, those living closest to a bare subsistence level, whose fertility is generally high and for whom the spacing of pregnancies is therefore especially important, were the first to be lost. These are the people for whom the increase of less than 1 cent per condom and 5 cents per cycle of pills represented an insurmountable obstacle.

Further, the terrible irony from the donor's perspective was that the cost per couple year did not go down. Despite the fact that the project was recovering more money per condom or per cycle of pills sold, the dramatic lowering of project beneficiaries meant that fixed operating costs became more of a burden due to the smaller scale of the program, and the incremental marketing efforts to overcome the price increase also increased overall expenses. So the cost per couple year of protection, the cost incurred for each couple served, actually went up slightly from $6.20 (1990) to $6.26 (1991). In other words, the only reason the donor was saving any money under this situation was because the project was serving fewer people. This was an outcome that no one desired.

After nearly two years of sluggish sales, everyone involved agreed that prices should be lowered. In February 1992 the price of Raja condoms was reduced to the level it had been in the late 1980s and, six months later, the price of Maya pills was rolled back to early 1980s levels.

The response was immediate. During the two years of increased prices, Raja condom sales had dropped from more than 100 million pieces per year to fewer than 80 million. In 1992, sales rebounded to 104 million pieces, and the following year, to nearly 125 million, reestablishing the condom sales trends that the price increases had interrupted. (See Figure 8.2.) Sales of Maya pills, with their new low price, reached 6.6 million cycles in 1992, nearly triple the figure in 1990. While this number fell in the following year because of a shift in emphasis to the Ovacon brand, total pill sales remained strong and have maintained a gradually growing level of more than 10 million cycles per year, versus 6 million cycles in 1990.

The results of price changes in Bangladesh were particularly dramatic, perhaps even beyond what might have been expected, because fifteen years of contraceptive marketing there had established certain expected price levels in the minds of consumers and retailers, and the new prices obviously violated those expectations. All the same, it is clear that exces-

Figure 8.2
Annual Sales of Raja Condoms, Social Marketing Project, Bangladesh,
1988–1993

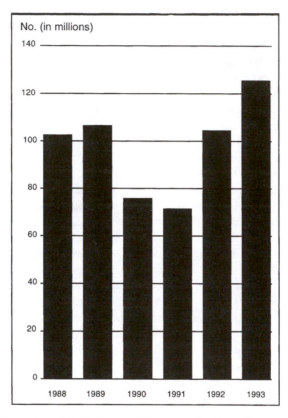

Source: R. L. Ciszewski and P. D. Harvey, "Contraceptive Price Changes: The Impact on Sales in Bangladesh," *International Family Planning Perspectives*, 1995, 21(4):150.

sively high prices worked against the most fundamental interests of contraceptive social marketing in Bangladesh during this period.

HOW SHOULD CONTRACEPTIVES BE PRICED?

We have noted that it is vital to provide retailers with a sufficient profit so that the commercial distribution system can be engaged, and I will address the trade margin issues shortly. First, some guidelines for *consumer* prices.

The experience cited here and other evidence from social marketing programs suggest the following rules for pricing condoms in social marketing programs.

Table 8.1
Per-Capita GNP and Purchasing Power Parity for DKT CSM Program Countries, 1993

	Per-capita GNP*	Purchasing Power Parity**(PPP)	1% of GNP	.25% of PPP
Brazil	$3,020	$5,470	$30.20	$13.68
Ethiopia	100	380	1.00	0.95
India	290	1,250	2.90	3.13
Malaysia	3,160	8,630	31.60	21.58
Philippines	830	2,660	8.30	6.65
Vietnam	170	1,040	1.70	2.60

Sources: *From Population Reference Bureau Population Data Sheet—1995 (GNP from 1993). **From World Bank, World Development Report 1995.

1. A year's supply should cost *less* than 1 percent of per capita of gross national product.[2] A year's supply is one hundred condoms (see Chapter 9). This means that if the per-capita GNP of the country where you are working is $350 per year, a year's supply of condoms should not cost more than $3.50, which means that the cost per condom to the customer should not exceed 3.5 cents. I believe this is the absolute maximum. For optimum sales prospects, I recommend pricing at or below 0.7 percent of GNP. In any case, 1 percent of GNP is the absolute maximum for condoms.

2. Check the Purchasing Power Parity (PPP) comparison figures from the World Bank. (See for example, the World Bank's "World Development Report 1995.") This index reflects a somewhat more sophisticated economic analysis of purchasing power, taking into account the prices of necessities and other goods in each country as well as the total amount of wealth in the economy. The PPP figures are typically 3 to 4 times higher than per-capita GNP for developing countries, and I recommend that condoms be priced below 0.25 percent of PPP for a year's supply. The differences between the two indices can sometimes be significant. For example, Table 8.1 shows per-capita GNP and Purchasing Power Parity for the six DKT programs operating in 1993. It shows that in India, Ethiopia, and Vietnam, the GNP and PPP figures are pretty much in line with each other. That is, if the < 1 percent GNP standard is met, the < 0.25 percent PPP standard (my recommendation) is also met. However, in Brazil and Malaysia, there is a noticeable difference between the two indices. In Brazil, the 1993 price for the Prudence condom (which was 18 cents per condom = $18.00 per year) is well under the pricing standard for per-capita GNP (0.6 percent) but is significantly over the allowable maximum on the PPP scale. This means that in Brazil, while per-capita GNP is much higher than it is in most developing countries, the cost of many necessities is also very high. So

purchasing power available to Brazilian citizens is significantly less than would be indicated on the basis of per-capita GNP alone. The same pattern holds in Malaysia, another relatively wealthy developing country where condoms could be priced at 30 cents on the GNP guideline but only 20 cents according to the PPP indicator.

Both the GNP and PPP yardsticks should be checked, if possible (PPP figures are not available for all countries) and prices kept at or below the lower of these two guidelines ($<$ 1 percent of per-capita GNP; $<$ 0.25 percent of PPP). A less conservative guide is to price between the two standards when they are significantly different.

3. Check prices of everyday consumer items purchased by ordinary people. If a cup of tea at a working man's tea stall costs the equivalent of U.S. 3 cents and low-income people are accustomed to routinely paying this amount, then this will help guide your decision about the pricing of condoms, which are also often purchased casually and in small quantities. What is the price of a single cigarette (or cigarettes, in the quantities normally purchased by low-income people)? A bottle of beer at an open-market kiosk? A box of matches? These are important indicators of what your target market can afford to pay for contraceptives.

4. What are the country's single coin units? If there is a common coin that represents the price of your condom packet, whether that packet contains two, three, or four condoms, this will facilitate purchase.

5. What are the margins necessary to involve the trade? The first four standards here help define the *maximum* price that can be charged. There is also a minimum. The consumer must pay at least enough to provide the retailer and any middlemen with an adequate profit margin to keep them involved and interested.

   However, there is seldom any conflict between pricing for maximum sales and pricing for adequate trade margins. For one thing, retailers and distributors appreciate the profitability of rapid turnover. They recognize that a low-priced product for which there is a demand, particularly if that demand is stimulated through mass media advertising, will result in brisk sales, and they are therefore likely to be happy with their normal margins even though the CSM products are very low-priced. Figure 8.3 gives some typical margin structures from selected social marketing projects. Note that for all of these margin structures the initial sale to the trade represents a significant portion of what the consumer pays—that is, none of these programs (and no program anywhere that I am aware of) has reduced the price to the first tier of trade to the level of insignificance. This seems not to be necessary to meet affordability guidelines. A general rule of thumb has been that the price by the project to the first trade layer is roughly half the price ultimately paid by the consumer. Another way to put this: if you sell your condoms to the trade for 2 cents each, the likely price to the consumer is 4 cents, with the difference providing appropriate margins to the trade.

6. A simplified summary of all these rules: if you sell your condoms to the consumer for a (U.S.) penny or less, your condoms will probably be affordable

Figure 8.3
Amounts Retained/Charged by All Parties in Three Social Marketing
Programs

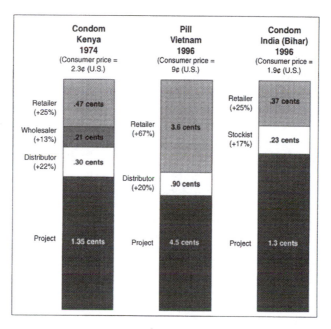

anywhere. In Asia, 2 cents per piece is probably safe, except for Bangladesh, Bhutan, and Nepal. For most of Latin America and the Caribbean, 10 cents is probably reasonable For Africa, check the charts.

It should be noted here that the contraceptives—especially condoms—will not always be sold at the price you set. Especially when condoms are sold outside pharmacies, retailers are naturally inclined to charge what the market will bear. It is generally true, for example, that the price of condoms at a kiosk outside a brothel at ten o'clock at night will cost significantly more than the same product sold under more routine circumstances. In some countries, marking the price on the package and advertising it is sufficient to keep the consumer price down to the desired level. But if you want to be sure what your customers are actually paying, send out "mystery shoppers" to various kinds of retail outlets, at different times of the day to make purchases.

PRICING ORAL CONTRACEPTIVES

Pills appear to be somewhat less price-sensitive than condoms. In general, the guidelines for GNP per capita and the PPP index should be observed, but with a little more flexibility. While condoms should be priced below 0.7 percent of per-capita GNP for a year's supply, 1 percent of per-capita GNP for pills seems likely to be acceptable. In Bangladesh, both Maya at 0.3 percent of per-capita GNP (for a year's supply of thirteen cycles) and Ovacon at 1 percent of per-capita GNP are doing well in the 1990s. In Vietnam, Choice pills sell very briskly at 0.7 percent of per-capita GNP. Colombia's Eugynon does just fine at 1 percent of GNP. Perle in Jamaica sells well at 0.9 percent. Microgynon in the Dominican Republic is priced at the high end of the range, 1.4 percent, but still does well.

Also relevant is the fact that the impact of the price increase on pills in Bangladesh, described above, was noticeably less dramatic than it was on condoms. Bob Ciszewski observed:

In recognizing the different effects of the price increases on condom versus pill sales, two factors are of primary importance. First, the condom is very often the contraceptive choice of the poor. It requires a small individual outlay (poor people are accustomed to buying a single cigarette, 100 grams of fish or meat, etc.) and is perceived as something which can be bought only when needed. Also, there is a much greater tendency for condoms to be purchased casually, on impulse, by people for whom the alternative to contraception (i.e., the possibility of a pregnancy) may not be perceived as a pressing or unduly negative prospect. Further, pill users may have a greater tendency to maintain use of the product because it requires both consistent motivation and a regimen which users may not wish to interrupt. Discontinuation of pills often results in physiological changes such as less regular menstruation, which may not be desired. The fact that women have a greater influence over pill purchases than over condom buying probably contributed to this trend. . . . Pill use overall, therefore, probably has a stronger built-in inertia to change than condom use. (Ciszewski and Harvey, 1994: 33)

PRICING OTHER CONTRACEPTIVES

A growing and substantial percentage of CYPs delivered through social marketing is being provided by IUDs and injectable contraceptives. The social marketing of IUDs was particularly and notably successful in Egypt prior to 1993; the social marketing of Depo-Provera injectables has likewise worked well in Indonesia. About one-fifth of social marketing CYPs was provided by these two methods in 1996. A small number of implants are also delivered via CSM.

The pricing of these methods is considerably more complicated because the consumer receives a service as well as a product. For IUDs particularly, trained medical personnel are required for insertion, and such personnel will normally expect a fee for their service and consumers often expect to pay such a fee. While many IUDs are inserted in clinics free of charge, social marketing is not amenable to that form of distribution; IUDs and injectables distributed through social marketing are always sold for a price.

That said, the foregoing guidelines are still relevant. If a consumer must pay significantly more than 1 percent of per-capita GNP (or one-quarter of 1 percent of the PPP index) for a year's contraceptive protection, there is likely to be price resistance, especially if the payment is loaded up front, as it is with IUDs. A quarterly Depo-Provera injection should not have been priced substantially above $1.75 in 1995 in Sri Lanka, for example (per-capita GNP = $700; four injections at $1.75 = $7.00 = 1 percent of per-capita GNP). An IUD insertion (including the cost of the IUD) in Sri Lanka could theoretically cost $18, because one IUD insertion equals 3 or 3 ½ CYPs. But in the case of an IUD, the 1 percent rule almost certainly must be modified downward, since the three-year cost must be borne all at once, and this high initial cost is likely to be a very substantial obstacle.

The price of an IUD with insertion in the Egyptian program was $5 to $7 (roughly 1 percent of per-capita GNP) during the most successful years of that program. A typical price for an injection of Depo-Provera was around $1.30 in Indonesia in the late 1990s (0.7 percent of per-capita GNP annual equivalent). Thus, the two largest social marketing providers of these long-term methods tend to support the validity of the "1 percent rule."

THE SELF-SUFFICIENCY "WARS"

The preceding section indicates what contraceptives in social marketing programs *ought* to cost. But frequently these rules are not followed. Contraceptives in social marketing programs generally tend to be priced higher (and, rarely, lower) than they should for two reasons: financial necessity in programs that are underfinanced; and political realities requiring pricing decisions that are meant to lead to eventual self-sufficiency for the program.

In the first category, DKT's Zaroor condom in Bombay in 1995 was somewhat overpriced at 0.3 percent of PPP and 1.1 percent of per-capita GNP because DKT had no donors to support the project at the time and was required, by financial necessity, to recover more than its cost from the price charged to the first tier of the trade. Similarly, Sri Lanka's condom, priced at 4 cents in the 1990s, was too high, because the Sri Lanka FPA had no source of subsidy for their contraceptives. In both cases the result has been less than satisfactory sales: only 0.1 condoms per capita in Bombay after five years and 0.4 condoms per capita in Sri Lanka after twenty years.

Other projects that have overpriced their contraceptives have done so because the donor insisted on moving toward financial self-sufficiency. We have seen one dramatic example in Bangladesh; there are many others.

"Self-sufficiency" and development

The idea that the industrialized nations should provide developmental assistance (foreign aid) to low-income countries in such a way as to lead to their financial self-sufficiency is, of course, an appropriate and worthy paradigm, originating in the Marshall Plan of massive economic aid to Europe after World War II. This approach to developmental assistance is designed to promote a future of profitable economic activity. When donors provide loans to farmers for fertilizer, or give assistance in the form of capital equipment, electrification, or the building of infrastructure, they have every reason to expect—indeed, to insist—that their investments pay off in economic terms.

What has not been recognized is that developmental assistance in the form of improved health is not designed, and should not be expected, to produce directly measurable economic gains. This reality requires that donors adopt a completely different mind-set when they "invest" in health care for poor people in poor countries. This is especially necessary in the area of preventive health care, and family planning is preventive health care of the most fundamental sort. (Abortion is an exception to this rule. Abortion is not preventive care, rather it is curative for those women who seek it, an emergency to be resolved. Women desiring to terminate pregnancies are therefore often willing to pay and/or be inconvenienced as much for an abortion as for the resolution of a life-threatening disease. This means that abortion programs, alone among all fertility control efforts in poor developing countries, can be and often are financially self-sufficient.)

As I stated in a 1991 paper concerning preventive health care costs:

The idea that we can recover from the world's poorest peoples a substantial portion of the costs of their own health care, particularly preventive health care, is based not in sound reasoning but in wishful thinking. We need to stop wishing and face a few simple truths.

First, low-income citizens of developing countries will always need subsidized health services, particularly in the preventive health care area and most particularly in the family planning area. . . .

For further evidence on this point we need only look at health services in the industrialized world. *All* of the world's wealthiest societies subsidize health care for their low-income citizens, most of whom are enormously affluent by less developed country standards. In light of this, to expect the poor of developing countries to pay the full costs of their health care seems ludicrous. (Harvey, 1991a:52)

In light of these facts, why have the self-sufficiency arguments been so potent? The first reason is probably the earlier noted imperative of having an exit strategy. Donors instinctively dislike the idea of a continuing presence in recipient countries, and the political pressure to have a "plan" for terminating assistance is therefore very intense. One of the most easily structured of such plans is to provide a blueprint for gradual assumption of the costs of a family planning project by the clients of those projects.

A second reason lies in the ability of bureaucratic decision making to create its own myths. I have often referred to the self-sufficiency syndrome as the conviction that we can spin gold from flax. Too many people actually propound the hypothesis that we can reach ever larger numbers of low-income beneficiaries in the world's poorest countries with contraceptives and, at the same time, put donor costs on a glide path toward zero by somehow charging these increasing numbers of clients ever more of their hard-earned incomes for the services and products provided. It is a zany hypothesis. But it has persisted in part because donors want to believe it, and also because it is given credibility by "experts."

Donors routinely hire accredited and expert consultants to advise them on matters of this sort, and they have a way of letting these consultants know what it is they are expected to say. Consultants like to go on consulting; that is how they earn their living. If a donor or major financial institution commissions consultants to write reports on the viability of self-sufficiency in family planning social marketing programs, and the donor or financial institution lets it be known (perhaps without actually saying so) that it wishes to get a report supporting this hypothesis (e.g, you *can* spin gold from flax), numerous reports by otherwise competent consultants will tend to confirm that this may indeed be possible. I am not making this up. It happens. Any science can be easily undermined by a group of experts whose continued livelihood requires that they bend, at least slightly, their scientific principles, and governments are particularly adept at commissioning this kind of science.

THE OTHER SIDE OF THE STORY: WHAT ABOUT MORE ADVANCED DEVELOPING ECONOMIES?

I have stressed the impossibility of achieving, and the disfunctionality of seeking to achieve, financial self-sufficiency for social marketing in low-income countries. But a substantial amount of social marketing activity takes place in more advanced economies where the goal of financial self-sufficiency is more realistic.

The mathematical analysis of this is relatively straightforward. Condoms cost about 3 cents apiece (unpackaged) on international markets in the late 1990s; pills cost around 20 cents per cycle. Injectables cost around $1 each for quarterly injection ampoules (with disposable syringe). This means that a year's supply of these methods costs from $2.80 to $4.00. Adding packaging costs for condoms and pills and allowing for an approximate doubling of these cost prices to provide trade margins, we arrive at a consumer cost for a year's supply of contraceptives of between $6 and $9 if we wish to fully recover the cost of contraceptive supplies (and trade margins) from the consumer. This means that, as a given country's economy begins to approach $1,000 GNP per capita, we can begin planning to recover these costs from the consumer. Virtually all of the countries of the Western Hemisphere qualify for this treatment. Some Asian countries, such as Malaysia and Thailand, also qualify easily, while other very important and populous Asian countries like Indonesia come very close.

So there are developing country economies where "self-sufficiency," at least to the extent of recovering the cost of the contraceptives from the purchaser, is indeed realistic. I have emphasized the other side of the argument in this book because I believe it is on the lowest-income developing countries that we should be concentrating our resources. (Despite this conviction, two of DKT's nine CSM projects in 1996, Brazil and Malaysia, were in wealthy LDCs.) But there is nothing wrong with working in the "in-between" developing areas and seeking a degree of financial self-sufficiency in those areas, particularly where economic growth promises to make consumer-paid socially marketed contraceptives more and more affordable as people generally become wealthier. In accordance with this principle, it is not surprising that social marketing in Colombia (per capita GNP $1,400 in 1995) and Costa Rica (per capita GNP $2,380 in 1994) have been financially self-sufficient for some time, and that other Latin American programs are moving in the same direction.

SALES, PREVALENCE, AND PRICES

Contraceptive prevalence is the indicator by which family planners assess the use of contraceptives in a given society (more fully discussed in Chapter 9). It is usually expressed as a percentage of "couples in union" or of "married women of reproductive age." In this book, I refer repeatedly to a "5 percent success" standard, which is calculated as 5 percent of 80 percent of all women aged 15–49. This is roughly the same as 5 percent of "married women," or 5 percent of "women in union," for most countries, and is a bit more objectively comparable across societies.

A society approaching 70 percent prevalence of modern contraceptive use has essentially arrived as a contracepting society. Most of Europe has contraceptive prevalence rates at around this level. When we take into account those couples who are trying to get pregnant or already are, those who are infertile and do not need contraceptives, and those who are not sexually active, 70 percent represents prevalence success.

It is the stated goal of most family planning donors and agencies to achieve ever higher levels of prevalence in developing countries, aiming toward this 70 percent level or something like it. This means that sales of contraceptives in social marketing programs should be maximized, which means, in turn, that prices must be kept at least approximately within the guidelines outlined here. It is that simple. Maximum prevalence means maximizing sales, and that means that the contraceptives must be priced accordingly. Condoms in Zimbabwe in 1995 priced at 2.5 percent of per-capita GNP, condoms in Indonesia in 1995 priced at 2.4 percent of per-capita GNP (Simplex) or even 1.5 percent (Dualima) are unlikely to achieve significant prevalence (in fact they have not, after many years). Similarly pills in the Philippines at 3 percent of per-capita GNP (Couples' Choice phased out at the end of the 1990s) were simply beyond the reach of low-income people and could never make their full potential contribution to contraceptive prevalence at those price levels.

In addition to all of the reasons stated earlier, it is desirable to price lower rather than higher because we save money by "stealing" customers from government give-away programs rather than from commercial contraceptive sales. In countries where the government provides free birth control services (and a great many of the larger and poorer developing country governments do), very low-priced social marketing contraceptives will tend to attract low-income buyers who would likely otherwise avail themselves of free government services (or none at all). This means that such persons, while paying only a fraction of the cost of their contraceptives, are at least paying something, whereas in the government program their family planning would be more expensive to the donor/government because the client pays nothing. If we price our social marketing contraceptives at a relatively high price, we are more likely to attract buyers who would otherwise avail themselves of fully priced commercial contraceptives. This is undesirable because such people will receive a degree of subsidy they do not need. Ross and Frankenberg note that "Programs that are directed primarily at higher income clients probably encounter more switching, since many such clients may have been buying at regular commercial prices" (1993:30).

SOAP, "BARE," AND THE MANUFACTURER'S MODEL

Many approaches have been discussed and tried in the effort to make social marketing (and family planning) less expensive to the donors who subsidize it. These have included plans for the development of profit-making businesses unrelated to family planning; the provision of contraceptive supplies to pharmaceutical distributors with the understanding that they add those contraceptives, sometimes unbranded and unpackaged, to their product line; and several ways to get companies that manufacture contraceptives more intensely involved in promoting their own products, particularly to expanded and lower-income markets.

One of the first recommendations in the "unrelated" business category was a soap factory for Nepal. A team of experts visited the Nepal social marketing program in 1987 and concluded that it would continue to require subsidies from the donor (USAID) for some years to come if affordable prices were to be maintained; therefore, it advised, the project should invest in one or more money-making enterprise. One suggestion was a soap factory. The following is what I wrote about this idea at the time:

The Nepal CRS story revives the old self-sufficiency shibboleth which seems to have haunted contraceptive social marketing programs from their very earliest days. We have pointed out before that there is simply no reason why social marketing programs, if they are providing contraceptives to needy people in needy countries, should be saddled with any greater financial self-sufficiency requirement than a vasectomy program or a community-based distribution program or a clinic program or any other kind of family planning program for which AID or other international donors provide support.

A recent report suggests, among other possibilities, that the Nepal CRS project might go into the business of manufacturing soap. No one disputes the virtues of soap. Further, if it is AID's policy to promote start-up businesses in areas like soap manufacturing in countries like Nepal, that would be perfectly worthwhile if done under its own rationale. Indeed, such activities were supported for many years by the Congressionally mandated Cooley loans. But what does soap manufacturing have to do with family planning? Why should AID's Office of Population, even indirectly through its support of a CSM program, be involved with making soap? The notion is simply unsupportable.

The evaluation criteria for any donor-supported family planning project should be this and only this: is the project benefiting large numbers of needy people at a reasonable cost? We have excellent measurement tools available to help answer that question in the contraceptive couple-year of protection (CYP) and in cost per CYP data, as well as contraceptive prevalence surveys.

If AID and its contractors are going to demand of contraceptive social marketing programs that they work toward financial self-sufficiency through such activities as soap manufacturing, or perhaps even more ominous, through charging market rates for their family planning products and services, then all AID-supported family planning programs (and perhaps other programs as well) should be given the same burden: develop a method, however remote it may be from the purposes of your program or your organization, to achieve financial self-sufficiency or face extinction. (Social Marketing Forum, 1987:2)

Fortunately, donor enthusiasm for this "investment" idea has waned. A number of family planning organizations were pushed into such unrelated activities as fish farming in the 1980s, with generally dreadful results. Such "investment" sideshows, which PSI president Dick Frank puckishly categorized as "Soap," have now taken their place in the pantheon of development horror stories, and there is little enthusiasm for their revival.

"Bare" on the other hand, still has its adherents. The idea here is to provide contraceptive supplies to a distribution company that has the capability of distributing and selling those contraceptives widely in a developing country economy, without packaging—"bare" contraceptives. The largest and most important experiment of this kind took place in Nigeria between 1987–1993. Unpackaged condoms (hermetically sealed in foil but not overboxed or otherwise branded) in foil strips of four, and plain blister-pack cycles of oral contraceptives* were made available to the Sterling Drug Company under a USAID-funded project. Sterling Drug, an international manufacturer/distributor of pharmaceutical products headquartered in London and with a fully staffed office in Lagos, Nigeria's capital, was to make these contraceptives available through their distribution network throughout Nigeria at reasonable, agreed-upon prices. These prices were low—65 kobo ($0.08) for a cycle of pills and 50 kobo ($0.06) for four condoms, prices well within the guidelines discussed in this chapter. But since Sterling paid nothing for the contraceptives, the entire consumer price could be applied to trade margins, primarily Sterling's and the retailers'. The project was overseen by a cooperating agency called Family Planning International Assistance (FPIA), an arm of the Planned Parenthood Federation of America, which had been created in the early 1970s to supervise and conduct AID-sponsored family planning projects in developing countries. FPIA was to maintain liaison with Sterling, help keep records, issue reports, and maintain the supply of contraceptives.

The project got off to a reasonably good start. It was indeed low-cost. USAID paid only for the contraceptives and for FPIA's participation. The contraceptives provided all the margins. In the early years, no consumer advertising or promotion was undertaken, though there was some limited promotion of the pills in trade journals. In 1986 the project delivered just over 100 thousand CYPs, not a bad beginning. Then it seesawed for several years, floundered, and finally died.

The fatal flaw, in my view, lay in the donor's and FPIA's inherent inability to maintain Sterling's interest over the long haul. Public-sector and non-profit professionals often find it difficult to accept that commercial companies must prioritize their activities in ways that maximize their stockholders' return. For most companies, the dissemination of family

*Oral contraceptives are normally packaged at the factory in "blister packs" of twenty-one active pills, sometimes accompanied by seven placebos or iron tablets to comprise a complete twenty-eight-day (monthly) cycle.

planning is simply not very high on the list. It is true that Sterling was allowed to keep a healthy margin on the contraceptives it sold, and this project was therefore, theoretically at least, a profitable activity for them. But they were not dedicated to this line of products as an organization, and when opportunities arose that appeared to be potentially more profitable than the contraceptives, they began to lose interest. They were also expected to do a good deal of extra work for the sake of accountability (perfectly reasonable from the donor's point of view, but bothersome and expensive to Sterling), and the costs of that extra work ate into their profit margins.

Fortunately, DKT and PSI had been doing closely related work in Nigeria and were able to take over Sterling's sales with branded products in the time-tested manner. The "bare" condoms were packaged, given a brand name (Gold Circle), and supported by advertising. The pills were identified by their original (U.S.) brand names, such as Norquest and Ovrette, and by their "blue lady" logo, an identifying mark for pills furnished to family planning programs. Oral contraceptives cannot be advertised to consumers in Nigeria, so the "blue lady" pills were promoted in medical journals and through talks given to professional associations of doctors and paramedical personnel. For the orals, this was not radically different from the approach under Sterling and FPIA.

The new (more traditional) approach has worked. Condom sales went from an average of less than three million per year in the late 1980s to twenty million in 1993 to more than fifty million in 1995 (but falling after this meteoric rise, in 1996). Pills improved from 1.5 million (1991) to 3.3 million in 1995. The Nigeria contraceptive social marketing program is now one of the world's largest, crossing the 5 percent "success" line in 1995 and nearly doubling contraceptive prevalence in Africa's most populous country. See Figure 8.4 for a graphic and revealing history of these two social marketing approaches.

The traditional approach worked not only because of the branding, packaging, and advertising of the condoms and the promotional efforts for the pills, though these steps were important. The crucial ingredient is the fact that the project is being supervised—including day-to-day management—by a (private) organization that is committed to making it succeed in terms of family planning, and because, at least during 1992–1995, the project was adequately funded. These two ingredients are the sine qua non of social marketing success.

A variation on the Sterling approach was also tried in Pakistan in 1986. USAID and the Pakistan government entered into a direct contract with Woodwards Pty Ltd., which at that time had very good distribution in Pakistan with a single product, their own brand of "gripe water" (an elixir for infants, designed to quiet crying babies with a sweetened antacid). Woodwards had a broad distribution network and a good sales staff. Their contract, which was funded by USAID, called for the

Figure 8.4
Nigeria, Sterling (1985–1992), DKT/PSI (1990–1996), CYPs (000)

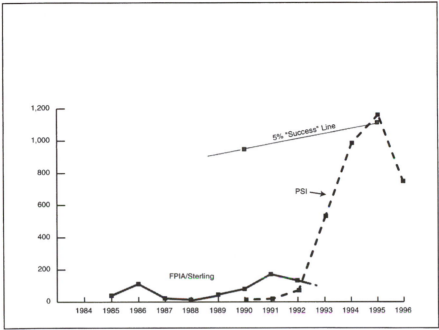

packaging of a USAID-supplied condom, later branded Sathi, a pleasant-sounding Urdu term that means companion. Planning was conducted jointly by PSI, Woodwards, and USAID and with participation by the government of Pakistan through a para-statal agency called the National Development Finance Corporation (NDFC). Woodwards' responsibilities included all subcontracts with commercial firms. PSI had a separate contract with USAID to provide technical assistance and to coordinate overall activities. However, PSI did not have the authority to direct Woodwards' actions; instead, it found itself in the position of having to suggest, to cajole, and otherwise attempt to bring about a consensus among all four parties (and the Pakistan Ministry of Population Welfare as well) in order to execute important decisions. Despite the diplomatic talents of PSI's representative, Frank Samaraweera, who had also played a role as the distribution company's executive in the Sri Lanka social marketing project in 1972–1973, the arrangement was fraught with problems. As John Davies, who succeeded Frank Samaraweera as project manager some years later, recalls:

Beginning in 1986, the governing committee consisted of representatives of five stakeholders: the Ministry of Population Welfare, USAID, Woodwards, the NDFC, which contracted with the Ministry to monitor the field work and process the financial claims of Woodwards, and PSI, which would provide social marketing advice. There was much friction among committee members. For example, Woodwards complained to USAID about PSI and found great difficulty abiding by the government's many rules. By 1990, it was clear to all stakeholders that five parties were too many, and furthermore, Woodwards, which was distributing Sathi condoms, lacked the experience to market the planned oral contraceptive pills. So a new set of contracts was agreed upon with four parties involved. The new contracts gave more responsibilities to PSI, including market research, oral contraceptive training, and monitoring. But the management by committee continued, as did the friction. Many meetings were held during 1991–1993 but few decisions were implemented. The oral contraceptive was dropped and USAID funding was discontinued in 1993. Not until 1995 did all of this get sorted out. (Davies, 1996)

At the end of the day, I think the Pakistan project suffered from the same problem as the Sterling project in Nigeria, plus a few others. Sathi became less and less attractive as a long-term commercial proposition for their company, and Woodwards began losing interest, particularly after USAID pulled out. The lack of clear authority resulted in friction, continually postponed decisions and inaction. Woodwards decided to bring in their own much higher-priced condom (Durex) with greater profit margins and better potential, from their perspective, for long-term return on investment.[3]

Woodwards withdrew from the project in 1994. This time PSI was already on the scene and could therefore have maintained Sathi sales with another distributor or distributors but unexpected events intervened. Pakistan had failed to convince the U.S. Congress that it was not secretly building nuclear weapons and all U.S. foreign aid to Pakistan was therefore discontinued under the Pressler Amendment in 1993. PSI and its new Pakistan affiliate, Social Marketing Pakistan, Ltd., struggled on for some months of plummeting sales, sending out distress signals to the international community. The German KfW came to the rescue in late 1994. Sathi sales began to revive that year and, by 1995 were on the way to full recovery.

THE MANUFACTURER'S MODEL

Several other variations on the design of social marketing programs have come to be known collectively as "the manufacturer's model," as first mentioned in Chapter 2. They are also called "partnership programs" (with manufacturers) and "third" and "fourth" generation CSM. Starting with heavily subsidized projects using donated contraceptives (first generation), the next two stages are based on progressively lesser levels of donor subsidy. The fourth generation is meant to be operated by a commercial company rather than a family planning organization and to require no subsidy at all by some foreseeable date. This approach pursues an "exit strategy" and the ideology of financial self-sufficiency. The idea is to provide a way for donors to work with the manufacturers of contraceptives (or, in a common variation, with distributors who already handle contraceptive products) in such a way as to make it possible for the commercial firms to seek and find wider markets for their contraceptives, hopefully to lower the prices of those products and to make them available to more and lower-income people than they would otherwise do.

In sum, the manufacturer's model (third/fourth-generation; partnership) approach has great theoretical appeal. It has a target date for termination of donor support. It relies on free-market commercial enterprises. It depends for programmatic continuity on organizations that are already in place and which are likely to remain in place for reasons independent of the project. All of these are enormously pleasing and potent attributes.

But, in practice, this approach just doesn't seem to work very well. Without the independent participation of an organization dedicated to the family planning goals of the project, entropy is likely to set in. As soon as commercial firms see areas of activity that are more promising from the point of view of return-on-equity than promoting contraceptives to lower-income markets, their attention will shift. This is perfectly right and natural. Commercial companies have a fiduciary duty to maximize return on investment and they should do so. But to promote the aims of a family planning (or AIDS-prevention) program through social marketing or otherwise, one must have the participation of an organization philosophically and ideologically devoted to that purpose. Only then do you have commitment for the long haul, and the continuity that comes from the focus on the family planning outcome rather than other outcomes that frequently—eventually almost always—come into conflict with the low-income-consumer focus of family planning goals.

Further, the "manufacturer's model" approach to social marketing is useful only in the more advanced developing-country economies. It has little to contribute in the truly low-income countries. Recognizing this, USAID and SOMARC have focused the development of this model on countries with per-capita GNP over $600, mostly on countries with over $1,000. (For further details and analysis of the manufacturer's model experience, see Appendix 1.)

The relatively poor batting average of these self-sufficiency designs (see Appendix 1) is not mitigated by the fact that this approach is new and may not have had time to demonstrate its utility. In the 1970s, the "traditional" approach to social marketing was also new, yet of the first eight social marketing projects started between 1968 and 1986, six were still in operation in 1998, delivering family planning on a highly cost-effective basis to substantial numbers of couples.

A critical component of successful CSM programs is the continuing involvement of a committed family planning/AIDS-prevention organization, preferably in an actual management role. Providing catalytic inputs to the commercial sector, while conceptually intriguing, does not appear to be an adequate model for bringing about long-term change.

NOTES

1. Another useful analysis of the pricing issue can be found in "The Effect of Contraceptive Prices on Method Choice in the Philippines, Jamaica, and Thailand," Schwartz et al., 1989.

2. See also The Population Council's "Findings from Two Decades of Family Planning Research" (Ross and Frankenberg, 1993:30): "In setting prices, a year's supply of contraceptives should cost less than 1 percent of the yearly household income of lower income groups."

3. This last step was facilitated by the fact that Woodwards was acquired (probably not coincidentally) by the owners of the Durex condom brand, LRC International.

9

Measuring Results: Sales, CYPs, Contraceptive Prevalence

One of contraceptive social marketing's great assets is the measurability of its results. It is difficult to overemphasize the importance of this point. International family planning is a nonprofit activity with humanitarian goals. Other activities in this realm, both internationally and within individual societies, suffer chronically from poorly defined goals and the great difficulty of measuring results. Unlike commercial enterprise, which is continually measured by its bottom-line profits, nonprofit[1] managers and staff members can stay busy on procedural and administrative matters for years without genuinely advancing their purpose. This happens all too often, and without adequate measurement tools, such inchoate activities may continue indefinitely.

There are many reasons why this happens. First, many nonprofit managers fear accountability. We all know professionals who are attracted to the nonprofit world because they think they can perform a useful service without being subjected to the harsh discipline of the bottom line. This is a mistake for all concerned. Nonprofit organizations need a bottom line too, and nonprofit managers must be held accountable for achieving it. (See Harvey and Snyder, 1987.)

Another reason for such ad infinitum activity is that the nonprofit world often has no mechanism for terminating faulty or completed projects. When a business makes a big mistake, it has no choice but to recognize it or go broke. But a nonprofit group may drone on for decades, accomplishing little but continuing to persuade its donors that it is "doing its best."

Nonprofits also fall into the trap of undertaking any activity for which money or other resources are available. U.S. farm subsidies and the lobbyists, companies, and farmers who benefited from them in the 1960s, contrived to promulgate policies that created "surplus" food, so CARE and Catholic Relief Services designed programs to use this resource. Such "donor-driven" activities take on a life of their own. Food and nutrition programs get dedicated, institutionalized, and photographed; the photographs are used to raise funds and, indirectly, to support the subsidies. The "programs" become desirable project activities for those who conduct them. But rarely does anyone seek to measure how much—or even *if*—they are improving the health of children in poor countries, and particularly if such "resource-driven" programs are as cost-effective as other approaches would be.

Some nonprofit managers fear that management science may replace romance: Won't hard-nosed evaluation undermine humanitarian instincts? The answer is no. For those who are truly concerned about serving people in need, a clearly defined set of goals and yardsticks to measure progress are very reassuring. You do not vitiate an idea by clarifying it, even when you subject it to statistical analysis. Rather, you render your ideas more doable. If the beneficiaries' needs are uppermost—as opposed to, say, the needs of donors, board members, or staff—then quantifying output can only improve the humanitarian results because all concerned will know when and to what extent they are making progress.

Unfortunately, nonprofit managers are compelled to spend a great deal of time on activities that do not further their organization's goals, even when those goals are clear. Meeting with donors, coping with reporting demands, explaining programs and policies to committees, placating and organizing volunteers, and fund raising all make heavy demands on managers. Board members and donors often accept descriptions of activity ("met with volunteers from 2–4 today; rescheduled training program for February; signed long-term agreement for computer service—excellent price!—with help from Board Member X") as substitutes for progress toward goals, permitting unfocused and fragmented activity to continue.

Nonprofits have no financial report cards to tell them how they are doing. In the for-profit world, balance sheets and profit-and-loss statements tell managers a lot about how close they are to meeting their objectives; a nonprofit organization's financial reports reveal nothing about its progress. The only useful information in a nonprofit audit or other financial report is how much money is coming in (and from where) and how much is being spent on what. This is important information, and nonprofit boards should pay close attention to it. But there is a chronic danger that board members (or donors) will confuse this information with the achievement of something useful. If income is up, the organization must be effective, they reason. But if an organization's goal is to improve the education of Peruvian children, then the only way to measure success is in the educational levels of Peruvian children—not the number of schools built or the number of teachers trained, and most of all, *not* the amount of money spent on or raised for this activity. Success only comes when the children actually attain higher educational levels. The confusing of intermediate activities with real goals is thus a trap for many donors and other nonprofit institutions.

For all these reasons family planners (and other nonprofits) must make a special effort to establish clear and measurable goals and to apply objective yardsticks to their activities to assess whether or not those (measurable) goals are being met. It turns out that family planning service programs* can be easily subjected to this discipline. When a contraceptive procedure—like a sterilization or the insertion of an IUD—is performed, we have a specific and concrete event that can be translated immediately into a measurable index, which permits us to track progress toward our goals. This is also true of contraceptive injections given and of oral contraceptives and condoms, when they are sold.

WHAT IS THE OBJECTIVE?

Most family planning professionals now agree that their overall objective is increasing contraceptive prevalence in the societies where family planning programs are implemented. Contraceptive prevalence rates simply measure the number and percentage of couples in a given society who are using contraception. A distinction is usually drawn between the "traditional" methods, like withdrawal and rhythm, and the modern (and much more effective) methods, which include, in approximate order of worldwide usage rates, sterilization, oral contraceptives (the Pill), IUDs, condoms, injectables, implants, and various vaginal barrier methods. Abortion, as it is not a method of contraception, is usually excluded. (For a summary of all common methods of birth control, see Appendix 3.) In the United States in the mid-1990s, contraceptive prevalence (modern methods) was 68 percent; in Nigeria it was 7 percent. Most family planning programs are designed to close the gap between these kinds of disparate levels.

If increased prevalence is our objective, then we must provide affordable contraception to the largest possible number of people. I have noted that we should emphasize low-income groups—the lowest-income target groups possible—in our programs: Our objective is to reach as many

*A "service" program in family planning means a program that actually provides contraceptive and/or abortion services to clients, the term service being used to differentiate these programs, which are readily susceptible to CYP analysis, from training or policy activities, which are not.

people as we can and, for CSM, that means selling as many contraceptives as possible. The pursuit of this policy will put our focus as a matter of course on low-income clients, because the largest numbers of people are in the low-income categories.

In many government programs large quantities of condoms and pills are given away free. Some give-away programs may be effective overall, but it is extremely difficult to track or trace the contraceptives so distributed in any meaningful way, and waste and misuse are highly likely. As noted earlier, in India, for example, where the government has given away billions of condoms over the years, it is common for them to be used for making automotive repairs (plugging radiator leaks) and fashioning toys and sandal soles. For this and related reasons the Indian government began phasing out its condom give-away program in 1995. Similarly, in 1992 the government of Bangladesh, a major provider of free contraceptives, began charging a small amount for its condoms.

When consumers pay a price—even a very small price—for contraceptives for their own use, there is a very high likelihood that they will be used as intended, and this is an important component of CSM measurability. The contraceptives in a social marketing program move through the distribution chain from the port to the warehouse to wholesalers and distributors to retail shops backed at every stage by a traceable, auditable flow of cash, a process that produces reliable and verifiable sales statistics.

In a typical social marketing program, for example, a three-pack of condoms may be sold to a distributor for U.S. 2 cents. The distributor will sell the packet to a retailer for 2 ½ cents and the retailer will sell it to the consumer for 4 cents (or a bit more if he can get it). Each of these transactions (except the final one) provides a traceable record. This means that we know, from monthly sales statistics, how many of which brands of contraceptives are in the hands of consumers[2] who are sufficiently motivated to use them, having paid their own hard-earned money for them.

CSM sales statistics are useful in several ways. From the first year a program is begun, for example, we have some sense of whether it will be successful or not from sales statistics alone. Assuming that not many sales are made on credit, we can get a sense of a project's degree of likely success in just a few months. Even with credit sales the chickens come home to roost fairly soon; credit sales can result in overstocking on retailers' shelves and even in storage areas, but they cannot go on for long if there is no consumer off-take.

A good example of this occurred in the African nation of Burkina Faso in 1991–1992. A fired-up sales staff enthusiastically sold very substantial quantities of Prudence condoms to the trade and persuaded retailers, with the help of liberal credit terms, to stock up on an enormous number of condoms. I remember an ebullient Sylvia Watts, PSI's Burkina program

Figure 9.1
Average Monthly Sales of Condoms (000), Burkina Faso, 1991–1996

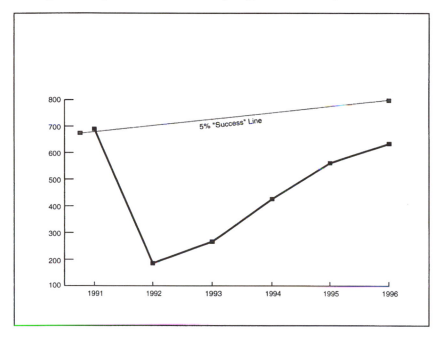

manager, returning to Washington to the equivalent of a ticker-tape pa-
rade early in 1992; she had sold over two million condoms in just four
months, and she was the envy of many of her peers. But reality soon set
in. (See Figure 9.1.) In 1991, retailers had purchased more condoms than
they could sell in a reasonable period of time and were badly over-
stocked. In 1992, monthly sales reflected this reality, dropping below 200
thousand. However, a satisfactory and sustainable pattern was then established and 1995 sales got back to nearly 600 thousand per month (0.6
condoms per capita), a commendable record for the fifth year in a very
poor African country.

   Allowing for such variations, we know in round numbers how many
condoms or pills should be sold relative to the size of the market in the
early years of a program, as well as in the later years. In an adequately
funded social marketing program for condoms, for example, a crude indicator of success in the second or third year is to approach a sales level
of 0.3 condoms per capita in the market being served. This is exactly
what occurred in Burkina Faso: 1993 sales of 3.2 million condoms represented just over 0.3 per capita that year (the population of Burkina
Faso was 10 million). In Ethiopia, a much more populous country of 55
million people, DKT achieved sales of 17.3 million condoms (0.3 per

Table 9.1
Uganda/DKT Condom Sales and Sales Per Capita, 1993–1994

Year	Sales	Sales Per Capita	Cost/CYP
1993	53,776	.003	$465
1994	655,088	.033	$ 29

capita) in its fourth year of operation, a year behind target, but still close to the mark. In Vietnam, the program reached 0.3 per capita, right on schedule, in the third year.

In the fourth, fifth, and sixth years of a well-funded program, sales should reach or exceed 0.7 condoms per capita. This is roughly equivalent to 3 percent prevalence—that is 3 percent of target couples are regularly using the product. Bangladesh and Costa Rica have achieved condom sales in excess of 1.0 per capita, a nice round figure referred to by one writer as the "Holy Grail" of social marketing. This translates to 5–6 percent prevalence for this method/brand, thereby achieving the 5 percent "success" level with just one product. Similarly, a successful level of oral contraceptive sales is about 0.1 cycles per capita, (achieved in 1994 in Jamaica [0.2], Colombia [0.16], and Bangladesh [0.1]), equivalent to about 4 percent prevalence. The prevalence measure itself, established through survey data as well as sales statistics, is our "bottom line."

Thus sales data alone give us important benchmarks, and we can use these benchmarks to assess the competence of managers, to decide whether to continue programs, expand them, or to close them down.

Such a decision was taken in Uganda in 1994. Sales of Gold Circle condoms by DKT began there in 1993. In a country of Uganda's size— 18 million—sales levels in the second year should have been approaching two or three million units per annum, that is, more than 0.1 per capita. Yet our sales had not even reached one million (see Table 9.1) and were showing no signs of taking off. In addition, a SOMARC project, operating in the same markets, was simultaneously coming to life and in 1994 sold 3.8 million Protektor brand condoms. It therefore seemed inappropriate to continue investing discretionary funds in a project of such limited sales when we were likely to achieve better results with the same resources elsewhere. DKT, therefore, closed down its Uganda Gold Circle program in early 1995.

An ethical point here: the improvement in SOMARC's program made the Uganda decision relatively easy. But what if there had been no SOMARC program? In a country plagued by AIDS at a truly devastating level, would DKT have had an obligation to stay, even though the relationship between the expense of its program and the number of condoms sold was unsatisfactory? I believe DKT has an obligation to invest its resources where they will do the most good, and that means investing in programs where the cost per couple year of protection is at least satisfactory, or very likely to become satisfactory in the immediate future. This means making hard-nosed decisions in the allocation of limited resources. If, for example, with the same funds, DKT can prevent more HIV transmissions by supplementing PSI's Zaire program (which already achieves acceptable cost-efficiency levels) than it can by continuing in Uganda, then it should shift its funds to Zaire. More starkly still, if, on a budget of $200 thousand per annum, which was our approximate budget in Uganda, we are able to prevent two hundred HIV transmissions in that country (the approximate number prevented by 650,000 condoms), and we can prevent three hundred HIV transmissions for the same $200 thousand in another country, then we should move to the other country. Some will say this means "abandoning" Uganda and that doing so is wrong. But it is not wrong if you believe that all human life is equal. A life saved in Zaire is equal to a life saved in Uganda, and if we can save even one more life in Zaire on the same budget, that is what we should do, even if it means "abandoning" Uganda.

An analogous event occurred when CARE was involved in the fight against famine in the east Indian state of Bihar in 1968–1969. CARE's job was to move massive quantities of milk powder and a fortified corn–soy-meal mixture to tens of thousands of primary schools throughout the state of Bihar, so that several million young children could be fed at least one meal a day. This program was a vital component in the fight against starvation in one of the most chronically deprived parts of the world. It involved a massive logistical operation, with thousands of tons of food moving along a variety of rail and truck lines in a complicated pattern throughout most of Bihar's 67 thousand square miles. Some of the American staff who came to India to help in this effort were so touched by the plight of the beggars in the capital city of Patna that they became distracted from their tasks; they felt they had to do something about the pitiable condition of the beggars. But doing so, worthy as such efforts might be, took them away from a more important task. Resources (their time and energy) were being misallocated. We needed everybody at work moving the bulk food to the schools so it could provide urgently needed nutrition to millions of kids. If that meant stepping over the beggars in the capital city—even letting them die—in order to keep the railcars moving, then that is what was required. One or two Americans actually had to be fired, for they were unable to accept this fundamental fact. Hard-nosed? Sure. But it was essential if we were to do the job of saving larger numbers of people. (See Harvey, 1969.)

In just such a way, goal-delineated yardsticks will remind us about how to allocate our resources for maximum benefit. They help us know when we must close weak programs, and when to shift additional resources to programs that show more promise.[3]

Compare these measuring tools to the relative blindness of agency executives engaged in social marketing where no product is sold, or in other kinds of development assistance. If DKT were simply putting on media campaigns for AIDS prevention with no sale of condoms, and spent a million dollars developing and broadcasting mass media messages on safe sex practices in, let us say, Sudan, then it still would have to do a massive amount of expensive surveying to ascertain the effectiveness of the campaign. And even then, uncertainties would remain as to how much people's behavior had actually changed. Such surveys are extremely useful and important, as we shall see later. But the social marketing of a *product* provides a great advantage because its sales are immediately measurable, and they quickly signal a change in behavior (purchase and use of contraceptives) without requiring surveys to document it.

COUPLE YEARS OF PROTECTION

All family planning service programs have very good intermediate statistical yardsticks. IUDs inserted, sterilizations performed, injections given at clinics, as well as social marketing sales, all provide excellent yardsticks by which to measure program success. A refinement, called a couple year of protection (CYP), takes this process one step further. A CYP consists of the provision of an adequate supply of contraceptives, or the provision of a contraceptive service, sufficient to protect one couple from pregnancy for one year. Thus, the sale of one hundred condoms, fourteen cycles of pills, or the provision of four quarterly injections are all considered equivalent to one CYP. A sterilization procedure is credited with about ten CYPs, as this is a permanent operation that will provide contraceptive protection for many years. The insertion of an IUD is credited with about three CYPs, as that is the average length of time these highly effective devices are left in place.

There is some disagreement over the conversion factors for these CYP equivalents and the range of estimates for each method is given in Table 9.2. A complete reconciliation of these figures is neither possible or terribly important for the CYP to be an effective measurement tool. The table shows that the mean and median figures for condoms are roughly one hundred, making it relatively easy to settle on that as the appropriate conversion figure for this method. Similarly, there appears to be a relatively strong consensus on pills: Thirteen cycles by definition are required for complete protection and the additional cycle is included to cover wastage and misuse. While there is a wider disparity among the experts on the other methods, the point is not that we reach precisely the "best" conversion number but rather that we apply a particular number consistently. Thus, if we are comparing the cost effectiveness of IUD programs in Egypt and Nigeria, for example, it doesn't really matter whether we use 3.5 CYPs for each insertion or 2.8 CYPs, as long as we apply the

Table 9.2
Estimated Measures of Contraceptive Protection Associated With Various Methods; By Source

METHOD	Hutchings & Saunders (1985)	IPPF (1988-1989)	Government of Pakistan (1990)	USAID (1991)	Davies & Louis (1977)	King et al/ Government of India (1964)	Chernichovsky & Anson (1993)	Trussel, et al, and the National Opinion Research Center (1995)	USAID (Shelton) (1997)	Mean	Median
NUMBER NEEDED FOR ONE YEAR OF PROTECTION											
Pill Cycles	14.3	13	13	15	—	—	13.9	—	15	14	—
Condoms	120	100	100	150	62	72	74.6	83	120	98	100
Spermicides	120	—	—	150	—	—	83.3	—	—	118	—
NUMBER OF YEARS OF PROTECTION PROVIDED											
IUD	3.6	2.5	2.3	3.5	—	—	2.3	—	3.5	3.0	—
Sterilization	7	12.5	7	10	—	—	9.9	—	8-10*	9.2	9.9
Norplant	—	—	—	—	—	—	—	—	3.5	—	—

* 8 in Africa; 10 in Asia and Latin America

References:
— Hutchings, J. and L. Saunders, "Assessing the Characteristics and Cost-Effectiveness of Contraceptive Methods," PIACT, Paper No. 10, Seattle, Wash., 1985.
— International Planned Parenthood Federation, IPPF Service Statistics Manual, London, 1988-1989.
— Government of Pakistan, Population & Welfare Division, Summarized in internal USAID correspondence, September 23, 1990.
— US Agency for International Development, unpublished memos, September 23, 1990, and September 13, 1991.
— Davies and Louis, 1977.
— King/GOI: see Indian Institute of Management, 1964.
— Chernichovsky, D., and J. Anson, "Cost Recovery and the True Cost-Effectiveness of Contraceptive Provision," International Family Planning Perspectives, Vol. 19, No. 4, December 1993.
— Trussel, J., et al, "The Economic Value of Contraception: A Comparison of 15 Methods," American Journal of Public Health, 85:4 (1995).
— USAID, 1997, undated memo, "1997 CYP Factor[s]."

Note: Pill, condom, and spermicide numbers assume that the products are sold, not given away.

Table 9.3
DKT International Costs and Results, 1994

Country	Year Started	Sales		CYPs	Total Costs	Cost Per CYP
Brazil	1991	11,568,009	Condoms	115,680	$797,251	$6.89
Ethiopia	1990	17,293,221	Condoms	172,932	$1,608,825	$9.30
Bombay/India	1992	2,272,183	Condoms		$595,402	$8.42
		564,408	OCs	70,588		
Malaysia	1991	5,653,440	Condoms	56,534	$382,544	$6.77
Philippines	1990	7,836,498	Condoms		$837,564	$9.56
		120,432	OCs	87,629		
Uganda	1993	655,088	Condoms	6,551	$190,641	$29.10
Vietnam	1993	7,202,088	Condoms	72,023	$497,292	$6.90
HQ Expenses					$394,090	
TOTAL				582,037	$5,303,609	$9.11

standard consistently. If we then derive a cost per CYP based on this factor, and take any other important circumstances into account, we have a fair comparison of the relative cost-efficiency of the two programs.

The availability of the CYP yardstick and the cost-per-CYP indicator permit us to examine this form of programming in ways that let us calculate our return on investment.

Table 9.3 shows the costs, CYPs, and cost per CYP, for DKT's six programs in 1994, information that reveals a great deal. First, the very high cost per CYP in the Uganda program suggests serious problems there. To be sure, the Uganda program is new, and new programs often have very high start-up costs. But sales are also low relative to the size of the market in Uganda. As noted earlier, we assessed other factors, but the high cost per CYP and the low CYPs overall were major reasons in DKT's decision to close down the Uganda program.

The table also gives us comparative information to suggest strength and weakness among the satisfactory programs. For example, the Vietnam program, despite being only two years old, is showing excellent results, which means almost certainly that it is being well run. The Philippine program, on the other hand, is in its fifth year and is falling a little behind. It turns out that this is the result of particular difficulties faced in the marketing of condoms in that country, but the statistical indicator sends a signal that we must, at the very least, check out the causes and satisfy ourselves that adequate progress is being made.

COMPARING FAMILY PLANNING APPROACHES

The CYP also gives us a means of comparing the efficiencies of one kind of family planning program with another. At least two reviews of this subject have been undertaken: Huber and Harvey, 1989 and Barberis and Harvey, 1997. Tables 9.4 and 9.5 summarize the cost/CYP results from these two studies. As can be seen, sterilization is (and has long been) the most cost-effective form of providing birth control because a single procedure provides so many couple years of protection, with costs often below $2 per CYP (and the method is more than 99 percent effective). The social marketing of condoms and pills is normally the second most efficient, providing couple years of protection in the range of $2 to $7 per CYP after five or six years of operation. Clinic-based services also have a wide range of cost effectiveness, from $5 to $25 per CYP, with community-based services falling near the higher end of that range. (Abortion has not been included in the studies that have examined comparative cost per CYP statistics. As noted elsewhere, abortion tends to be highly cost effective because even very poor women are prepared to pay all, or nearly all, of the cost of the service so that not much subsidy is required.)

This method of comparing program efficiencies has aroused some controversy. One author has asked, "What's wrong with CYP?" (Shelton, 1991). But even those who stress the shortcomings of this approach gen-

Table 9.4
Cost per Couple Year of Protection by Mode of Service Delivery

Delivery mode	Cost/CYP ($)	
	Average	Range
Social marketing	2	<1–6
Sterilization clinic	2	1–5
Full service clinic + CBD	9	1–17
Mini-clinic + CBD	8	3–14
Full service clinic	13	1–30
CBD alone	14	5–19

Source: Adapted from Table 4, Huber and Harvey, 1989.

Table 9.5
Weighted Average Cost per Couple Year of Protection by Mode of Service Delivery

Method/Mode	Weighted Average Cost/CYP
Sterilization	$1.85
Social Marketing	2.14
Clinic-based services, excluding sterilization	6.10
Community based distribution	9.93
Clinic-based services with sterilization	3.89
Clinic based services & CBD	14.00

Source: Summarized from Table 5, Barberis and Harvey, 1997.

erally agree that it is a very useful device for analyzing intermediate feed-back on the effectiveness of family planning programs.

PREVALENCE VERSUS SALES VERSUS CYPS

As noted, contraceptive prevalence rates, or the percentage of adult couples using contraceptives in a society, is generally accepted as the ultimate yardstick for family planning programs. Success stories point to the increase in contraceptive prevalence in Thailand, from less than 20 percent to more than 50+ percent in just a decade; in Bangladesh from around 12 percent to more than 40 percent between 1980 and 1995; in Indonesia to 50 percent by the mid-1990s. (Remember that 70 percent is about as high as prevalence ever gets, or needs to go. So 50 percent for modern methods is getting in range.)

Of course, contraceptive prevalence also has gone up rapidly in certain countries that have no family planning programs, and it can sometimes be difficult to assess the impact that a program has had. This is particu-larly true when socioeconomic indicators like wealth and education are rapidly rising at the same time. In South Korea, for example, contracep-tive prevalence has gone up to a current level of 70 percent during a period of rapid overall socioeconomic improvement. The family planning initiatives undertaken by both private and government parties almost cer-tainly helped boost this improvement along, but it would probably have taken place in large part anyway. Similarly in Brazil, there has been little large-scale family planning activity, yet contraceptive prevalence there also has increased to 70 percent, higher than that of the United States.

This difficulty in assigning credit for changes in prevalence to particular programs is one reason why the Bangladesh effort, with its "control" population in Pakistan, is pointed to with such frequency. Because prev-alence in Bangladesh has increased dramatically without any significant changes in educational levels (particularly the educational level of women), or much improvement in socioeconomic status, it appears al-most certain that the government and CSM family planning programs have been the primary cause of the prevalence change. There is simply no other reasonable way to explain the improvement in Bangladesh (to around 40 percent), while prevalence in wealthier Pakistan (of which Bangladesh used to be a part) has remained below 15 percent. In Paki-stan, there has been no government family planning program and, until recently, only very limited social marketing activity.

WHAT ABOUT BIRTH RATES?

Family planners are often asked to justify their efforts by pointing to falling birth rates as well as to contraceptive prevalence. Here, the link may be too tenuous to be useful. While birth rates are unquestionably lower in populations where the use of contraceptives is higher, falling birth rates are not really required to justify the impact of family planning. As we have noted earlier, the impact of contraceptive availability is, first and foremost, humanitarian, and secondarily economic at the family level. For these objectives to be achieved, no drop in birth rates is required (though they almost always occur anyway). (The arguments, pro and con, on the importance of birth rates and population growth and their relationship to economic growth are discussed in Chapter 12.)

In general, then, the current consensus among family planning professionals that contraceptive prevalence is the appropriate "bottom line" for family planning is correct. We need not go beyond it to know whether we are succeeding.

HOW IS PREVALENCE ESTABLISHED?

The only way to assess the prevalence of contraceptive use is to go out and ask people whether and what contraceptives they have used or are using. This is an expensive and time-consuming process and it offers considerable room for error, but there is simply no other way to do it. For the past decade the world is fortunate to have had a highly professional group, Macro International (formerly Westinghouse Health Systems) conducting these surveys in countries around the world. The work is funded by USAID, and the results they have produced are referred to as the DHS surveys (Demographic and Health Surveys).[4] Surveys that provide data purported to be representative of the entire population must be executed with carefully drawn scientific samples and performed by small armies of well-trained interviewers, and the DHS surveys are done about as well as they can be. The prevalence rates quoted throughout this book are based on DHS data.

THE RELATIONSHIP BETWEEN SALES AND PREVALENCE

Contraceptive sales data ought to match up with prevalence statistics, and they sometimes do. If, for example, we are selling oral contraceptives in a country of 100 million people with 20 million sexually active couples, and we sell 14 million cycles of pills per year, that should translate into 5 percent prevalence being provided by our program's pills: fourteen million cycles equals 1 million CYPs, and 1 million CYPs (couples) equals 5 percent of the target population.

Nevertheless, when we are measuring two different statistical phenomena through two such different means, there is plenty of room for error. This is particularly true in determining the relationship of sales to prevalence for condoms. Error can occur on both sides of the ledger. Sales statistics can be misleading and so can survey data. Some problems on the sales side:

- The expected number of contraceptives (one hundred condoms; fourteen cycles of pills) may not be the number actually used on average by the couples in the population being examined;

- Some contraceptives may be misused;

- Some contraceptives may be smuggled out of the country where the project is taking place; and

- Some sales may be made to couples who switch from other methods or from other brands of the same method.

Obviously if couples are not using the number of condoms by which we translate sales into CYPs (normally one hundred condoms per year), there will be an error in the transposition of sales data into prevalence figures. If our formula uses 100 condoms per couple per year, and in fact couples are only using 75, or 125, that will mar the comparison of the two sets of data. Adjustments may need to be made to allow for this variable, a factor that is not normally a problem with pills and other contraceptive methods whose use does not vary with frequency of intercourse.

Some misuse also occurs with condoms, which have been used as party balloons in Egypt and Bangladesh and probably in a few other countries, and to repair sandals in India. This is not normally a widespread problem in CSM programs because the contraceptives are *sold*, not given away. Program managers must keep an eye out for this kind of misuse, but anecdotal evidence usually surfaces very quickly and corrective action—such as training retailers not to sell condoms to children—can be taken. There are no economically interesting alternative uses for oral contraceptives. There have been rumors of OCs used as plant fertilizer in Bangladesh but such instances, like the use of contraceptive foam as shaving cream (Chapter 6) have been short-term, aberrational phenomena.

Smuggling also occurs. Social marketing products from Bangladesh are found in both India and Burma, for example. There is undoubtedly smuggling of social marketing condoms across borders in southern African and between Nigeria and some other western African countries. When this takes place on a limited scale and the smuggling is between developing countries where the products are badly needed, few serious objections are likely to be raised. However, if the smuggling becomes significant, it will have an impact on statistics that compare sales/CYP data with prevalence data, because survey data are collected exclusively within the borders of the country concerned. If, for example, as has been estimated, 10 percent of the contraceptives sold in the Bangladesh CSM find their way to neighboring countries, then sales/CYP data must be reduced by 10 percent to arrive at our expected prevalence equivalent. If smuggling becomes pronounced, it must be monitored and controlled. Unexpectedly high sales levels near port or other transit cities may be a tip-off.

For both smuggling and misuse problems, pricing may need examination. As long as prices meet the guidelines outlined in Chapter 8, it may be worth considering small price increases to help control either smuggling or misuse (or both) if these are deemed to be problems in any particular project.

Finally, there is the problem of substitution of one method or one brand of contraceptive for another. If social marketing pills are being purchased by couples who have chosen to no longer avail themselves of pills at a government clinic, or if project condoms are being used by couples who previously bought a commercial condom brand, the sales figures must be adjusted accordingly when translating them into expected prevalence. An AID official has correctly pointed out, for example, that the sale of a million units of a new brand of condom in India will have far less impact than the same number of condoms sold in a "virgin" market like Ethiopia. This is because India has had, for years, a large number of competing, relatively low-priced condoms on the commercial market, as well as condoms provided through the government social marketing program and through four private social marketing programs. So the introduction of a new brand in that environment is likely to get many of its customers from those who were purchasing other brands, providing little incremental improvement in overall contraceptive prevalence. In Ethiopia, on the other hand, where essentially no other brand of condom is available at an even remotely affordable price, the CSM Hiwot line of condoms is likely to have a very substantial incremental impact on prevalence because very few consumers will be switching from other brands or methods. In any event, this substitution factor must be allowed for when predicting prevalence from sales (or CYPs).

Beyond the issues of substitution, misuse, and smuggling, CYPs and cost per CYP do not tell us anything about quality of service. This issue is generally more important for clinic-based programs than for social marketing, but it matters for both. Sales and CYP data, for example, do not describe education about use. If women who receive injectables or IUDs are inadequately informed about the possible side effects of those methods, they may discontinue using them when such side effects occur. While this will eventually show up in sales (and prevalence) statistics, it can distort short-term analysis.

Sterilization presents a special quality of service issue. As the procedure is essentially irreversible, anyone undergoing it must be adequately informed about this and related facts so that the decision to have the operation is based on a full understanding of the procedure and its implications. While such information is the norm in family planning programs, failure to provide it is an extremely serious problem that violates fundamental human rights. Adequate counseling and education prior to the performance of sterilization procedures are therefore imperative.

For social marketing programs, the most important quality-of-service issue is education about the use of oral contraceptives. When IUDs and injectables are marketed through social marketing mechanisms, the source of information and education will normally be the provider of service to the end user, a medical or paramedical practitioner. But with oral contraceptives, over-the-counter sales in social marketing projects are commonplace, and the CSM project itself must be careful that women—and where appropriate, their husbands—are adequately informed about proper use. Oral contraceptives are the most easily misused of all contraceptive methods. Women who take a few pills and then stop, or women who believe that they can get adequate contraceptive effects by taking pills only when they have sex, will be ill-served by any program if such misperceptions are not corrected. Social marketers have a special obligation to ensure that their pill customers adequately understand side effects, contraindications, and correct usage so that the method is effective. Failure to provide adequate information will not be revealed in sales/CYP statistics for some time and must be provided for independently.

In terms of education, condoms are not much of a problem. The condom seems to be universally understood; people everywhere seem to know how the method works, and misuse appears to be rare.[5]

PREVALENCE SURVEYS

If additional information is required to be combined with CYP information in order to assess the effectiveness of social marketing programs, what about the effectiveness of surveys? Prevalence surveys have the great advantage of bypassing virtually all of the problems just discussed. Substitution doesn't matter since we are asking people directly what method they are using; misuse and smuggling are essentially irrelevant since we are speaking only with persons living inside the boundaries of our target country, and therefore misused products would not in most cases, be counted. The surveys themselves can include questions that reveal whether pill users are using the product properly.

The problem with surveys is that they depend on consistently accurate answers to questions about the most intimate aspects of couples' private sexual lives, and the questions are usually asked by complete strangers who may also be from a different tribal, ethnic, or socio-economic group. So people frequently give inaccurate answers, not only because all of us have a tendency to tell interviewers what we think the interviewer wants to hear, but because sometimes people simply lie in answering such questions, and sometimes give incorrect answers because they haven't adequately understood the question or lack the knowledge to answer it accurately. Here is a list of other sources of error in survey data (from Fowler and Mangione, 1991):

SOURCES OF ERROR IN SURVEYS

A. The Samples Are a Source of Error:

1. When the sampling frame, or list from which the sample was selected, does not include everyone in the population to be described. . . .

2. Because there is some probability that by chance alone a sample will not perfectly reflect the population from which it was drawn; and

3. When those selected to be in the sample do not provide answers either by refusing to participate altogether or by selectively refusing to provide answers to specific questions.

B. Questions Are Sources of Error:

1. When they are misunderstood;

2. When they require information that respondents do not have or cannot recall accurately; and

3. When respondents are not willing to answer accurately.

C. Interviewers Are a Source of Error:

1. When they do not read questions as worded;

2. When they probe directly;

3. When they bias answers by the way they relate to respondents; and

4. When they record answers inaccurately.

D. Data Reduction Is a Source of Error:

1. When coders inconsistently apply coding rules or use faulty judgment about the appropriate codes to apply; and

2. When data are entered incorrectly into computer-usable files.

So surveys have problems too, and their fallibility is too often underestimated. Indeed, in one of the few cases in which discrepancies between sales/CYP data and prevalence data have been studied in detail, it was found that a substantial part of the problem lay in the surveys rather than in the sales/CYP data. This disparity was referred to in Bangladesh as the "condom gap," the gap being the difference between the number of couples expected to be using condoms on the basis of condom sales, and the number who appeared to be actually using condoms on the basis of the interview data (Ahmed et al., 1987).

The analysis revealed that wives in Bangladesh significantly and consistently underreported condom use, especially when they were interviewed alone. Husbands interviewed alone also underreported condom use, but less so than their wives. When couples were interviewed together the incidence of condom use (based on survey numbers) miraculously increased! The authors of these studies surmise that both men and women in the Bangladesh culture were embarrassed about this product and were therefore reluctant to report its use. When interviewed together, prevarication and evasion by either partner became more difficult, and more accurate data tended to emerge.

Despite these problems, surveys are still by far the best way to measure contraceptive prevalence. As noted, the DHS surveys are carefully conducted and the results generally reliable. Nevertheless, scientists tend to denigrate sales and CYP data when such data disagree with surveys.[6] The results of the "condom gap" problem in Bangladesh teach us that when there is a disparity between survey data and sales data, both sides of the equation need to be examined.

All of this is to show that the interim yardsticks we use in social marketing—sales, couple years of protection, and costs per CYP—are not perfect or all-inclusive, but they remain an astonishingly good and accurate measurement of program success, particularly if we allow for the variables discussed above.

It is worth stressing again how important the availability of such objective yardsticks is. Useful programs from feeding children to building schools to sinking tube wells all appear praiseworthy and often are. But unless we define specific goals for such programs, we are likely to fail. Schools that are built may not be used. Tube wells may flow briefly and then fail. Feeding programs, if too extensive, can undermine local farmers' crop prices as well as create distorting dependencies. But when programmatic goals are defined in measurable output units like CYPs, we can have reasonable confidence that we will know when we are getting somewhere. Our program managers can be held accountable to the discipline in our system, and we can celebrate victories based on objective criteria—like a new monthly sales record or an outstanding sales performance by a staff member. In short, we have a "bottom line," much like a commercial business. We derive our sense of worth by setting explicit, quantifiable goals that allow us to *measure* what we are accomplishing.

THE SIZE OF THE MARKET

Finally, our cost-per-CYP calculations permit us to analyze important variables like the relationship between cost efficiency and market size. Since it has become clear over the years that social marketing programs in big countries tend to be more cost-efficient than programs in smaller ones, I examined this correlation systematically. I calculated costs per CYP for all social marketing programs in 1994 for which those costs were

Figure 9.2
Costs per CYP and Size of Population, Selected Social Marketing Programs, 1994

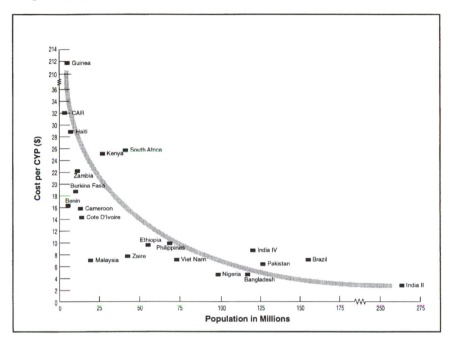

Note: All programs in operation for three years or more.

available and plotted those efficiency figures against the size of the countries (in India's case, states) in which the projects were taking place. The result is Figure 9.2. You will see that the correlation is quite powerful. The lowest costs per CYP (vertical axis, with lowest costs near the bottom) are in markets like India, Bangladesh, and Nigeria, countries near to or exceeding 100 million population (population is delineated on the horizontal axis). The highest costs per CYP are in countries like Guinea and Haiti where the population is under fifteen million.

There are many reasons why social marketing works better in bigger countries. First, there are economies of scale. When the number of beneficiaries is limited, fixed costs must be spread on a relatively small sales base. The cost of management, the expense of operating a vehicle fleet, and many administrative costs are relatively fixed. An overhead of $200 thousand per year means an additional $4 per CYP in a country like Benin, where 50 thousand CYPs is a good performance. In Nigeria, the overhead might be twice as much—$400 thousand. But CYPs in Nigeria are around 1 million, so the larger overhead adds only 40 cents—one-tenth as much—to the cost of serving one couple. Mass media tend to cost more as the number of listeners/readers/viewers goes up, but the differences are frequently not proportional. National TV coverage in Bangladesh reaching perhaps seven million viewers sometimes costs little more than national coverage in Guinea or the Ivory Coast, where the viewership is likely to be fewer than one million people.

The bigger the market the more cost effective the social marketing program is likely to be. We should focus our efforts on countries like India, Ethiopia, Nigeria, and Vietnam—countries that are both populous and poor. It would appear to be particularly inefficient to fund and operate social marketing efforts in tiny countries like Swaziland, Barbados, and Guinea-Bissau.

NOTES

1. I include here as "nonprofit" all those activities that are sponsored by governments and private groups in pursuit of social goals. Some are conducted by for-profit companies on contract.

2. CSM sales statistics usually reflect sales to retailers, or other levels of the trade, because sales to consumers are too difficult to count. However, consumer off-take very soon must become equal to sales to retailers; shopkeepers simply will not go on buying the product (with *their* own money) if consumers do not buy from them.

3. Government donors often do not have this luxury. The amount of funds available for a given country is usually the result of a lengthy political (and bureaucratic) process, and program funds tend to get allocated accordingly. Cost-effectiveness measures hardly mattered, for example, in Pakistan in 1994, when the U.S. Congress pulled the plug on all aid to that country because of its presumed nuclear weapons program.

4. The word "surveys" in this phrase is redundant but is generally included anyway.

5. There is a classic tale of condom misuse that bears repeating. A family planning worker visits a remote Indian village and demonstrates the proper way to unroll the condom on the penis by using a bamboo stake stuck upright in the ground. When the worker returns a few weeks later, there are condom-covered bamboo stakes sticking up on display outside the entrances to half the huts in the village.

6. Scientists, in this case meaning people who examine and measure things for a living, tend to trust survey data because it is scientifically derived (probabalistic samples, cross tabulations), and, I suspect, because it is so expensive to collect. They tend to dismiss sales figures as too "simple." This is, of course, scientific folly.

10

Running a Program

A contraceptive social marketing program is a major undertaking. In order for such a program to be successful, it must have certain components and characteristics, which are discussed in this chapter.

A CSM project requires:

- funding,
- a competent manager,
- contraceptives,
- advertising, usually an advertising agency,
- a distribution system,
- market research capability, and
- a reasonable institutional environment.

PROJECT FUNDING AND BUDGETS

All projects must have a budget. Even a project that is designed to become financially self-sufficient must have start-up funds. For the kind of social marketing project recommended in this book, a budget of $600 thousand (1997 dollars) per year for two years is a reasonable minimum in a normal less-developed country (LDC) setting. This is enough to buy contraceptive supplies equivalent to about 100 thousand couple years of protection. Cost: about $300 thousand with the balance of the budget ($900 thousand) going for operating expenses, including salaries and

Table 10.1
CSM Budget Estimates by Size of Program

Annual CYPs	1997 US Dollars Cost Per Year (000)	Cost/CYP
<50,000	$500-900	$10-50
50,000	$500-900	$10-18
100,000	$600-1,200	$6-12
300,000	$1,200-2,000	$4-7
500,000	$2,000-3,000	$4-6
1,000,000	$3,500-5,000	$3.50-5.00

advertising. If 100 thousand CYPs are provided for a total cost of $1.2 million over a two-year period, the cost per CYP would be $12. This is quite satisfactory for a start-up.

It should be emphasized that this is a minimum start-up amount for a serious program. The definition of an *adequate* budget depends on the size of the country and the cost of mass media there, but begins at about $1 million per year. This amount permits some useful market research, the purchase of needed vehicles, and a little breathing room.

Media cost can make a big difference. In Ethiopia and Vietnam in the mid-1990s, for example, DKT's media cost is less than $100 to reach 5–10 million listeners/viewers for sixty seconds. Comparable national coverage in the Philippines costs over $4,000; in Brazil over $30,000. These differences are partially (but only partially) offset by the fact that your contraceptives can be priced higher in the wealthier markets. For longer-range budgetary planning, you can figure the cost per CYP will drop from $12 to about $5 as the project expands. Table 10.1 gives a rough guideline for these figures.

In a low-income developing country—which is where, I have stressed, our efforts should be focused—the cost per CYP cannot fall much below $3.50, because contraceptives cost $2.50 to $3.00 per CYP (depending on source and quantity) and the consumer can pay only a small part of this. There will always be some marketing, selling, and administrative expenses as well.

As noted earlier, funding for social marketing programs is most commonly obtained from major international donors like USAID, the German KfW, or the British, Dutch, or Swedish governments. The Ford Foundation has funded the start-up of at least one CSM project, and DKT funds many of its own.

Because the government of India routinely subsidizes the cost of condoms and pills to bona fide social marketing ventures, social marketing projects can be operated at a lower cost in India than anywhere else. The subsidy reduces the cost of contraceptives there to a fraction of their cost (condoms < 1¢ each; pills about 3¢ per cycle). Four private CSM organizations benefited from this subsidy in the mid-1990s. The GOI's generous policies cannot always be counted on, however. In 1995–1996 the government failed to renew its contraceptive supply contracts and all four social marketing projects in India cut back on sales or were forced to hustle to buy on the open market at much higher prices.

A GOOD MANAGER

Social marketing managers are an eclectic lot. They vary by nationality, background, education, and many other characteristics. There are no hard and fast rules about qualifications. Business experience is useful, as is some experience with the marketing of consumer goods, but some international experience with donors and governments seems to be even more important. Having made a living in the business world for twenty years, I have a strong pro-business bias myself, but I must admit that social marketing managers whose background has been *only* in the for-profit world frequently do not take well to social marketing management. For one thing, I believe they find it difficult to understand why any organization should go on selling products at a loss. To a businessperson this is a kind of through-the-looking-glass world—"the more we sell the more we lose"—that they can never quite get comfortable with.

Marketing expertise is useful, but not essential. People who have good diplomatic skills and who have run projects that do not directly involve the application of marketing techniques can often learn the marketing aspects quickly and, even if not, the good ones usually manage to hire the necessary marketing expertise, either through an agency or on their own staff. In any case, a competent manager eventually must develop a good marketing "sense."

The ideal manager is one who has had some business background in marketing consumer goods in an international context and has also served in some capacity that required liaison with donors and with local governments. He or she should have worked as a professional in a developing country, dealt successfully with government counterparts, and have some sense of donor needs and interests.

Because the manager is responsible for commissioning advertising and supervising promotion, he or she must believe that marketing can bring about useful social change. I hired one otherwise qualified manager for Bangladesh some years ago and learned, after he had been on the job several months, that he believed that advertising was actually immoral.

Perhaps most important, the prospective manager must be dedicated and enthusiastic. Devotion, determination, and persistence are the secret ingredients in all successful projects (and practically everything else in life), and they are key attributes in a good manager.

Finally, managers must be willing to be measured against the success or failure of the project in pure family planning/AIDS-prevention terms. They must accept the CYP (or equivalent) as the yardstick by which they, personally, will be measured. They must *want* to sell.

Expatriates versus Local Managers

Other things being equal, I favor expatriate managers for social marketing projects for several reasons. Expatriates are relatively free from local communal and political pressures, and they have a high degree of motivation by being "in the spotlight" in the countries where they serve, there being no other reason for them to be there except for the project itself. Self-selection helps here—people will not go to faraway places where living is usually less comfortable unless they are fired up about what they propose to do. I favor the international exchange of personnel on general principles anyway. As mentioned elsewhere, when people live and work in other countries and cultures, they usually bring the world closer together in positive, creative ways. Just as international commerce is served by Japanese managers in Tennessee, and by Filipino executives in Malaysia, and by Americans in China, so are social marketing aims furthered by cross-cultural exchange of working managers. One reason I have always felt that the international exchange of citizens is good and useful is based on my experience serving on the Fulbright review committee when I lived in Bombay. At that time Fulbright scholarships were offered to graduate students in many countries, providing financial assistance for their studies in the United States. This program, named in honor of the U.S. senator from Arkansas who championed it, was based on the worthy assumption that the international exchange of people from different countries and cultures would improve our understanding of one another, would enrich the lives of those who studied and worked abroad, and would also enrich those with whom they met and interacted. As a participant in the process, I came to believe in it.

There have, on the other hand, been some outstanding local managers of CSM projects, and their record is generally as good as that of the expatriates. While expatriates may be free from many local communal pressures, they also lack the networks that well-connected local managers may have.

Local CSM managers in Colombia, Costa Rica, and Egypt have been notably successful. Expatriates have served with distinction in Bangladesh, Sri Lanka, Nigeria, Zaire, Pakistan, Kenya, and Vietnam, among others.

Nationality doesn't matter. Outstanding managers from Canada, the United States, Britain, Sri Lanka, the Philippines, and others have turned in first-class performances as expatriate managers in foreign countries. As far as I can tell, sex doesn't matter either. There have not been many women managers of CSM projects, but the performance of those few has been fine.

Next the manager must:

- locate and acquire contraceptives,
- identify and commission an advertising agency,
- conduct at least some market research,
- identify and contract with a distributor or otherwise arrange for distribution of the contraceptives.

CONTRACEPTIVES

There is a good competitive international market for contraceptives. The best price and quality for condoms is usually found in Malaysia or Thailand, sometimes Korea. Indian manufacturers are becoming more competitive as to quality and their prices have always been good as well. Unpackaged condoms in foil strips meeting the international ISO 4074 standard (generally accepted by the U.N. agencies and others) can be purchased for U.S. 3 to 3.5 cents each in the late 1990s. Attractive packaging in printed cardboard three-packs or four-packs adds about 1 cent per condom. So the fully packaged contraceptive cost per condom is roughly U.S. 4 cents.

Pills cost U.S. 17 to 25 cents per cycle (late 1990s) in unpackaged blister packs. This price includes seven placebos or iron tablets accompanying the twenty-one hormone tablets in the normal cycle of pills. Manufacturers in Europe and the United States vie for this business along with LDC companies, some of which are subsidiaries or partners of the U.S./European firms (e.g., Wyeth/Suaco in the Philippines, Schering/Indonesia). Pill tableting is done in dozens of countries—from India to Indonesia to Mexico.

Depo-Provera and Noristerat as well as other injectable contraceptives are available to international family planning organizations for around $1 per ampoule injection, including disposable syringe. Depo-Provera is manufactured in the United States and Europe by Upjohn and by Upjohn subsidiaries in other countries. Noristerat is manufactured by Schering in Berlin.

Copper T IUDs are available for about $1 (including sterile package and inserter) from Finishing Enterprises in the United States. The Multiload IUD is available from Organon in the Netherlands and from the Organon factory in China.

ADVERTISING

Advertising is a crucial component of any social marketing campaign. An advertising agency is normally a must. In today's increasingly market-oriented world, all but the smallest of developing countries usually have at least two or three ad agencies.

The selection of an agency can be extremely important. In addition to the creative talent that most agencies bring to a project, and their familiarity with local cultural and linguistic norms, a good agency can be a catalytic partner. They will work with your manager (or you) in seeing to it that advertising campaign concepts and slogans are carried through with the distributor sales staff or with project sales staff. They can provide important advice for packaging and countertop presentation containers. They may help you settle on pricing structures and on pricing "deals." But while energy and initiative are crucial attributes of a good agency, they are also the qualities most often missing. Your account is not Coca-Cola or the national airline, and the agency may do little more than what you demand of it. If so, you are not getting your money's worth. Find an agency with key people who are enthusiastic about your project, who will assign one or two individuals for whom your project is their most important job (preferably their *only* job), and who generally exhibit the kind of dedication that you and your staff exhibit to make your brands household words in the country where you operate.

DISTRIBUTION

One of the linchpins of social marketing is the availability of affordable products in many thousands of retail outlets that are convenient to the everyday lives of the majority of the people. No project can succeed unless the contraceptives are available in many thousands—usually tens of thousands—of retail shops. A good distributor can make an enormous difference, and distributors that already sell products in, say, twenty thousand outlets can get your contraceptives into those same twenty thousand outlets relatively quickly and easily. Their salespeople are already calling on these shops and on the wholesalers that serve them. Their transportation infrastructure already exists and is already operating. Particularly if a distributor calls on both pharmacy and non-pharmacy outlets, it may enable you to get your product into most of the places you want in short order.

There are several variations on the distributor/sales staff arrangement in social marketing programs. The first is simply to hire a distributor, pay him a percentage of the selling price, and monitor the performance based on sales and on audits of the retail outlets where the product is supposed to be. The DKT project in Brazil, for example, for its first three years, provided the Biersdorf Company, which distributes Nivea skin cream and other products throughout Brazil, a 35 percent mark-up for the Prudence condom; in exchange for this mark-up (which provided them about $500 thousand per year pre-expense) Biersdorf saw to it that their sales staff aggressively promoted and distributed the Prudence condom. Project management provided Biersdorf with sales aids and with special advertising from time to time in response to the sales staff's particular requests. An example of the latter was several ads run in 1992 specifically addressing the issue of condom quality. There had been some bad publicity in Brazil about defective condoms, and the Biersdorf sales staff was encountering resistance from retailers as a result. The salesmen and -women felt that they had to reassure the trade that Prudence met strict international quality standards, so we ran an ad in several São Paulo newspapers reminding the public that *"Prudence* condoms are tested in conformity with ISO 4070 and ASTM D3492 [standards]."

A similarly straightforward distributor relationship was a characteristic of the Sri Lanka project in 1974. Distribution was the responsibility of Reckett & Coleman, a distribution company that reached essentially all of the important retail outlets of that island nation with its own brand of shoe polish and a popular analgesic called Aspro. The inclusion of the analgesic assured that Reckett's staff would visit most pharmacy outlets, and the shoe polish took them to many general merchandise stores. The addition of condoms and oral contraceptives to their line seemed to fit especially well, and the results were quickly satisfactory.

I remember being especially impressed with the ubiquitousness of the distribution when I first visited Sri Lanka in 1974. Square metal shop signs for Preethi had been provided to Reckett & Coleman, and these Preethi signs jutted out from the fronts of thousands of shops. It looked like Preethi was the new Coca-Cola! Everywhere I traveled the signs were in evidence.

Because socially marketed contraceptives usually sell for such a low price, however, many distributors give them insufficient attention and often need some extra push. This has resulted in at least two other variations on the project-distributor relationship.

The commonest variation is a hybrid arrangement in which a distributor's sales organization is abetted by a few direct-hire project employees—sales representatives or area sales managers—who serve both to prod the distributor's field people and to do some direct selling themselves. These supplementary sales staff can monitor and push the distributor; they also may serve particular areas and markets that the distributor tends to neglect. They may call on low-volume outlets that represent priority targets or which are of particular interest to a donor. This is frequently the case, for example, with nontraditional sales outlets for condoms in AIDS-prevention programs. Project sales representatives may call on brothels and motels, bars and nightclubs where the availability of condoms may be especially important for the prevention of AIDS, whereas a distributor's salesstaff would not normally call on these outlets at all.

Project sales staff have the additional advantage of being exclusively devoted to project products, so they are not distracted by the need to sell other (usually more profitable) ones in the distributor's line.

In the Philippines the DKT project followed this hybrid system. Craig Darden, DKT Philippine project manager during 1991–1995, described the process:

When DKT began operations in the Philippines in 1990, there already existed national distributors of packaged consumer goods who could warehouse, sell, and deliver products. This is significant in that the Philippines is a large archipelago made up of over 7,000 islands with no cheap or efficient highway or road network connecting even the main islands.

However, within a short time after our condom launch with one of the major distributors, Metro Drug, it became increasingly obvious that we would not meet our distribution objectives. While it was quick and easy to achieve a national distribution for our newly-launched brand because of the reputation and reach of the distributor, our Trust condom sales were confined to drug stores and health clinics. Also, field reports from DKT sales management showed that the limited group-type training for the sales reps which was conducted by Metro was inadequate in overcoming retailers' objections and for addressing the salesmen's embarrassment over selling condoms.

I was with one of the Metro salesmen shortly after we launched Strawberry Flavored Trust. We were working the street on his normal sales route. After we left one drug store, we were walking down the street and we passed another pharmacy, but the salesman didn't stop in, and kept on walking. I asked him why we didn't visit this pharmacy, since there were a lot of people at the counter and it seemed like a popular pharmacy, right on Osmena, the main street. He replied that it was a pharmacy which belonged to the Catholic Hospital, which was run by nuns who were very conservative. I insisted we enter however, and we asked at the counter if they had condoms or other contraceptives, which they did (the competition!). The person at the counter told us to see the purchaser upstairs, as she had received several inquiries about Trust.

We went upstairs and asked to see the purchaser, a rather large lady sitting behind a desk stacked full of papers, and surrounded on all sides by her accounting staff, working at their desks with calculators. She asked the salesman, "What do you want?" "I've come to offer you a new product" he replied. "Well, what is it?" asked the purchaser. To this, the salesman whispered in a very low voice "Condoms." "What is it you say?" she asked. "Condoms," he again whispered, this time a bit louder. "I'm afraid I can't hear you, young man, tell me what it is you want to sell or get out of here, since as you can see, I'm very busy!" said the lady. The salesman bent down to the lady and whispered in her ear, "Condoms. I have Trust condoms for sale." "Oh! Trust Condoms, eh?" she shouted, which raised a few heads from the accounting staff. "I've been wondering when you would be coming around here! We've been getting lots of customers asking about them, haven't we girls?" "Oh, yes, yes," they replied in unison. "Especially the flavored ones!" they giggled. The salesman, shocked that his preconceived notions were so far off base, nonetheless had the presence of mind to pull out his order pad and conclude the sale.

Our early experience—events like this one and many others—convinced us that we must design a distribution model which would complement and improve the effectiveness of our distributor's salesforce, augmented by our own sales and promotion teams. In coordination with the distributor, we mapped out sales territories for the new DKT reps which would complement Metro's coverage. Each of the DKT reps was assigned the task of opening new accounts in his or her respective territory, with an emphasis on motels, massage parlors, discotheques, and other establishments associated with the "entertainment" industry, as well as opening supermarkets and grocery stores of all sizes, as these outlets weren't being covered by Metro Drug either. Furthermore, each DKT rep had the added duty of coordinating regularly scheduled companion visits with the distributor's sales reps to provide on-the-job training for the distributor's personnel.

The result of this collaborative effort was a dramatic increase in the number and type of outlets served. The two largest motel chains, Victoria's Court and Anito Lodges, eventually became DKT's largest direct purchasers. (These Philippine "motels" are interesting places for sexual assignations. Victoria's Court has "theme rooms" for lovers' rendezvous. There are "'60's rooms," complete with a bed shaped like a '57 T-Bird and piped-in Buddy Holly music, a "Jungle room" with bird sounds and Tarzan calls, an "Oriental Suite" with bamboo and a rock garden and Japanese music, and the "lover's suite" with heart shaped bed and mirrors on the ceiling and low mood music, to name just a few.)

It's also worth noting that the period of 1992–93 was the time when we had our best sales to these motels. You may recall that during '92 and '93, the Philippines, and especially Manila, was experiencing an energy crisis, with "brownouts" occurring every day for 8–12 hours daily. This was a result of former President Aquino's complete dismantling of the Department of Energy, which she associated with deposed President Marcos and his excesses. In these dark and very hot years, the Manila motels, which had their own generator-supplied electricity, did a booming business. It was hard to find a room, especially on sweltering Manila afternoons and evenings. By 1994, the energy crisis was basically a thing of the past, because President Ramos (who succeeded Corazon Aquino in 1992) placed a high priority on increasing the energy supply, and he was successful in turning the lights back on (and the air-cons!). Thus the irony, that President Aquino, whose fealty to the Church hierarchy made her a staunch opponent of condoms, was the driving force behind increased *Trust* condom sales, at least for a while.

As for our distributor's renewed efforts, after just a couple of years, our dependence on pharmacies for condom sales, which represented 95% of sales in 1991, fell to 68% (and dropping) in 1995, as sales to all the other outlets soared. Pharmacy sales grew too, as the distributor tried to match our own pace. (Darden, 1995)

Distribution Without a Distributor

Another design option is for the distribution function to be conducted entirely or almost entirely by sales staff on direct hire with the project. This transpires either because there is no adequate distributor available or because the available distributors simply cannot be adequately motivated to pay sufficient attention to the project's products. (An example of the latter is described in Chapter 6.)

When the DKT project first began in 1989 in Ethiopia, on the other hand, there simply *was* no distributor. The country was just emerging from a Marxist-oriented, centrally directed and woefully moribund economy. Selling to retailers (even in communist countries, there are retailers!) was therefore undertaken from the beginning by sales staff employed by the project. This was an imaginative and energetic crew. They had to travel on bicycle, jeep, and mule back to reach widely dispersed markets. A lot of travel was of the good old shoe leather variety as these sales reps created their own routes and calling cycles in a country of very poor infrastructure. Some two- and four-wheel motor vehicles were purchased in the mid-1990s, but bicycles continued to be important modes of distribution. Jim Myers, who started the Ethiopia project, reports on the imaginative use of one defunct vehicle:

We had a Land Rover that was rolled over several times and no longer cost effective to repair, so we pulled the engine (sold the parts), packed the vehicle with HIWOT condoms and then towed it to different parts of Addis Ababa each day where it served as a mini-warehouse for the bicycle boys (so they didn't have to come back to the office all the time) and simultaneously served as a HIWOT [Hiwot means "life" in Amaharic, one of Ethiopia's principal languages] condom kiosk. It was painted with HIWOT logos and had lots of Amaharic sayings promoting condom use. (Myers, 1995)

Ethiopia presented plenty of sales and distribution challenges; sales had gotten under way in the midst of the long civil war. In one of the more dramatic episodes, a DKT sales representative was given permission to fly into rebel-held territory in Asmara (now in Eritrea), only to be greeted by a nearby hail of bullets as passengers disembarked from the plane. Opportunities being where you find them, the rep made his first condom sale under a desk in the airport waiting lounge.

Other efforts were born of energy problems in Ethiopia. For example, in the early days, program staffers passed out AIDS brochures and the HIWOT shopping bags to motorists waiting in gas lines, which often extended for one or two kilometers. In one ninety-minute stint at a single gas line more than three thousand condoms were sold.

There is no rule for the "best" distributor arrangement. If a social marketing project has a good distributor, a great deal of time, expense, and effort can be saved. If the distributor (or distributors; sometimes it pays to use more than one) performs satisfactorily, the project may have to contribute only catalytic inputs to the distribution function. If a hybrid arrangement works, stick with it. If all else fails, a project manager must do whatever is necessary to see that the distribution function is adequately carried out, even if all distribution must be conducted by project staff. We have seen why this was necessary in Bangladesh and Ethiopia. It also seems to be a growing tendency with social marketing programs generally. In the late 1990s, CSM projects in the Philippines and Brazil switched over to staff distribution, as did one of the projects in India. So, despite the fact that distributors can do much to get a project launched, more and more CSM managers are finding that independent distribution companies do not have what it takes to keep a project growing over the long run. If that happens, roll up your sleeves and do it yourself.

MARKET RESEARCH

The importance of market research in social marketing varies considerably from project to project. While one simply cannot operate a social marketing program without products, advertising,[1] and distribution, it does appear possible to do so with very little advance research. Part of the reason is that in a well-run program, managers are adept at making mid-course corrections and they are normally in a continuous mode of refining the project's marketing messages, getting feedback, and making appropriate adjustments. This form of trial and error marketing may itself be, technically, a method of research, but that is not the way supporters of market research normally think of it.

Western marketing experts probably rely too heavily on preliminary research and insufficiently emphasize the importance of continuous learning, feedback, and refinement (at which the Japanese are particularly adept). Even if you develop brand names with carefully selected focus groups, try them out on scientific samples of the population, pre-test your advertising messages, including testing a half dozen messages and themes against each other, you will almost never come up with a combination that does not need amendment. All campaigns must be continuously redefined and, for this reason, starting off with very little knowledge is perfectly feasible. For example, as long as I had ascertained that the brand names did not have some negative connotation in the local language, I would not hesitate to start a social marketing program with Trust brand condoms and Microgynon brand pills in a new market virtually anywhere in the world. I would further be comfortable using colorful and attractive point-of-purchase display material that stresses that the condoms are reliable, meet international standards of quality, and are effective protection for men and women. Initial ads could promote Trust as a reliable and safe method of family planning. Similarly, Microgynon pills could be promoted to the medical profession and to the pharmacy trade as a low-dose, safe, minimal-side-effects, highly reliable method of family planning that is completely reversible when the couple wishes to have a child.

Assuming that the local government did not object, I would be prepared to take this approach to marketing in any country, and figure that it might work pretty well. Once feedback began to come in—for example, to the effect that pill users were concerned about the association of pills with cancer, or with interference with the "natural" menstrual cycle— these issues could then be addressed.

Let me be clear: going out blind like this is not my preference. Market research can reveal a great deal of extremely useful information, particularly about the positioning of your product. But it does seem possible to start and operate a social marketing project with very little research, and this has been done on a few occasions with quite satisfactory results. In the Vietnam project, for example, one of social marketing's more recent success stories, very little research was conducted prior to launch, though the project was able to take advantage of some very useful research that was already available. (See Chapter 11.)

Do perform some basic research if you can. For guidance on this and on research priorities, see Alan Andreasen's (1995) excellent description of "backward research." Andreasen makes the point that, at the very least, we should not do research unless we know in advance how we will use the results. The first step in backward research is to determine what key decisions are to be made using the research results, and then to determine what information will best help management make those decisions. In other words, don't go looking for "interesting" information just because it is interesting; stick to the generation of data that will help you make your most important decisions. In the social marketing of contraceptives, the varying beliefs that people hold about birth control and about specific contraceptive methods are usually the most important areas to investigate.

In India, for example, market research conducted by PSI revealed widespread concern by women about the side effects of oral contraceptives and particular concern about possible difficulties in getting pregnant after discontinuing use of the Pill. Having this information enabled project managers to address these concerns directly in advertising for PSI's Pearl oral contraceptive. In some circumstances the information revealed by this kind of research can be of great importance.[2]

Andy Piller reports from his work in Vietnam that:

The lack of any condom brand awareness in Vietnam [in 1993] meant that we pretty much had a wide open field for establishing a product image which we were able to develop from our rudimentary research along with the research done by others.

We didn't do very much pre-testing for advertising either because of the low production costs (initially about US$700 to produce a 30-second spot). At that price, it was cheaper to develop an ad (based on the information already available) and see what kind of response it got. This has worked fine. (Piller, 1995)

Once Trust condoms and Choice pills were launched in Vietnam, it was clear that there was a strong demand for high-quality branded contraceptives; because sales were so brisk, there has not seemed to be any need for research subsequently. This may change as the project progresses. But for at least four years, keeping adequate supplies in the distribution pipeline was a bigger problem than product positioning or message refinement. In such circumstances sophisticated or extensive research is a postponable luxury.

Similarly, the Hiwot condom in Ethiopia has been successful with minimal market research. When the marketing systems in a country are at a very rudimentary level of development, brand-awareness advertising and advertising that simply stresses the most obvious advantages of a product are often sufficient.

The Ethiopia CSM experience also illustrates an important point about how easily an outside force can override market research results. In 1990 research showed that Addis Ababa consumers strongly preferred the condom brand name Gasha, meaning "shield," accompanied by a shield design. But this name was vetoed by the Ethiopian government as being too "military" and perhaps too reminiscent of the deposed Emperor Haile Selassie, who, as "the Lion of Judah," had often employed traditional shields among his symbols of power. Jim Myers, who was DKT's Ethiopia program manager from 1990–1993, gives the flavor of conducting market research there, and a mini-course on keeping research in perspective and adjusting as you go along.

Late in 1989, when I first went to Addis, all that Ethiopia had, by way of advertising, was one man who owned and operated Lion Advertising Agency, the only show in town. Lion Advertising was a one-person operation and more of a PR group than an ad agency. The "studio" featured an old Aiwa reel-to-reel tape recorder, which produced "world class" quality radio spots, complete with traffic noises for background because the studio, with broken windows that faced a noisy street, also served as the reception and office. Graphics and creative departments were "in the planning stages." Under the circumstances, we decided to go it alone.

Marxism, and central planning, had two good things going for them: vast numbers of statues depicting the suppressed, and later freed masses, and every "service" occupation had its correct central location. One simply had to drop by the bus repair garage and you had every mechanic in the country who was trained/skilled in bus repair, all under one roof. Same held true for furniture makers, matchstick makers, and what have you. Now we had our focus groups, even the high-risk [for sexually transmitted diseases] groups like truck drivers, very conveniently collected in one place, at no cost to us.

Country liquor shops (Tej Bets), as traditional as English high teas, provided yet another source of high-risk groups for conducting market/consumer surveys. It really wasn't hard to find people to talk to and no "stratified samples" were needed.

We identified possible logos by looking at the various statues dotted around the city. I liked three or four, all of which had a common theme . . . the GASHA (shield). I asked the graphic artist girlfriend of a UN volunteer living in Addis to make a few sketches. I wanted at least one sketch to include a woman, because I felt strongly about women taking charge in contraceptive use. Also I had plans to advertise that "it was o.k. for women to buy condoms." (We also ended up with a female salesperson for condoms. She was, and perhaps still is, one of the best sales people we employed.)

In addition to the "Gasha" sketches we also had some symbols of Ethiopia's rich cultural history . . . the Lion's head on the back of a 10-cent Ethiopian coin, a man in traditional Ethiopian dress. And then we had Prudence condom packets from Zaire. The focus groups, all sexually active men, quickly jumped on the GASHA logo as something they wanted to see on "their" condom packets, for all the usual macho reasons. Prudence didn't even get a second look.

We did our market research by visiting those massive workshops (after obtaining administrative approval to do so, not easy, by the way), identifying the foreman of each repair section (brakes, transmissions, injectors, etc.), and explaining to him our purpose. DKT was going to provide good-quality condoms for the prevention of HIV/AIDS, and would sell them at various locations, including their workshop if they would like, and we wanted to design a packet, with an Ethiopian name, and thus wanted their ideas. Through a Ministry of Health employee, who was translating into Amharic for us, we asked six or eight questions. We first explained that we wanted to develop a name for the condom, so that people wouldn't have to say the big "C" word each time, and listed a few, including the Amharic terms for LION, SHIELD, SPEAR, etc. Then we showed them the various sketches and noted their comments and remarks. We then "researched" price by asking "would you pay Birr $1.00 for a condom? would you pay Birr $1.00 for 3 pieces? and so on till we got what seemed like a reasonable consensus. The number of pieces per packet was approached the same way. We also tied the number of pieces per packet to the amount of "available change" they had for the purchase of condoms. (The 2-piece HIWOT Trust packet developed in year two of the program, which sold for 15¢ Ethiopian (half the price of original HIWOT four packet) was launched because students, our special target audience, only had about 15¢ "extra cash" to spend on condoms and they didn't want their parents to catch them with condoms in their pockets, so two pieces was ideal.)

As is often the case once you get an idea finalized and a logo and brand name settled, something happens. I was never sure if there was a place to register products/brand names. One probably didn't discuss such things under a Marxist society, but the Council of Ministers, the folks in power during those days, decided that GASHA was a slam against the military (who were the ones really in power) and GASHA would not be permitted. I often wondered why the Council of Ministers, who were fighting a losing battle against the rebels in the late 80's, had to approve the name of our condom . . . seems they would have had more on their minds, but GASHA was out. Until that time, we had been thinking about names that offered protection (because of AIDS prevention, etc.). We then started throwing about other names, and HIWOT (meaning "life") was one of those names. The artist, who had since broken up with her boyfriend, was about ready to head back to the UK, but before leaving did a few more sketches for us. One of the things that came out of the research was that they didn't want the logo to appear to be too Ethiopian, whether it was the shape of the GASHA or the faces of the people. Our artist did some black and white silhouettes of people, who could have been Ethiopian, they could also have been Sudanese or Somalian. We threw in the sun, which was originally planned to be a moon! (night-time and sex and condom use concept), but because the condom was called "life" this couple was depicted to be looking off into the sun (future) and they would have a future because they were using HIWOT condoms and saving their life together.

It seems to me that extensive market research is often a waste of time and money. The Liberians say "too much book is not good" . . . and they are right!

In more sophisticated economies, more research is likely to be required, but there is much wisdom to the minimal approach.

Actually as I think about it, our service to the trade—free delivery, regular delivery with no kick-backs, understanding and willingness to listen to the shop owners, was probably as important to our success as anything else we did. (Myers, 1995)

Running the Organization

With all of the above components in place, it is still easy to run a bad program. You must hire good people, who not only share your enthusiasm for birth control and AIDS prevention but will also take real pleasure in advertising, selling, and distributing. And you must delegate to those people. The worst organizations in the world have bosses who want to keep their fingers on all the strings. Don't be one of those.[3]

The size of the staff of a social marketing project can vary all the way from just two or three people to several hundred. If you are fortunate enough to have a good distributor, a good and enthusiastic advertising agency, a competent market research firm, and reliable suppliers, you should need very few people on your own staff. There is little relationship, by the way, between the number of staff and overall project efficiency, though "lean and mean" is always a good rule, other things equal.

MANAGEMENT: AUTONOMY, GOVERNMENTS, DONORS

The best institutional arrangement for conducting a social marketing program is private management with appropriate support from the donor and the local government. A near ideal arrangement is one in which the donor signs an agreement with an implementing agency like SOMARC or PSI, spells out what results, reports, and financial accountability it expects from the implementing agency, and then leaves the day-to-day operation of the project to the private organization. The local government extends its permission for the activity and facilitates it through necessary visa approvals, product registrations, import permits, and, where applicable, duty and tax concessions.

Surprisingly, this ideal arrangement, or something very much like it, is not all that rare. DKT's relationship with the German KfW and the government Health Department in the Philippines pretty well fits this model. Several of PSI's and SOMARC's programs also come pretty close.

The addition of a private counterpart organization may complicate the pattern slightly, but is effective in many countries and often helps provide continuity. SOMARC's arrangement with PROFAMILIA, the local family planning association in the Dominican Republic, fits this design, and has worked well. The Society for Family Health in Nigeria and the Pakistani NGO, Social Marketing Pakistan have also functioned smoothly as PSI counterparts.

However, the institutional relationships in CSM programs are often more complicated than this and many are beset by problems. I have mentioned elsewhere that the relationship between USAID, PSI, the Woodwards (distribution) Company, and the parastatal NDFC in Pakistan in the early 1980s was an institutional nightmare. AID funds went directly to Woodwards whose bills had to be approved by the NDFC, while PSI was expected to design advertising and other aspects of the project. Even worse was the Egyptian CSM episode that took place when the "musical chairs" of directors and executives at Family of the Future, the private organization that started the project, resulted in a Health Department takeover of FOF's board (see Appendix 2). The process decimated FOF, which had run one of the world's best projects for nearly ten years.

Simple arrangements, with clear authority vested in the (private) implementing organization, work best. Because family planning historically has been part of government-to-government foreign aid, many donor governments and host governments still need to become comfortable with private-sector CSM management. Enormous progress has been made in this area in the past decade. When Peter King and his colleagues were designing the world's first contraceptive (social) marketing project in India in 1964, it was simply assumed that the government would be a key player and that any funds provided by outside donors would be provided to the Indian government. Today, it is quite common for donors to supply funds directly to private grantees, be they family planning associations or international private organizations (always, of course, with permission from the host government).

As detailed earlier, private management of day-to-day CSM operations is essential. The payment of commissions to sales staff is one good example of the kind of time-tested business practice that makes this kind of social marketing particularly inimical to government supervision. Virtually none of the sixty-three programs operating in 1997 were managed by governments. One, in India, is traditionally a government effort, but is becoming increasingly privatized. Another, in Jamaica, worked remarkably well under government supervision for a decade or more, but it too was turned over to a private company in 1994.

Social marketing projects succeed best when the implementing organizations have a sense of ownership of the projects that they are managing. This means that they should be involved in design and policy matters, as well as project administration. The best projects (Colombia, Bangladesh, Vietnam, Costa Rica) were designed and have been nourished, refined, and expanded by the same organizations that manage these projects on a daily basis. This is one of the reasons that the submission of CSM management contracts to a competitive bidding process has not worked well. Bidders cannot normally be involved in the early design phases of the projects.

IS THIS EASY?

The number of social marketing programs that have been started with at least modest success in the past twenty-five years—more than fifty programs—suggests that starting and operating such a program is not a terribly difficult task. In many ways this is so. Social marketing managers are asked to use time-tested techniques to sell branded consumer products that are of high interest to the great majority of the world's adult population, with no need to make a profit! In theory, it shouldn't be hard, but it often is. The imposition of new organizational designs that turn out to be cumbersome and ineffective, the unexpected defunding of projects in mid-stream (as happened to Mexico's PROFAM project in 1981 and Sri Lanka's CSM project in the late 1970s), the loss of interest on the part of a key player like Sterling Drug in Nigeria in 1990, the simple entropy that seems to have taken over with regard to Mexico's Protektor condom, and political/organizational snafus can all wreak havoc with otherwise good programs. The key component seems to be a management unit that is dedicated to the long-term success of the program, based on its commitment to family planning and/or AIDS-prevention goals. When there is such a unit, whether it is a family planning association as in Colombia, an international implementing agency like PSI or SOMARC (when SOMARC directly manages its own programs) or DKT, or a specially created organization like ASDECOSTA in Costa Rica, these projects are remarkably durable. Of twenty-one CSM programs started between 1970 and 1986, seventeen were still operating in one form or another in 1995, with an average duration of more than fifteen years. (And of the four that were terminated, one—Kenya—was replaced after a fifteen-year hiatus; another—Sterling in Nigeria—was folded into PSI's project, only two projects have actually ended.)

The projects in Colombia and Bangladesh have not missed a beat for nearly twenty years. Colombia's PROFAMILIA is *committed* to its family planning objective. So are PSI and the SMC in Bangladesh (PSI stepped down from its role in Bangladesh in 1997. That project is now entirely in the hands of the local Social Marketing Company.) The Bangladesh project is particularly notable for having survived repeated political up-heavals, including the assassination of three heads of state and tumultu-ous government successions. Other projects have survived de-funding. Mexico's PROFAM kept going on a small scale for at least twelve years after a funding cut-off. The Sri Lanka project similarly carried on after a de-funding process (though at a predictably reduced level) because the FPA in Sri Lanka is dedicated to the goals of CSM in that country. The Central American projects have sailed along pretty smoothly under the tutelage of the organizations created to run them (or already existing Family Planning Associations), for an average duration of more than four-teen years. And, if funding continues to be available, there is every reason to believe that the twenty relatively new projects in sub-Saharan Africa will be carrying on at increasing levels (and at decreasing costs per CYP) ten or fifteen years from now.

When they are run by committed organizations, CSM projects have real staying power.

NOTES

1. Some projects, e.g., Thailand in the early 1980s and India's Nirodh project for several extended periods, have even tried to get by without advertising. To my mind this defeats at least half the purpose of social marketing—informing and educating people about contraceptives. The advertising budget should be cut off only during dire emergencies.

2. Market research is *always* important in a generic (non-brand-oriented) cam-paign. When one is attempting to affect behavior change with information and persuasion (no product) alone, research becomes more important because there is no feedback from hard sales data.

3. See "The Boss Who Won't Let Go" (Harvey, 1994a).

11

Advertising: The Fuel of Social Marketing

When Aeschines spoke, they said, "How well he speaks." But when Demosthenes spoke, they said, "Let us march against Philip!" I'm for Demosthenes.

—David Ogilvy

Good social marketing advertising for contraceptives has the same characteristics as good advertising for margarine or mouthwash. It appeals to a sense of something people want and promises that the product will satisfy those wants in important ways. There is one important difference, however: While commercial advertisers are most frequently engaged in efforts at building or maintaining market share, CSM marketers must expand the total market—for contraceptives and for the practice of family planning generally. The overall impact of social marketing advertising should therefore be to persuade people who would not or might not otherwise practice birth control to buy and use contraceptives. This decision by consumers is an important one, likely to affect their family, their future, and their physical, emotional, and economic well-being. Whether they choose brand A soap or brand B soap is much less likely to impact their lives in such basic ways.[1]

WHAT DO WE HAVE TO OFFER?

The things that people want in life have not changed much over time. The following is Victor Schwab's 1950 list of things people wanted:

- better health,
- more money,
- greater popularity,
- improved appearance,
- security in old age,
- praise from others,
- more comfort,
- more leisure,
- pride of accomplishment,
- business advancement,
- social advancement, and
- increased enjoyment. (Simon, 1965, p. 110, citing Barton (ed.), 1950)

These wants appear to be virtually universal, varying only in the ways they are sought and prioritized from one culture to the next. A farmer in Bangladesh seeks these things, as does a housewife in Amsterdam.

Those of us who advertise contraceptives are fortunate that contraceptives can satisfy more of these wants than almost any other product. Contraceptives enhance the pleasures of sex (increased enjoyment) by removing the fear of pregnancy. Planned pregnancies mean better control of the family budget and thus "more money" available to the family unit; spaced births lead to better education for a family's children (pride of accomplishment); spaced pregnancies lead to "better health" for both children and mothers; a less crowded household means "more comfort" and "more leisure"; even "improved appearance" and "security in old age" can be the result of practicing birth control—the desire of young mothers to maintain a youthful appearance is greatly abetted by not having too many pregnancies too close together. And the improvement in family finances may result in greater old age security, even to the extent of offsetting any diminishment that results from having fewer sons in cultures where they are expected to provide that security.

So CSM advertisers have a double advantage: they can use advertising techniques developed over many centuries to promote products that usually satisfy only one or two human needs, to promote a product that satisfies quite a large number of them. Two of the world's biggest advertisers, Coca-Cola and Pepsi, must appeal to just one item on Schwab's list—increased enjoyment—albeit a particularly powerful one, especially when one envisions the prospect of an ice-cold sweet drink on a very hot day. And therein lies Coke's big advantage and the challenge for family planning advertisers: immediate gratification. The payoff for contraceptive use is usually many months, or at least a few weeks ("I'm not pregnant *now*"), away.

PROMISE A BENEFIT

When I send someone off to run a social marketing program in another country, I provide him or her with a copy of David Ogilvy's book, *Confessions of an Advertising Man* (1963). Ogilvy conveys the importance of listening to the consumer, of doing the research that will enable you to position your product for maximum sales and profits, and the importance of creating ads that promise the consumer a benefit. This last point seems self-evident: if an ad does not hold out a benefit to the consumer (postponed pregnancy; whiter teeth; tastier meals) it is unlikely to inspire people to purchase the product advertised. But it remains as true today as when Ogilvy first started writing copy in the 1950s that millions of dollars are wasted on ads that fail to promise a benefit or even to provide necessary information.

An extreme example was an "ad" run in *Forbes* magazine in March 1996. It consisted of eleven consecutive pages, five of which, at perhaps $30 thousand each, were completely and intentionally blank! The remaining six pages said: "All of the space . . . We're wasting in this magazine . . . is nothing . . . compared to what American businesses . . . are wasting . . . in their offices" followed by a brief pitch for "use of space and furniture" services. What a waste! Over $300 thousand on a message that need only have cost a tenth that much. There ought to be a law against throwing away money on such "creative" ads!

Of course, not all promotional activities consist of benefit-promising advertisements. In building brand awareness social marketers have made good use of imprinting contraceptive logos and brand names on T-shirts, baseball caps, keychains, boat sails (see Figure 6.1), billboards, score cards, calendars, and shopping bags. These promotional strategies are often effective in making people aware of your product and its name.

But when your agency sits down to write an advertisement, they should do so with the understanding that the ads must promise the consumer a benefit unless there is a very good reason (such as censorship considerations) for not doing so.

THE VIRTUES OF DIRECT RESPONSE

A direct response advertisement is an ad that provides the consumer with the opportunity to respond directly to it, either by filling out and mailing in a coupon, or by calling a telephone number to request information or to purchase the product offered. The largest volume of direct response advertising is in the form of direct mail—catalogs or other mailers sent to people's homes or businesses offering products or services. But a great deal of direct response advertising is also run in newspapers and magazines with coupons and phone numbers, and a growing body of advertising on television is also entering the direct response category with toll-free phone numbers to call for information on (or to purchase) a whole variety of products. The most common television direct response ads in the United States are for music CDs—often collections of "golden oldie" songs that appeal to very broad audiences—exercise machines, and "relationship" videos.

Direct response has the dramatic advantage of telling the advertiser almost immediately whether his ads are effective or not and, if so, exactly how effective they are. The ad in Figure 3.1, for example, ran in the *New York Times* on June 6, 1997. Within two weeks, those of us who created and ran the ad, knew we had a successful placement. The ad space in the *Times* had cost $10,158. One hundred and seventy-one orders, totaling $8,140 had been received, and we could project with a high degree of certainty that about 250 more orders would be received in the weeks immediately following, based on prior experience with response patterns in the *New York Times*.[2] If, rather than offering the videos directly in the ad itself, we had run the same headline and the same copy followed by an imprecation to the reader to visit his or her local video store to purchase the videos at retail, then reading the results—that is, reading the cost effectiveness of the advertisement itself—would have been vastly more difficult. While one could measure increases in the sales of these videos in the stores in the general area of the *New York Times* readership, the extent to which those sales were prompted by the ad, as opposed to, say, a change in the positioning of these videos on the store shelves or an increase in store traffic resulting from unrelated promotions by the stores, would be virtually impossible to assess. Difficulties in weighing these many variables in advertising effectiveness is what has led several advertisers to complain that "half the money I spend on advertising is wasted, and the trouble is I don't know which half" (Ogilvy, 1963:59).

Another advantage of direct-response advertising, and of special importance to family planners, is the psychological boost it gives to the advertiser. When those coupons start pouring in, or the toll-free number starts to ring, you have tangible proof that people out there are *interested* in your product, that there is a real thirst for information about family planning (for example), and that what you offer is needed. I remember the dozens of heart-rending letters we received in Colombia in 1974 after a direct-mail campaign. PSI had teamed up with PROFAMILIA to promote attendance at PROFAMILIA clinics. We mailed a booklet ("Guide to Family Planning"), accompanied by a coupon good for a free first visit to any of the clinics listed in the brochure, to a mailing list of rural and urban adult women in selected areas of Colombia. Despite the fact that we did not request any mail response (the reader was urged to take the coupon to a clinic), we got lots of letters from women clearly desperate for conception control. One wrote (in Spanish):

Truthfully, I don't know how I am not pregnant, not having used any method of birth control. However, I will say that sometimes I use a douche of vinegar, but not always. I am working and I always worry about whether or not I am pregnant, and I am frightened of having an abortion done, which I haven't had done often, but the last time was the beginning of 1972, and I recovered reasonably well.

Please advise me what I should do to avoid a pregnancy, but I forgot to tell you that I have five children, one girl 25 years old, a son 22 years old, another son 19 years old, a son 14 years old and the last one 12-½ years old, so it would be terrible to get pregnant now. I also wish to tell you that my husband is quite irresponsible and this is the reason I still have to work, and have worked 27 years, to look after my children.

I believe that it isn't appropriate to use a pessary at my age. Please advise me as to the best method of avoiding a pregnancy. I am grateful and await your prompt reply.

This kind of feedback provides both useful information and a sense of the importance of one's work.

Despite such advantages, very little direct-response advertising has been used by family planning providers in developing countries, and that is a great pity, for what little work has been done in this field appears to have worked pretty well. George Cernada (1970) reported on a number of direct-mail programs for family planning in South Korea, Taiwan, and India. Other direct-response promotions were examined by Wilber Schramm (1971). Among other things, Schramm pointed out that direct mail can be effective even among populations of very low literacy. "One of the interesting findings of family planning campaigns in Asia has been that direct mail can be effective even among families unable to read: It is so unusual and exciting to receive a letter that the recipients make sure they find someone to read it to them" (Schramm, 1971:4). John Davies has pointed out that "it is a common sight in Sri Lanka to see one person reading a newspaper to several others" (Davies, 1978).

More recently, a carefully controlled series of direct-response couponed ads were run by the Bangladesh CSM project in two newspapers. One purpose was to get information about what advertising themes would appeal to Bangladeshi readers. All the ads offered a free brochure about family planning with details about contraceptives, and the copy in each ad was the same. The headlines, however, were changed to present one of three overall themes: The first was concerned with the bread-and-butter issues ("Is there enough space in your house for another child?"; "Can you feed another mouth?"). The second theme centered around family health ("Can you afford the health needs of your family?"). The third theme focused on the wife ("How much more money will she need?"; "Will she really be happy?"). The coupons came pouring in and the free family planning booklet was mailed out to nearly five thousand respondents.

The most effective headlines were overwhelmingly the economic themes. Indeed, as measured by information requests, the economic themes were an astonishing seven times more effective than the health themes or the wife-focused themes in generating responses (Harvey, 1984).

Not only did this experience provide us with a good deal of important information about writing contraceptive ads, it also provided important information about the circulation and readership of the two newspapers. A newspaper called *Ittefaq* was responsible for eliciting by far the largest number of responses overall relative to the cost of the ads in that publication. The average cost per response in *Ittefaq* was only U.S.65 cents, as opposed to $2.83 per response in the other paper (*Sangbad*). This means that *Ittefaq* almost certainly delivers more readers for the advertising dollar (or advertising taka) than the other paper and would probably represent a good investment for future print advertising for Raja condoms or Maya pills.

Any consumer goods advertisement, including contraceptive advertisements, can carry a coupon at the bottom which permits interested consumers to get further information about the product. ("For a free brochure about family planning and about Trust condoms and Choice pills, fill out the coupon below and mail it to us today.") Such a tagline in no way detracts from the ad's power behind the branded product being advertised. And, if the product itself is not being offered through the mail but, instead, the offer is only a brochure or booklet, retailers will not object that the couponed ad is taking away from in-store sales. For condoms I favor a free sample as well; this doesn't bother retailers. A few people will complain about access by children, but I have never known a child to be harmed by a condom.

So why don't more social marketers use the direct-response device? The most often cited reason is that mail services are unreliable in many countries and that people will therefore be reluctant to request even something for free. In my experience, this is not so. The mails in south Asia, for example, and in many African countries, are fast and reliable.

Another reason may simply be that direct-response advertising has not gained a major foothold in very many developing countries and, therefore, most ad agencies are simply unaccustomed to dealing with it. But family planners should take the lead in doing more of it, because it offers a valuable tool for fast and inexpensive market research as well as an excellent way to get your message out.

DO WHAT YOU CAN

A firm rule of contraceptive advertising in social marketing programs is, of course, to do what you can. Contraceptives are controversial in all cultures and, as noted elsewhere, governments usually control the airwaves and can dictate the content of your ads in the broadcast media and often in many of the most important print media as well. This has, at times, necessitated toning down ads to the point that the benefits offered largely disappeared. As previously noted, Sathi condom ads in Pakistan could not, in the early going, use the word "condom" or "Sathi." The best PSI could manage was to get a photo of the box and logo on the screen with vague references to family planning. If that is the best you can do, it may still be worth doing. In some societies there is so little competitive advertising that even relatively bland ads for your product may prove a good deal more effective than nothing at all.

Stress Basics

Don't get too "creative." David Ogilvy (1963) used to forbid new copywriters to use the word "creative" to describe their functions at his agency. He quotes Bernard Berensen as having noted that "the only thing the Etruscans added to the art of the Greeks was 'the originality of incompetence.' " There are no creative or noncreative copywriters, says Ogilvy, only good admakers and bad. So keep it simple. Straightforward approaches are almost always the best way to begin. Condoms can be promoted as reliable and trustworthy and of the highest possible quality. All contraceptives can be promoted on the basis of child spacing ("Until you want another child, rely on Preethi"). The idea of having a choice in your life is not a terribly controversial one; simple ads can emphasize that customers can better control their lives by planning their families.

Don't let your ad agency try to win prizes. You don't want your ads to be admired, you want them to sell your product. David Ogilvy defines a good advertisement as "one which sells the product *without drawing attention to itself*" (1963:90, Ogilvy's emphasis).

This is a very difficult lesson to learn. We all want our work to be admired, and social marketers, particularly, will have their ads remarked upon by colleagues in the professional community, by donors, by government officials, and by others. If your advertising is on national networks or nationally circulated print media, it is inevitable that representatives of these "establishment" groups will see your advertising and comment on it. But when everyone is full of praise, look out! It is very likely that you are pandering to the elites. This is often done by using ads that show simple "culturally correct" rural life, which is almost always a bad idea. Most rural villagers aspire to the modern amenities of the city. Despite this, there are admittedly times when it may be wise to run an ad or two solely for the impact it will have on donors and/or government officials. This should not be beneath you. Politics is part of the game. Do not fool yourself that such advertising will also work with your target market.

Instead, keep trying your ads out on ordinary people. As I have repeatedly mentioned, and as revealed particularly well in Jim Myers's description of market research in Ethiopia, these do not have to be formal focus groups. But they do have to be people who are reasonably representative of your target market. They are the ones whose opinions count, though even their opinions as to how "good" the ads are need to be tested against marketplace realities. What really counts is whether your advertising sells the product, and that is why David Ogilvy (and I) place such a heavy emphasis on direct-response testing. In a direct-response ad, customers talk directly to you, often with their own money. This is something you can believe.

TEST EVERYTHING

Pretest your ads and, if possible, test more than one idea. Pre-testing advertising slogans and concepts is quick, easy, and inexpensive. Rough-up two or three storyboards and show them to a focus group (or even to some people in the market, or to taxi drivers waiting for fares). If you have the time and budget for it, produce some spots that can be interspersed with program footage so that focus group participants are not aware that they are judging only the contraceptive ads. Being a little less focused on the ads themselves, they may be less biased and more forthcoming when the subject of the ads is eventually introduced.[3]

The reason for testing more than one advertising idea or concept is, again, to help eliminate bias. When we sit down with our agency and get fired up about an idea, we just "know" that we have a terrific advertising concept—a concept that will revolutionize advertising in this decade. It can't miss! It can be very sobering to listen to the members of a focus group pick apart your brilliant concept and indicate their strong preference for an alternative concept that you may have very well thought was mediocre. Testing works. David Ogilvy says: "Test your promise. Test your media. Test your headlines and your illustrations. Test the size of your advertisements. Test your frequency. Test your level of expenditure. Test your commercials. Never stop testing, and your advertising will never stop improving" (1963: 86).

GENERIC CAMPAIGNS

Social marketing managers sometimes regard generic family planning campaigns or AIDS prevention campaigns with skepticism. They shouldn't. A well-designed generic campaign will almost always lead to increased sales of all contraceptives, and the low-priced contraceptives of a well-run social marketing project are very likely to be the primary beneficiaries.

The skeptical feeling comes from the view that it seems somehow wasteful to invest substantial funds in advertising campaigns that do not mention your brands. Issue advertising—that is, generic family planning or AIDS prevention—seems somehow "soft" because it doesn't ask the viewer/listener/reader to go out and buy condom Y or pill X; the results of a generic campaign cannot be promptly read in the sales statistics of particular products.

I already have noted the advantages of promoting a brand as opposed to promoting an idea. But idea advertising can be of tremendous importance. Two excellent examples are discussed in this book. One is the AIDS prevention campaign in Zaire (below); the other is the two-year generic campaign in the PSI Bangladesh project designed by Dan Lissance (Chapter 6). Both were accompanied by before-and-after research involving interviews with very large numbers of people. This method of evaluation is expensive, but it tells us a great deal more than we can learn from sales statistics alone about people's attitudes and intentions as well as about their actual practices. Generic campaigns can also engage audiences in ways that brand advertising seldom does. Soap operas that draw the audience in and create sustained interest have been effective for PSI in Zaire, Bangladesh, and Côte d'Ivoire, among others. The Population Institute has successfully assisted in the design and airing of soap operas with family planning themes in India and Kenya. Similar communications work has been conducted by the Population and Communications Section at Johns Hopkins University. Entertainers like Mpopo in Zaire are often willing to take part in multimedia activities promoting an idea—in his case the prevention of the dreadful scourge of AIDS—whereas they would not take part in the promotion of a particular contraceptive brand.

So social marketers, welcome generic campaigns! Even if you have little or no control over their design, they are highly likely to result in increased sales of your products. I have never heard of a generic family planning or AIDS prevention campaign so badly designed that it actually interfered with the sale of contraceptives, though this is theoretically possible. If a generic campaign is designed by professionals who want to help, it will far more likely be a real boost to all your project performance statistics.

VIRGIN MARKETS

The advertising of contraceptives in developing countries that are at a very early stage of economic development is a special challenge but also a special privilege. The story is told of a French advertising executive who spent a two-year sabbatical in French-speaking Côte d'Ivoire in West Africa. On his return to Paris, he was asked to discuss at a meeting the principal differences between advertising in France and advertising in Côte d'Ivoire. "The first difference," he said, "is that, in Côte d'Ivoire, everyone reads our ads. The second difference is that everyone believes them!'' This is an oversimplification, of course, but it makes an important point. When CSM contraceptives, the national airline, and government invitations to bid for water and sewage projects are the only advertisements in a publication, the contraceptive ads will get a good deal of attention. Furthermore, advertising rates are apt to be very low, as the purchasing power of the readership (or listenership or viewership) is likely also to be low in these circumstances. This means that a contraceptive advertiser can get a great deal of attention from very large segments of the public for a relatively small investment.

In many ways this is an ideal environment for the social marketing of contraceptives. We are, after all, trying to reach low-income consumers with a subsidized, low-cost product. While all other advertisers are focused primarily on the most affluent markets in any society, social marketers aim at the *least* affluent. This means that, in these relatively virgin markets, we can reach very large numbers of our prime target audience for an astonishingly modest cost. This is undoubtedly one of the reasons why the Vietnam social marketing project was able to achieve the equivalent of nearly 3 percent contraceptive prevalence in just four years, a remarkable record in a country of more than 70 million people.

A DYING ART?

Social marketing start-ups in Bangladesh in the mid-1970s and Ethiopia and Vietnam in the early 1990s took place in relatively untouched media markets into which large-scale contraceptive campaigns were introduced. There are very few large countries left in the world that are comparable in this respect. As economies around the world liberalize, as the world gets richer, consumer goods advertising will become more and more commonplace everywhere. So, while social marketers will not have many more opportunities to launch their products in such relatively virgin markets in the future, it is for the best of reasons that this is so.

Vietnam

DKT's Vietnam program manager (1992–1997),[4] Andy Piller, reports:

When Trust condoms were introduced in Vietnam in August, 1993, advertising in the mass media was still in its infancy. Most ads were very plain and were for local watch or gold shops and a few guest houses. The most "interesting" ads were for MSG. There were also a few ads for things like pens, detergents and shampoos. Most ads for other (locally made) products generally included a shot of the factory followed by shots of the management talking on the phone. (Piller, 1995)

In this environment, Andy and his colleagues recognized that the simple creation of brand awareness for the Trust condom would probably spur significant sales growth. They therefore began with a campaign designed to create that awareness.

Our first ad for Trust was intended to make people aware of the Trust brand name, to mention some of the benefits of condoms/Trust and to show Trust available in different outlets. Scenes of Trust being purchased in a doctor's office, in a pharmacy, at a general goods store and from a street vendor, were coupled with the statements (in order) "international quality," "no side effects," "easy to use" and, "not expensive." These shots were followed by a scene with the couple watching television and Trust coming out of the TV with the couple commenting, "available everywhere." Our slogan was simply, "Trust—International Quality." (Piller, 1995)

Early feedback from this campaign suggested a further issue relating to shyness, for which increased brand awareness might also be particularly helpful. As in most cultures, talking openly about sex or sex-related products is not considered "polite" in Vietnam. Having a brand name and a recognizable logo created a more comfortable and open atmosphere within which condoms could be promoted: one of the early Trust ads approached the issue of shyness in a somewhat humorous way with the slogan (picking up from the campaign in the Philippines) "Don't say condoms, just say Trust." This slogan was widely repeated on television and Andy believes it to be largely responsible for the fact that Trust became a generic term for condoms in Vietnam in a very short period of time.

Additional special opportunities that were presented at the time Trust was launched were:

- An existing awareness about family planning;
- An intensive government campaign to increase awareness of AIDS;
- A recent sharp increase in television ownership and viewing;
- Favorable ad rates for television and radio (television ads ranged in cost from U.S.$10–75 per thirty-second spot depending on time and station. Estimated television viewership is 15–35 million people. Radio spots are around U.S.$10 per one-minute spot for a nationwide audience, comparable to, or larger than the television audience).

Andy Piller continues:

Less than a year after introducing Trust, we conducted a brand awareness survey. The results exceeded our expectations. Eighty-nine percent of the men interviewed (in both urban and rural areas) mentioned Trust when asked to name the first condom they know; 79 percent of those men who knew of Trust said that they had learned about it from television.

The fact that we were even allowed on the air had more meaning than we anticipated. Everyone in Vietnam knows that the government controls the airwaves. That the government approved our ads by allowing them to be aired provided substantial legitimacy to the product.

However, there were no guidelines for contraceptive advertising and this may have been helpful. If we had pushed the federal government for clarification of guidelines or regulations, some officials would have tried to enhance their authority by creating their own guidelines. Once involved, these officials would create an additional layer of bureaucracy. To avoid this, we simply chose not to seek official rules about advertising. Instead we proceeded as if the general approval we had received to implement a social marketing project, plus the government's well-known strong support of family planning, meant we had all the permission we needed.

There were no advertising agencies capable of developing a coherent national media campaign. When we asked one firm about developing our Trust campaign, their recommendation was to concentrate exclusively on the use of billboards, despite the extraordinarily favorable TV rates. So we decided to contract directly for the services we needed. This included independent producers who produced our TV spots, and, importantly, individual TV station managers. This strategy had the great advantage of diffusing decision-making and avoiding any single authority who might have tried to control the contents of our entire advertising campaign.

"CULTURALLY CORRECT"?
All social marketing organizations make much of the fact that their advertising and promotion will be designed by marketing professionals who are sensitive to local cultural preferences and sensitivities. I have always been as strong a proponent of this policy as anyone but, in Vietnam, we encountered some ironic circumstances.

First, the Vietnamese government was convinced that consumer goods, particularly condoms, would not be popular in Vietnam unless they carried the patina of imports. In fact, the condoms distributed by the government had a photograph of a foreign woman and two children on the package and instructions in English on the back. Nowhere on the box was there any indication that the condoms were made in Vietnam (though they were). Our own initial focus group discussions confirmed this preference for products with a foreign image.

Since our first condom was an imported one, this part seemed straightforward. However, I felt very strongly that brief instructions on condom use in Vietnamese should be included in the package. I finally decided to compromise by including instructions in Vietnamese (with drawings) on the inside of each three-piece pack with English the exclusive language on the outside. When I presented the sample pack to government officials I was told that no one would buy them because of the Vietnamese writing inside. Some dilemma! Here was a foreigner insisting on the use of local-language instructions on a product which would, in fact, be imported, while local government officials were insisting that the product would sell better if there was nothing local about the packaging at all. Fortunately our government counterparts did not insist on this point and we went ahead with the inside-the-pack instructions in Vietnamese. The fact that the product quickly became popular and has sold well subsequently has convinced most of the same officials that some "Vietnamization" of our packaging is not a serious impediment to sales.

Another cultural issue arose over our New Year's ads. Each year DKT produced a Vietnamese New Year "Tet" TV advertisement which we broadcast for about six weeks just before and after the new year. According to Asian tradition, each year has a particular animal associated with it. For the Tet ads, we showed the animal for the old year leaving the screen followed by an animal representing the new year entering the picture. The *Trust* condom logo is prominently displayed throughout and at the end of the ad a narrator says "Trust condoms wish everyone a happy and safe new year." The purpose of these ads is to present Trust condoms as a sort of "corporation" that is respectful to the most important holiday in Vietnam, but with a slight sense of humor.

Somewhat to our surprise, TV station managers at three of the fifteen stations that broadcast our ads refused to carry these New Year's spots. Their explanations for refusing were clearly contrived and sometimes even trivial (one manager didn't like the music), and sometimes very imaginative (one word for pig in Vietnamese sounds like a slang word for pornography and a station manager objected to the association). But it was clear that these station managers really did not like the idea of condoms being linked so closely with such an important part of Vietnamese culture. Since these managers had carried other Trust ads, we realized that "culturally correct," in some cases, means avoiding cultural associations altogether.

AIDS, FAMILY PLANNING, AND TRUST

Another decision we made early in the process was that mass media advertising would promote Trust condoms for both family planning and the prevention of AIDS. This "combined" message in the mass media was supplemented by educational materials such as leaflets, comic books, and a 25-minute videotape drama. The use of the combined-purpose approach was made thoughtfully. We knew that there were proponents, particularly among family planning professionals, of the two-product strategy, calling for one condom brand for family planning and a different brand for AIDS prevention. But, reassured by two intercept studies from Africa which reported that users of a single condom brand typically used it for both purposes and noting that U.S. condom advertisers seemed quite comfortable in combining both messages [See Chapter 7; Harvey 1991b; Kodjo et al., 1991], we felt that the combination strategy was appropriate. In the event, it has worked quite well. (Piller, 1995)

The Vietnamese campaigns produced remarkably quick results. From launch in mid–1993, condom sales zoomed to 7 million in 1994 to 31 million in 1996, reaching nearly 2 percent prevalence in a remarkably short period. An oral contraceptive, Choice, was introduced in 1995 and sold nearly a million cycles that year.

AIDS PREVENTION—ZAIRE

Perhaps the most successful use of advertising in a program for AIDS prevention took place in Zaire in 1988–1990.[5] The project combined a classic social marketing effort for condoms with a multimedia educational and motivational campaign. The campaign was unusually imaginative and took advantage of many special communications opportunities.

Julie Convisser reports that the mass media campaign began with an examination of the lives, needs, beliefs, and behaviors of the target population. Project staff in Zaire spent long hours in the shady corners of market squares, under village Talking Trees [big shade-providing trees where people gather to talk], in school classrooms, on river barges conducting focus groups, listening carefully to the concerns and realities of people at risk. Results of these discussions were analyzed in terms of the motivations related to sexual behavior and risk-taking, and for information on media habits, preferences, and consumer behavior. This information then became the basis for the content and style of messages, and the selection of media channels and spokespersons. In addition, members of the target population, whether they were schoolgirls or men cruising nightclubs for women, were actually involved in the development of ads, posters, songs, and radio and television dramas, not just at the testing stage, but throughout the creative process. By including actual consumers in the media development process, the project ensured that the intended audience could identify with the messages, the characters or spokespeople delivering them, and their intended outcome.

The first part of the campaign was a series of television spots designed to undermine some destructive myths about AIDS. These were produced and aired in Kinshasa, Zaire's capital and principal city. Before and after surveys revealed that the message was getting through. For example, there was a decrease of fourteen points in the percentage of those who responded "yes" to the question, "Can you avoid getting infected with the AIDS virus simply by avoiding contact with people who look sick?" after that issue was addressed in the television spots.

But the campaign quickly began looking for other ways of getting the AIDS message across. Zaire boasts some of the world's most talented and highly visible musicians. The project sought to enlist this community of eloquent and persuasive performers, which had already been forced to confront AIDS. Not long before the project began, Zaire's most famous musician, Franco-Luwambo, had released a song about AIDS nine months before dying of the disease. Franco's song and startling death paved the way for the project to motivate other popular musicians to raise their voices against AIDS.[6]

The project selected three AIDS songs after sponsoring a contest among Zaire's leading bands. The songs were released in four-month intervals during a year and were guaranteed daily play time through agreements with national and regional radio stations.

The public response was extremely positive, "Step by step/hand in hand/let's all fight AIDS . . ." the refrain of the first-released song, by the well-known Empompo Loway, could be heard on the lips of rural schoolchildren and sophisticated Kinshasa residents alike. In a Kinshasa post-test six months after the song's release, 65% of a target audience sampling had heard it. Of these, 90% could sing a verse or two on request. Most importantly, 93% of those who had heard the song retained its key AIDS messages and 85% of the same group said it affected their behavior.

Of the latter group, one in three said it discouraged them from having multiple partners. One in four said it encouraged abstinence and one in six said it motivated them to be faithful to a single partner.

Buoyed by the response, the project sponsored a World AIDS Day concert in 1989, where Empompo sang his song. When a video of a performance was released just three weeks later, Empompo was already dead of AIDS.

Five more songs soon joined the original three—each addressing a slightly different population segment by selecting musicians with different styles and appeals. Similarly, the messages evolved over time. Due to the growing AIDS awareness, later songs veered away from the basic do's/don'ts and stressed more emotional appeals to change behavior patterns. For example, one song avoids the word AIDS altogether. Instead, a man and woman sing to each other of their marital trespasses and—in the face of "the dangers all around us today"—renew their love and commitment to mutual fidelity.

For the 1990 World AIDS Day (December 1), the project sponsored a nationally broadcast concert featuring live renditions of six AIDS songs by the original artists. Excerpts of the moving and persuasive five-hour performance were edited into five music videos, with cuts of musicians and other popular figures giving advice on AIDS prevention. The video-clips were later broadcast on a rotating schedule on TV and cassette tapes were distributed to AIDS prevention groups throughout the country.

THE ZAIRE RADIO/TELEVISION CAMPAIGN

Working with Zaire's best-loved drama group, Troupe Nzoi, the project produced a four-part radio/TV series aimed at the "prospective parents" group. Its underlying behavioral messages: (1) avoid having multiple sex partners; (2) practice mutual fidelity; (3) use a condom if you have sex in a high-risk situation.

The drama, about a young woman who learns after her wedding night that her husband has AIDS, was the first mass media treatment of many socially significant and sensitive AIDS-related issues in Zairian culture. They include widespread marital infidelity and the link between the economic and social plight of women and widespread prostitution. Moreover, two specific scenes provided a first-time opportunity for an explicit televised discussion of the advantages of condom use for AIDS prevention.

The public response to the drama's realism and sensitivity was overwhelming. Follow-up research verified that presenting messages through a culturally relevant radio/TV drama effectively motivates individuals to adopt safe practices. Four "day after" surveys among a representative sample in Kinshasa showed that over two-thirds of the intended audience watched each episode on TV. Of these, two-thirds could recount the plot of the episodes they watched.

By the end of the project's second full year, Zaire's 13 million urban residents were receiving an average of 10 minutes a day of consistent and effective AIDS messages. Now, radio was added to cover more remote areas. Four of the country's 11 regional radio stations in high priority areas were selected to broadcast AIDS prevention messages. After several initial visits, two producers from each of the four radio stations were invited to a workshop, then asked to submit a year-long action plan for an AIDS radio campaign.

By the end of the first year of formal collaboration, the regional radio stations had produced and broadcast in over 13 local languages 28 AIDS feature programs, 22 spots, eight AIDS radio dramas, two songs and five AIDS-knowledge radio contests. In all, audiences in the four regions received an average of 20 minutes a day of AIDS messages via their local radio stations.

CAMPAIGN RESULTS

The following results from the second phase of the Longitudinal Program Impact Study, conducted in August 1990, indicate the impact on the target audience in Kinshasa:

Awareness increase regarding asymptomatic carriers. The ratio of people who think "you can avoid getting infected with the AIDS virus simply by avoiding sexual contact with people who look sick" dropped from 56% to 42%.

Increase in abstinence and mutual fidelity for AIDS prevention. When asked "How have you changed your behavior in the face of AIDS," 16% more people spontaneously responded "by becoming mutually faithful" in the second study than in the first (an increase from 28.9% to 45.7%).

Increase in knowledge and acceptance of condoms for AIDS prevention. Those who named condoms as their first mode of AIDS prevention increased from 5% to 13%. The ranks of those who had ever heard of condoms increased by 11 percentage points.

Increase in condom use for AIDS prevention. When asked how they changed their behavior in the face of AIDS, five times the number of people responded "By using condoms" (18.8% vs 3.6% in the first survey). Indeed, annual sales of condoms offered through the Condom Social Marketing Project increased by more than 1,000% over the two and one-half years in the media campaign—from 900,000 in 1988 to 18 million in 1991, a record that has not been equaled since.

According to an equation developed by AIDSTECH, a project of Family Health International, the 18 million condoms sold in 1991 prevented nearly 20 thousand HIV transmissions in Zaire that year as noted by Convisser. More recent estimates (see Appendix 4) put the figure at around four thousand cases, still a very impressive figure.

These reports from the field indicate that "doing what you can" ranges widely in CSM campaigns, depending on the setting. And when dedicated project managers are in charge, they are usually up to meeting the challenge.

NOTES

1. The battle for market share does influence behavior. A classic example is the massive market share battle between Coca-Cola and Pepsi in the United States. The huge advertising budgets fielded by these two companies in support of their brands (frequently positioning each product as "better" than the other) has consistently resulted in increases in per-capita consumption of soft drinks overall. Distant runner-up Dr. Pepper, for example, has almost always benefited from the Coke and Pepsi wars because as Americans consume more and more soft drinks, Dr. Pepper's sales follow Coke's and Pepsi's on an upward path.

2. The success of a direct-response ad depends, of course, on the cost of the product being shipped (about 25 percent of the selling price in this case) and the projected "back-end" profits from a new mail-order customer; after buying from a magazine or newspaper, customers will be mailed catalogs, generating additional profitable sales.

3. For more on this, see Andreasen, 1995.

4. After the nightmare of America's war in Vietnam, it was a special privilege to go to that country in the 1990s to do something helpful. At one meeting with Andy in our Hanoi office, he proclaimed: "We're going to bomb Haiphong with condoms!" I almost hugged him.

5. This description of the Zaire project is drawn largely from Julie M. Convisser's article "The Zaire experience: Using mass media to battle AIDS in Africa," *Family Planning World* (Sept./Oct.), 1991.

6. Julie Convisser adds: "I can only say how surprised I was then, in Zaire, and even more grateful now, back in America, for the willingness of Zaire's most famous and talented artists to work with us on spreading the word. Part of that, I know, was financial need, but the superstars' genuine commitment to their fellow citizens, and to doing what they could to help prevent the further spread of HIV, was inspiring" (Personal communication 5/8/96).

12

The Population Wars

Certainly the health impact of family planning on low-income families and the expanded economic and personal freedom that the ability to plan and space pregnancies provides is sufficient reason for delivering these services on an urgent, priority basis. But in my view contraception's impact on birth rates and on population growth rates seems now to be a secondary consideration (I have not always held this view; when prevailing arguments in the 1960s suggested that population growth impeded economic growth, I was a strong proponent of that position). If strong scientific evidence were to demonstrate that lower birth rates (and, therefore, probably contraception) have a deleterious effect on societal well-being, I would certainly question the work that we do; if the evidence showed that lower birth rates contributed to the health of societies, beyond the elements noted above, that would be just one more reason for helping people plan their families.

A considerable amount of ideological and intellectual warfare has been waged over this question. On one side are those who are absolutely convinced—and believe they can prove—that increasing human numbers represent a threat to the environment, to economic advancement, and to the per-capita availability of necessary and useful resources. On the other side is an increasingly credible group insisting that, on the available evidence, natural resources are becoming less scarce rather than more so, that population growth does not impede and may actually help economic development, and that increasing numbers of people mean more ideas, better technology, and better control over our environment.

Figure 12.1
Per-Capita Income & Population Growth, 1970–1981 (annual percent)

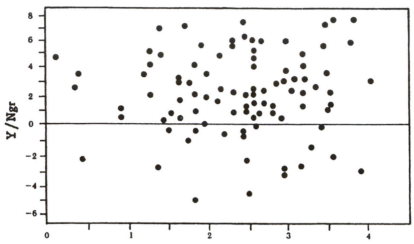

Source: Reproduced by permission of the World Bank, from *Population and Income Change (Discussion Paper #249)*, by Allen C. Kelley and Robert M. Schmidt, 1994.

The doomsayers have intuition on their side. After all, the earth is finite, and we are likely to have to go on inhabiting it fairly exclusively at least for a few hundred more years. The number of human beings cannot grow forever without running out of, literally, space. This suggests rather strongly that things like fish and farmland are likely to be increasingly in short supply as our numbers and our prosperity (which increases consumption per capita) increase.

There are good common sense reasons for believing that high birth rates also impede economic growth. Ansley Coale and Edgar M. Hoover (1958) argued persuasively in the 1950s that high birth rates in India (and countries like India) would increase the dependency ratio by rapidly expanding the number of young children relative to the working adult population. This in turn would place great strains on societal resources like schools and health care facilities for all these millions of new children. The result would constitute a major impediment to economic growth.

But intuition and even common sense reasoning do not always pan out. A growing body of evidence suggests that resources are becoming less scarce and less expensive, and that the correlation between population growth and economic development is not negative. Some would argue that it is positive, but the evidence of the twentieth century, at least until the 1980s, suggests absolutely no correlation at all.

Figure 12.1 is a "representative example" of the correlation between population growth and economic development in a recent review by a group of economists at the World Bank, whose dispassionate evaluation is as comprehensive and balanced of any I have recently seen. The vertical axis represents economic growth, the horizontal axis, population growth. As can be seen, there is no correlation between these two variables for the countries and the period (1970–1981) here examined. The World Bank points out that there *has* been a negative correlation between population growth and economic development in the 1980s, especially in poor countries, but not prior to that time; the 1980s may have been an anomaly, they assert. In any event, it is only for this most recent period that there is any correlation at all.

It is instructive also to note recently published views on this subject of the UN Population Fund (UNFPA). "The record of history has told a mixed story" about the relationship between population growth and economic development. The population and the economies of the Western industrialized countries have grown simultaneously and, "[m]ost studies of today's developing countries found no connection between the growth rates of population and per-capita incomes up to around 1975," says the report, further asserting that more recent data do suggest a negative correlation since 1975. Even then, "faster population growth is a handicap, like extra weight carried by a racehorse. It is not an insuperable obstacle" (UNFPA, 1992). These are significant concessions because the UNFPA has a powerful vested interest in maximizing the number of reasons for governments to contribute to family planning programs.

As to natural resources, Julian Simon of the University of Maryland, one of the leading and most vocal proponents of the optimistic camp (whose voice was tragically silenced by his death in early 1998), has demonstrated with massive and convincing evidence that the price of most resources, most tellingly food and energy, has been dropping in real terms for many decades and is likely to continue dropping in the future. For example, Figure 12.2 from Simon's book, *The Ultimate Resource*, tracks the price of wheat (top) and electricity relative to wages over two centuries. As can be seen, both are dramatically cheaper than they used to be.

The principal reason for this, of course, is technology: We get better and better at making efficient use of those resources we have, at finding new resources, and creating new and useful things from abundant resources. The silicon in microprocessor chips, for example, is almost infinitely abundant relative to foreseeable human needs.

Simon also argues persuasively that the availability of agricultural land is increasing, not decreasing, through land reclamation, irrigation, and conversion of forests. Indeed, confounding the pessimists, available food per capita has been going up year after year even as the human population has exploded from one billion to more than five billion in the past

Figure 12.2
The Price of Wheat Relative to Wages in the United States

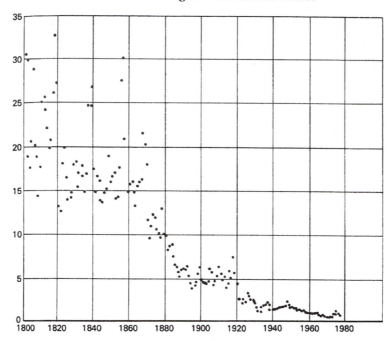

The Price of Electricity Relative to Wages

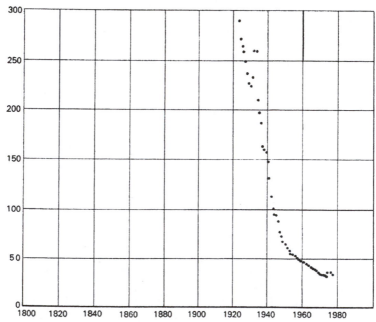

The cost of food and energy keeps dropping, clearly showing that these (and most other) resources are becoming less, rather than more scarce.

Source: Simon, Julian L. *The Ultimate Resource*. Copyright © 1981 by Princeton University Press. Reprinted by permission of Princeton University Press.

century. We are just learning how to grow food more efficiently and more productively.

THE DOOMSAYERS OVERDID IT

This much is now clear: the most vocal and pessimistic of the doom and gloomers were certainly wrong in the early rounds. In 1968 biologist Paul Ehrlich wrote a book called *The Population Bomb*, predicting that the population explosion would cause a massive die-back of millions of people in the 1980s. He was wrong.

Hugh Moore was another early crusader. He created a pamphlet (called "The Population Bomb," which was the source of Erhlich's title) and mailed it to over 1.5 million influential Americans in the late 1950s and early 1960s. The mailings were followed by near-hysterical advertisements in the *New York Times*, the *Wall Street Journal*, and other influential publications, which attributed everything from urban decay to crime and violence to war on the growth of population. Just to be sure nothing got left out, Moore headlined one ad: "Whatever Your Cause, It's a Lost Cause Unless We Control Population." He knew that these claims were exaggerated but he felt the hyperbole was justified to get people's attention. These views were reflected in the name of an important advocacy organization founded by General William H. Draper, a colleague of Moore's—The Population Crisis Committee, created in 1965. (The PCC changed its name to Population Action International in 1994.)

The media have always been happy to go along with the pessimists, of course. Bad news is good for readership and boosts ratings. "If it bleeds it leads," is the television news cliché of the 1990s, reflecting the media's propensity for death and violence. Predictions of disaster are the next best thing to disaster itself, so those who have foreseen cataclysmic fallout from the "population explosion" have seldom lacked for space or airtime. Disappearing forests make better headlines than the discovery that some rain forests are actually expanding. Food shortages—even just *possible* food shortages—make far better copy than the fact that food is more abundant, per person, than it has ever been before.

So the doomsday predictions will continue. And despite having been wrong on these issues so often in the past, Paul Ehrlich continues, in the mid-1990s, to sign fund-raising letters that warn of the "ominous danger signals of over population . . . in Los Angeles and Phoenix, where air pollution abounds." (The air in both these cities, like most American cities, is cleaner now than it was ten years ago.) Ehrlich even asks "how will we tell our children that they will have to wait in line for food, or water? How will we explain that we might have acted to prevent a future population nightmare, but did not?" (ZPG, 1996). This is, of course, nonsensical. If our children have to stand in line for food or water, it will not be because of birth rates!

Another notable early (1967) doomsday book was William and Paul Paddock's book *Famine '75*, which mirrored Paul Ehrlich's belief that population growth would inevitably lead to famine in the 1970s. The Paddocks suggested a system of triage in which the United States would have to decide to provide food assistance only to countries that already showed signs of steady development and growing agricultural production, leaving the really poor countries to die off and disappear! They were wrong too. There is a point of philosophy here, or perhaps theology or ethics. Those who advocate "writing off" certain poor countries, those who suggest that certain countries or societies are "going down the tubes," appear to have a view that life is not worth living below a certain level of poverty. In the 1960s, for example, when I was in India, those who said that Bangladesh (then East Pakistan) was doomed to simply "fail" never really articulated their definition of failure: Would everyone die? Or would life just be so miserable that it would not be worth living? Such views suggest that any society below a certain level of prosperity is simply not worth being concerned about, the lives of its citizens "down the tubes." This is deeply flawed reasoning. By historical standards, the average citizen of Bangladesh does pretty well today. Yet Bangladesh is still considered a basket case by many Western thinkers. In terms of human-life-worth-living one wonders why; life expectancy in Bangladesh in 1995 was fifty-five years—about twenty years less than the average for the rich countries, but six years more than life expectancy in the United States at the turn of the twentieth century. Life expectancy in the United States has generally been as good as anywhere else in the world, and America, I think, has never been written off as a basket case, even when people there were dying, on average, at a younger age than they are in Bangladesh today.

If it is true that one human life equals another human life, then it does not now and never did make the slightest bit of sense to dismiss any country or any group of people, or indeed any person, as deserving of being "written off."

I do not mean to suggest that the pessimists—those who are convinced that population growth and increasing levels of consumption are going to create tremendous, even cataclysmic problems for humanity—are in any way lacking in compassion for the poor. They are not. I review the exaggerated predictions of the past both to point out that they have generally been wrong—at least so far—and to suggest that they may have insufficiently valued the lives of poor people (I refer here specifically to the Paddock brothers) in the process.

Most of today's pessimists are more thoughtful. They are perhaps best exemplified by Lester Brown and his colleagues at the World Watch Institute, an organization that has provided numerous thoughtful studies on such matters as fisheries depletion, trends in agricultural production and land use, and related matters. Many of the World Watch studies are persuasive. Our ocean fisheries, in fact, are in serious trouble in a great many places as a result of overfishing, and it does appear unlikely that current levels of fish consumption can be maintained. This is also an area where human beings continue to surprise, however, fish farming is on the rise. Not only catfish and carp but Atlantic salmon are now raised in substantial quantities, just like chickens and cows. Huge salmon "pens" dot the coast of Norway (and Maine, and Canada), and salmon has become one of our most abundant (and least expensive) fish. This probably will not make up for the loss/shortage of all other species of fish, but it is a good example of how human ingenuity can solve problems in unexpected ways.

Where does that leave us? I think it leaves us in a world in which the quality of human life is likely to continue improving, at least gradually, even as the number of humans continues to increase.[1] It appears quite likely that human numbers can level off somewhere between eight and twelve billion, and that that number will be sustainable at an increasing level of prosperity. But I sympathize with those who worry about such huge numbers. At the very least this is uncharted territory, and as long as we are not able to inhabit other planets, twelve billion humans is an enormous number.

In any case, birth rates are coming down, populations are actually declining in a number of demographically important countries like Germany and Russia (the Germans and Russians are not particularly pleased about that), and, as the twentieth century comes to a close, birth rates are falling in virtually all areas of the world, even where economies are stagnating. The "explosion" is beginning to level off.

If population growth does not impact economic growth, what does? The principal determinants of economic growth appear to be government policies that permit (or do not permit) businesses to operate freely, including policies that permit open trade, both within and between countries. The demise of the Soviet Union and subsequent events have led to a near-universal recognition that prosperity requires open markets; all rich countries have open markets (and many of these are very poor in natural resources); most poor countries have stifling government restrictions on trade—internal, external, or both.[2] Compared to economic policies, birth rates appear to have an insignificant influence on economic well-being.

It is worth remembering that many of the crowding and environmental problems we intuitively attribute to population growth are really a result of rising prosperity. America's national parks are crowded because so many Americans (and others) can afford to visit them. European and

North American streams and lakes are less secluded than they used to be not because of population pressures per se (North America, for example, is not crowded in this sense at all), but because tens of millions of ever more prosperous people can afford longer and more expensive vacations, including vacations during which they impose upon themselves many of the primitive living conditions that less affluent people are trying to leave behind!

The fact that the resources needed for ever-improving human life are becoming more abundant is counter-intuitive and very difficult for many people to accept, but it does appear to be the case. Here is another of those philosophical dilemmas: Is seclusion, quietness in wilderness places, becoming more scarce as more people can afford to visit such places? With more visitors, of course, the quietness is less complete. Yet, if more people can enjoy it, is there really less of this resource?

While population growth's impact on economic development appears to be negligible, its impact on the environment is less clear. The growing human population continues to encroach on wildlife habitat, for example, and conflicts continue between those who feel that all human needs should be met first and those who feel the imperatives of protecting endangered species and other wildlife. I have sometimes indulged in a cruel-seeming mind experiment on this subject and I invite you to join me in it now.

Suppose you are forced, by some diabolical tribunal of the future, to choose between killing the last pair of elephants on earth or a single human. To make it even harder, suppose that the human has no family to mourn her. Or him. Which would you choose to kill?

There's no way out in the mind experiment, but there *is* a way out in the real world. The environment is improved not by diminishing the number—or even slowing the growth of the number—of humans but by prosperity and commitment. It is this road that saves species. Environmental cleanup costs money, a lesson we are learning all over the world as Western Europe and North America get cleaner air and water and Bangkok and Bombay get worse. The most dire environmental tragedies took place in the Soviet Union—where, incidentally, birth rates were and are among the lowest in the world.

So numbers do impact the environment, but in unpredictable ways that remain unclear. On balance I have to think, other things equal, that a reduction in the growth of human population will benefit the environment, but this is by no means certain.

In his 1995 book, Joel E. Cohen, a biologist, addressed the question of how many people the earth could sustain. A reviewer derived the following conclusions:

[t]he number of humans the earth can durably support lies somewhere between one billion and one trillion; . . . the number changes over time and with technology; and . . . the factors determining the number are a complex and poorly understood interaction of land, water, social institutions and ingenuity. (*New York Times*, 1996a:12)

However, Cohen notes that, "The human population of the earth now travels in the zone where a substantial fraction of scholars have estimated upper limits on human population size" (*New York Times*, 1996a:12, citing Cohen, 1995). This warning should not be lightly dismissed.

So we really don't know. We will probably do all right with ten or twelve billion people, which now appears to be the point where we will level off, but we would be okay with a smaller number, too. Numbers much bigger than twelve billion, I must admit, make me nervous. We have never been there, and the consequences of such large human numbers are simply unforeseeable.

It is worth repeating that none of these issues are crucial in assessing the priority of family planning services. Because contraception has such an immediate and substantial humanitarian impact, because contraception enhances human freedom, especially the freedom of women from the tyranny of unwanted and frequent pregnancy and childbirth, because family planning saves lives and makes human life better, the impact of birth control on other things, while interesting and while perhaps providing additional motives for funding family planning services, matters very little in terms of the effort, energy, and money we should put into family planning programs.

There are still those who oppose the spread of birth control. Some people believe that the availability of contraceptives increases sexual activity among those who should not be having sex. But there is no credible evidence that this is so. The ready availability of and aggressive publicity about contraceptives in Bangladesh, for example, has done little or nothing to change the conservative sexual views and practices of that country. There are also those, as in the Philippines and among Roman Catholic clergy generally, who would restrict the availability of condoms to discourage nonmarital sex. This is both silly and immoral. Silly because condoms are widely used throughout the world in marital as well as nonmarital sexual relations, and because numerous studies have shown that the availability of contraceptives does not increase sexual activity.[3] Immoral because withholding from a person something by which he or she may save his or her life and protect the lives and safety of others is, on its face, wrong. It is almost indisputably wrong in the absence of any proof that the availability of condoms has negative consequences, sexual or otherwise.

While the spread of voluntary birth control appears to have virtually no negative effects, it has many positive ones: lives saved, freedom enhanced, human welfare improved. If contraceptives were not associated with the pleasures of sex, they would probably be regarded as a "silver bullet" of human well-being and happiness.

NOTES

1. There will be setbacks and reversals in the positive trend. Life expectancy in several African countries has dropped since 1985 because of deaths due to AIDS. Economic development in fourteen African countries was negative during the period 1985–1994—that is, these people are getting poorer (Gwartney et al., 1996).

2. The strong correlation between economic growth and liberal economic policies is well documented in "Economic Freedom of the World" (Gwartney et al., 1996; Gwartney and Lawson, 1997).

3. See, for example, Furstenberg et al., 1997; Schuster et al., 1998; and Frost and Forrest, 1995.

Appendix 1

The Manufacturer's Model

Here are a few examples of variations on the manufacturer's model.

1. Depo-Provera, Indonesia. As part of the Indonesian government's "Blue Circle" (and later "Gold Circle") campaigns, locally manufactured Depo-Provera injectable contraceptives were advertised and promoted using donor funds. The primary "providers" were government-recognized midwives who have been part of Indonesia's national family planning program since the early 1980s. The manufacturer, Upjohn/Indonesia, agreed to reduce the price of the injections (about $1.15 in the late 1990s) in exchange for promotional inputs by the donor.

2. PSI and Wyeth-Ayerherst, Philippines, 1974. In this early experimental project, PSI, using funds from the Population Council, negotiated an agreement with Wyeth, a leading manufacturer of oral contraceptives, to try new approaches to the promotion of its Ovral brand in the Philippines. Mothers giving birth in selected hospitals were provided with free samples of Wyeth weaning food along with a free plastic measuring scoop that could be redeemed for two cycles of Ovral at a local pharmacy. The donor paid for the expenses involved in redeeming the free cycles and for some advertising efforts to publicize the project.

3. Schering/SOMARC/Dominican Republic. In 1985, the German company Schering had a brand of oral contraceptive "on the shelf" in the Dominican Republic that they were neither promoting nor expecting to continue selling in that country for very long. SOMARC saw an opportunity to persuade Schering to revive this brand (Microgynon) in exchange for marketing and advertising inputs. The result was a substantial boost in oral contraceptive sales.

4. Micropil/DKT/Philippines. This "pure" manufacturer's model experiment was initiated by DKT with a Filipino pill manufacturer, Pascual Pharmaceuticals, in 1991. DKT agreed to promote the company's Micropil and detail it to doctors and pharmacies. ("Detailing" is the term used by pharmaceutical marketers to refer to sales calls on doctors and other medical personnel.) The product was already on the market in several cities, and DKT agreed to introduce it in new geographical areas. In exchange, DKT got a royalty for each cycle of pills sold in these new areas.

5. The Turkish pharmaceutical distributor, Eczacibasi signed an agreement with SOMARC to promote and distribute the three already leading brands of oral contraceptives in Turkey: those of Wyeth, Germany's Schering, and the Dutch firm Organon. Each of those firms agreed to lower the consumer cost of their oral contraceptives in exchange for a substantial advertising input by SOMARC using USAID funds.

6. Oral contraceptives in the Philippines (SOMARC). In the late 1980s SOMARC and AID negotiated an agreement with the three leading oral contraceptive manufacturers/importers in the Philippines, the same three companies with whom the deal was worked out in Turkey: Schering, Wyeth, and Organon. An advertising strategy was worked out under which Wyeth's Nordette, Schering's Microgynon, and Organon's Marvelon would be "umbrella branded" under the theme name Couple's Choice. Couple's Choice advertising would promote the virtues of oral contraceptives and specifically promote the oral contraceptives that carried the "Couple's Choice" logo (see Figure A1.1). All three companies agreed to reduce their prices somewhat, but the price was still a commercially viable one.

There are many other variations. The experiment with Sterling Drug in Nigeria (Chapter 8) is itself a variation on the "manufacturer's model."

The most important characteristic shared by nearly all manufacturer's model (or "third/fourth generation") social marketing programs is that the project is not intended to be managed, at least over the long term, by a separate family planning or AIDS-prevention organization. Instead, the implementing organization is a commercial firm, a for-profit company, either a local one or a local branch of an international firm. This company is—or is intended to become—a normal component of the commercial landscape in the project country. The intermediary organization is to provide a temporary catalytic boost with technical assistance and marketing budgets for two or three years—perhaps up to four or five years in some cases. The commercial companies, so this approach assumes, will then carry on, after the catalytic input, selling more contraceptives without additional donor support.

Eliminating the need for an ongoing intermediary organization appears at first to be a great virtue. It has considerable appeal because the implementing commercial companies already exist for other purposes and need not be "created" by donors who will then be asked to maintain

Figure A1.1

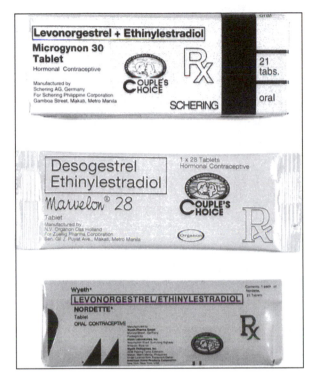

"Umbrella" branding is a frequent feature of manufacturer's model CSM programs. Here the Couple's Choice logo is superimposed on commercial brands of pills in the Philippines.

them. Schering has been active in the Dominican Republic and the Philippines for many years and expects to be active in those countries for a long time to come. Wyeth is a permanent presence in most developing countries. Eczacibasi is a well-established Turkish company whose continuing existence can reasonably be assumed, regardless of any donor inputs. This appears to be a big advantage, but it turns out also to be the Achilles' heel of this approach, because the continuing involvement of a dedicated family planning organization appears to be a sine qua non of CSM success. (See Chapter 8.)

The second common characteristic of manufacturer's model social marketing projects is that *the customer must pay enough to cover the cost of the contraceptives and all trade margins*. The contraceptives cannot be donated or otherwise subsidized, at least not for long. This is an absolute requirement for the "pure" manufacturer's model and for

all variations that are designed to become financially self-sufficient. Theoretically the "bare" variation tried in Nigeria could be continued with
free (therefore subsidized) contraceptives indefinitely, thus permitting
below-cost sales, but no program today takes that approach. Rather, the
typical manufacturer's model involves promoting, (sometimes) repricing,
plus advertising or otherwise helping increase the sales of products the
contracted companies are already in the business of selling. Alternatively,
a contraceptive may be added to the multiproduct line of a distribution
company. The catalytic inputs may also involve policy changes, like the
elimination of import duties or other taxes on contraceptives and/or helping break down barriers to mass media advertising of contraceptives. In
any case, the underlying assumption is that the commercial firm will be
able to make a reasonable profit on an ongoing basis, without need for
a continuing subsidy. The customer must, therefore, pay enough money
to cover the purchase/manufacturing price of the product (including
profit) as well as all trade margins.

The proponents of the manufacturer's model are not absolutist in their
views on these issues. Santiago Plata, who was head of SOMARC from
1987 to 1995, for example, points out that "sustainability should be more
than just financial returns. It is developing managerial and programmatic
capability as well. If the system is successful in setting up a project that
. . . can manage itself and recover most of its administrative costs, then
that is a measure of success" (Plata, 1996). On this, I am happy to agree.
But Santiago also insists that SOMARC has always tried to avoid "setting
up artificial systems that require a subsidy to survive." Since the largest
programs in the poorest countries will always require such subsidies, this
policy differs markedly from my own position.

The fact that manufacturer's model projects must normally charge
higher prices for their contraceptives than do the traditionally designed
social marketing projects has given rise to some confusion because some
of the traditional projects have, for one reason or another, begun charging higher prices in order to reduce the need for subsidy or, indeed, to
become completely financially self-sufficient. The most conspicuous example of this is PROFAMILIA's project in Colombia. By design and history,
this is a traditionally constructed project. It has been entirely under the
management and supervision of a not-for-profit family planning association, perhaps the best and best-known of the International Planned Parenthood Federation's affiliates. But because per-capita GNP in Colombia
is a relatively high $1,900, and because PROFAMILIA is well positioned
to sell imported contraceptives at a mark-up in the Colombian economy,
it has actually earned a profit on its social marketing sales for the past
several years. Similarly, the Family Planning Association in Sri Lanka was
forced to raise prices following a drastic reduction in its funding in the
1980s. It has now reached a point where it just about breaks even on its

social marketing activities. Another example is DKT's Prudence project in Brazil. Because Brazil, like Colombia, has a relatively high per-capita GNP, DKT is able to sell the Prudence condom in that country at a small mark-up and still remain within the consumer pricing guidelines outlined in Chapter 8. This large project will probably be financially self-sustaining before the end of the century.

But the fact of charging higher prices or achieving financial self-sufficiency does not make a "manufacturer's" or "fourth-generation" model. Rather, these are traditional social marketing programs that, because of the increasing affluence of the markets in which they operate, are able to charge high enough prices to cover their costs. They are properly characterized as traditional social marketing programs that have or may achieve self-sufficiency, rather than manufacturer's model (or partnership) projects, because their designs are fundamentally traditional, particularly insofar as they continue to be managed by non-profit organizations with social goals and motivations.

HOW HAS THE MANUFACTURER'S MODEL WORKED SO FAR?

One of the first problems with the manufacturer's model programs is that they have been oversold. This applies particularly to the cost-effectiveness measurements of these projects. As noted elsewhere, the pervasive tendency among those donor and NGO representatives who want to believe that these new self-sufficient partnership programs can deliver the goods to poor people, as well as to more affluent ones, has let wishful thinking replace objective assessment of the evidence.

A case in point is the favorable citation in Alan Andreasen's book (1995) of several SOMARC assertions concerning the "success" of SOMARC's early efforts toward financial self-sufficiency through manufacturer's model programs. "[R]ecent evidence suggests the exciting possibility that it is possible to make contraceptive social marketing (CSM) self-sufficient. In an extensive 1992 study of projects in seven countries, the Futures Group's SOMARC program found that projects in four countries were producing total cost recovery." Andreasen then approvingly cites SOMARC's authors (Stover and Wagman, 1992):

In four of the longest running projects—Mexico (condom), the Dominican Republic (orals), Indonesia (condom), and Barbados (condom)—long-term sustainability is already assured. In Mexico the Protektor condom project became operationally self-sufficient in 1990 and purchased its first commercial supply of condoms in 1991. In the Dominican Republic, sales and associated marketing activities of the oral contraceptive are totally self-sufficient. Marketing of the original Dualima red condom in Indonesia is also being completely supported by the

Figure A1.2
Percentage of Market Reached, Four Condom CSM Programs, 1988–1996

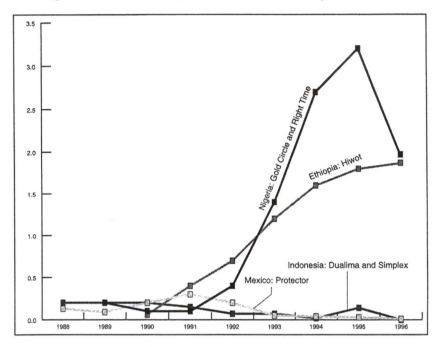

Note: Market defined as 80 percent of all women aged 15–44.

commercial sector. In Barbados, the Panther condom project has achieved complete self-sufficiency, and the distributor purchased the first commercial supply of commodities in late 1991 using project generated funds. (1995: 294)

When Stover and Wagman first published the preceding quote they could be forgiven their surge of optimism and lack of stress on project results, particularly in light of the fact that the projects being examined were all still operating in 1992. However, the uncritical repetition of these claims in 1995 by a respected peer impels me to observe that these assertions are, to put it kindly, overblown.

Of the four projects cited in the quotation—condom projects in Mexico, Indonesia, and Barbados and the pill project in the Dominican Republic—only one (Dominican Republic) can be characterized as successful. The others have all stumbled, faltered, or collapsed. (See Figure A1.2.) The condom project in Mexico has collapsed without ever having achieved significant sales. In Indonesia, the condom project has kept going but has never sold enough condoms to make an impact. These two projects have never achieved even a 1 percent market penetration

Table A1.1
Cumulative Costs per CYP, Barbados Condom Project

Project start date: 1987		Cumulative Cost/CYP
Total costs including overheads:	$640,000	
CYPs through 1991:	6,370	$100.50
Expected cumulative CYPs through 2000:	13,360	$47.90

Source: Derived from Stover and Wagman, 1992.

and their sales in the late 1990s were falling (or defunct), not rising. Compare (Figure A1.2) the market penetration of those two projects with the more traditional condom programs in Ethiopia and Nigeria, which were started a few years later and thus had less time to make their mark (all data through 1996).

It does little good to achieve "self-sufficiency" (i.e, no more donor funds) if the result is the end or continued lackluster performance of a project. This is the triumph of theory over substance. Similarly, the highly praised condom project in Barbados is both small and very costly. Indeed, the small size of the Barbados project, reaching only 1,800 couples at its peak in 1993, has made the initial investment so high relative to the projected benefits of the project that SOMARC's own cost/benefit analysis suggests that it will take several decades to reach an acceptable level of cost-effectiveness, even though the project is self-sustaining on a current basis. (See Table A1.1.)

A project that takes more than thirty years to reach an acceptable cost per CYP, as this one will, must be counted a failure, at least in cost-benefit terms. This is a good illustration of how difficult it is to make a very small project cost-effective (see Chapter 9). Social marketers should not permit themselves to be drawn into such tiny markets.

That leaves the orals project in the Dominican Republic, which has been notably successful, albeit on a modest scale. Cumulative cost per CYP was $14 in 1991, projected to drop to a very reasonable $4 by the year 2000, based on phasing out donor inputs after 1990. The fact that donor contributions resumed in 1991 might push this figure back up to $5 or $6, but that is still a reasonable amount. Note, however, that the Dominican Republic project includes one very important element of the traditional CSM project design: the active involvement of a dedicated family planning organization, the IPPF affiliate *Profamilia*, which has supervised project activities throughout, making this a "mixed" design program.

Andreasen also takes note of SOMARC's 1994 report that manufacturers' model projects in Morocco and Turkey had "achieved complete self-sufficiency" (295). These programs fared better than Dualima/Simplex in

Indonesia or Protektor in Mexico, but they are hardly worthy of emulation. The condom project in Morocco was delivering only 20 thousand CYPs in 1996, less than 0.4 percent of the market. In Turkey sales reached 10.5 million condoms in 1996 after six years of effort, representing 0.8 percent of market, the best of this group. But compare this to traditional programs started at about the same time (1990–1991): Côte d'Ivoire (5.0 percent of market), Ethiopia (1.9 percent), Haiti (3.8 percent), Burkina Faso (4.1 percent), Philippines (0.8 percent). Except for the Philippines, all of the traditional programs outperformed the highly praised manufacturer's model programs.

Excessive claims of success about these "new breed" programs, while they may be good for fund-raising in the short run, are bad for social marketing over the long haul. Just as the population problem doomsayers, like Paul Ehrlich, have destroyed their own credibility by exaggerating the problems they address, so has the credibility of "self-sufficiency" proponents been eroded by the excessive claims they have made for this approach. More realistic expectations, including the fact that this design has not ever proved effective in low-income markets, will result in both a more realistic picture of what this kind of social marketing can do and a more selective (and better) application of the manufacturer's model in field programs.

There are additional reasons to be skeptical. PSI's experimental project with Wyeth in the Philippines (and another 1974 experiment with Schering in Thailand) must also be categorized as unsuccessful. These were interesting experimental undertakings at the time, but they simply did not lead to anything more substantial, nor did they result in the sale of significantly more oral contraceptives over the long haul. Likewise, I must characterize DKT's partnership project with Pascual in the Philippines in the mid-1990s as barely worth the effort. Again, it has been interesting and both parties have learned something from the relationship, but the maximum number of pills sold through this manufacturer's model partnership program was only 125 thousand in 1995. DKT sold several times that number of pills when it introduced its own oral contraceptive a few years later, following the traditional subsidized approach.

So the batting average for these projects is not impressive. In the process of achieving self-sufficiency, a significant portion of manufacturer's model projects have substantially reduced the service they provide or failed to reach satisfactory service levels in the first place.

WHAT ABOUT COSTS?

Cost information for individual programs is notoriously difficult to come by. However, Stover and Wagman (1992) have provided some un-

Table A1.2
Cost-Benefit Figures: SOMARC Programs, 1991

	1991 (000) CYP*	Cost/ CYP 1991**	Years in Operation	Cum Cost/CYP**
Barbados	1	$4.20	5	$100.50
Bolivia	11	24.80	4	93.90
Dom. Republic	54	1.30	7	13.70
Ecuador	32	11.90	4	19.90
Indonesia	59	1.50	6	3.80
Mexico	56	1.40	5	16.40
Morocco	18	13.40	3	37.50
Zimbabwe	20	15.40	4	24.50
TOTAL/AVG (unweighted)	251	9.24	4.8	38.78

Source: Stover and Wagman, 1992.

Notes: *Based on 100 condoms; 13 cycles of pills. **Based on 76 condoms; 14.5 cycles of pills.

usually detailed cost data for eight SOMARC programs that are, on average, just under five years old. We also have comparable data for six DKT programs that, in 1995, had been operating for about the same length of time: four and a half years. (The age of a CSM program is one of the strongest correlates with cost-efficiency. Older (and therefore larger) programs nearly always cost less per CYP than newer ones.) The DKT programs are almost entirely "first generation," that is, traditional programs with donor-subsidized products, while the SOMARC projects have moved away from this design in the direction of the manufacturer's (or "third-generation") model. Comparing the cost-efficiency figures of these two groups of projects, therefore, gives some indication of the relative efficiency of each approach.

As can be seen in Tables A1.2 and A1.3, there is very little difference in the two design models based on current cost per CYP. However, on a cumulative basis, the traditional programs are significantly better. Current cost per CYP in 1991 for the manufacturer's model (and mixed) projects ranges from a very creditable $1.30 in the Dominican Republic to just under $25 in Bolivia (which is characterized as a second-generation project). The range for the DKT projects is narrower ($5 in Vietnam to just under $13 in the Philippines). The average for the DKT projects, at $7.89, is better than the average for the SOMARC projects ($9.24), but this difference is probably not significant.

However, the "manufacturer's model" programs are burdened with very heavy start-up costs relative to the service they deliver. The cumulative costs per CYP (Tables A1.2 and A1.3 include all overhead costs of the respective organizations) average more than three times the cumulative costs per CYP of the DKT programs. Even if we eliminate the very small Barbados program already discussed, the average for the SOMARC

Table A1.3
Cost-Benefit Figures: DKT Programs, 1995

	1995 CYP (000)	1995 Cost/CYP*	Years in Operation	Cum. Cost/CYP*
Brazil	183	6.44	5	10.95
Ethiopia	198	9.82	6	10.49
Bombay	115	7.57	3	11.06
Malaysia	72	5.89	5	10.00
Philippines	100	12.68	5	15.17
Vietnam	271	4.92	3	7.20
TOTAL/AVG (unweighted)	939	7.89	4.5	10.83

Source: DKT sales & financial records.

Notes: *Based on 100 condoms; 13 cycles of pills.

programs is still much higher than the comparable figure for the first-generation programs.

Apart from cost efficiency, a major difference between these two groups of programs is volume of service delivered. I have discussed elsewhere the efficiencies of social marketing that are realized by higher volume operations. Because the second-, third-, and fourth-generation CSM approach generally keeps contraceptive prices high, the volume of service remains low and the start-up costs keep the cumulative cost/CYP stubbornly high.

PILLS VERSUS CONDOMS

An interesting fact to emerge from these comparisons is that condom social marketing through the manufacturer's model appears to have fared quite badly, while this partnership approach to the marketing and sale of pills has worked much better. This is dramatically illustrated in Morocco and Turkey where pills, introduced into those programs after condom sales were under way, were already doing much better just two or three years later. On a CYP equivalent basis in 1995, pills were outselling condoms by fivefold in Morocco, and twofold in Turkey. Pills have also done much better than the ill-fated Dualima in Indonesia.

There are several reasons why this may be so. First, as noted in Chapter 6, condoms tend to be more price sensitive than pills. Because of this, programs that set or keep their prices (relatively) high, as is usually demanded by the manufacturer's model approach, may have more deleterious consequences for condoms than for pills. In addition, pills are a bit less expensive inherently. Manufacturers can make a decent profit selling pill cycles to the trade for less than 20 cents a cycle, meaning that 40–50 cents per cycle is a reasonable commercial retail price in many markets.

This makes the average annual cost of using such pills ($6 to $7) affordable in any country with per-capita GNP in the $600 range. Commercial condoms cost somewhat more, $3–$5 per 100, resulting in an unsubsidized retail price of $7–$10. In practice, $10 (10 cents each or more) is the norm. India and China are important exceptions. Commercial prices in India start at around 7 cents; in China at about 3 cents. This is possible in part because both governments provide indirect subsidies.

I asked Santiago Plata for his views as to why the manufacturer's model approach seemed to work better with pills than with condoms. His reply:

- The OC is a known quantity, it is a pharmaceutical; there is an active distribution and promotion network already in place.
- A cycle of OCs is probably perceived as cheaper than the equivalent number of condoms.
- Governments have traditionally backed the OC more than the condom. Health services were more likely to have pills than condoms available for their clients.
- OC manufacturers are more comfortable dealing with governments in their traditional business. (Plata, 1996)

I agree with Santiago that the pharmaceutical companies that make OCs may be more comfortable dealing with donors and project contractors. Pharmaceutical manufacturers must deal routinely with a plethora of regulatory and other government agencies, and they may find donor government and host agency requirements less onerous, or at least more normal, than do the less regulated condom companies. However, I think the most important reason is that pills are less price sensitive, as Santiago suggests in his second point.

MORE AFFLUENT MARKETS

The manufacturer's approach has focused, as I believe it should, on the more affluent developing markets. In 1993 Turkey, Mexico, Morocco, and the Dominican Republic all had per-capita GNP in excess of $1,000. The Philippines ($830 in 1993) and Indonesia ($730) are less wealthy, but are nonetheless above average for the developing world. The manufacturer's model approach has not even been tried in very poor societies like Vietnam, Ethiopia, or Nepal where per-capita GNP is below $300.

This makes sense. An approach to family planning service delivery that requires financial self-sufficiency is much more likely to work in richer developing countries than in poorer ones. This, I believe, constitutes a second fundamental flaw in this approach (the first being their failure to achieve substantial market penetration, that is, prevalence). There is nothing wrong with providing family planning assistance to the more advanced developing economies, but surely these countries constitute a less urgent priority for assistance than the truly poor countries like those of sub-Saharan Africa and much of south and southeast Asia. If, as I have argued elsewhere, low-income people in low-income countries are the highest-priority target groups for our family planning dollars (or sterling or deutsche marks), then we should focus first and foremost on those countries, and in those poor countries, the manufacturer's model just doesn't work.

WHAT ABOUT OTHER MEASURES?

It can be argued that prevalence and related CYP measures are not the only true yardsticks for the effectiveness of CSM programs. What about the catalytic effects? While very small (or terminated) projects have little permanent impact, it is possible that the catalytic efforts engaged in to further the better third- and fourth-generation programs will have made some useful and significant changes in the societies where they operate. This includes such matters as lower tariffs for contraceptives and better access by contraceptive advertisers to mass media. To the extent that the initiatives undertaken on behalf of manufacturer's model programs have succeeded in achieving these results, they are to be commended; they have made useful and lasting changes. However, there is nothing in the manufacturer's model per se that facilitates this type of change any more than other approaches. Just as the partnership approach works better in a climate of good media access for contraceptives, so likewise does the "traditional" approach. Indeed, it can reasonably be argued that the two approaches are essentially equal in this regard, and that long-term subsidized CSM projects may be even more successful than the manufacturer's model in bringing about permanent institutional changes because they are on the scene lobbying for longer periods of time.

THE INDIAN VARIATION

India has been trying a new approach, an interesting combination of contraceptive subsidization and the manufacturer's model. The Indian government provides a subsidy to private organizations, including commercial contraceptive manufacturers in India, for the social marketing of condoms and pills. Under this arrangement, the companies and social marketing organizations get condoms for less than 1 cent each, pill cycles for 3 cents.

To the extent that this system is used with contraceptive manufacturers, it is a variation on the manufacturer's model, and a unique one. But, excepting the government's own Nirodh and Mala D brands, the largest share of these subsidized contraceptives is sold by non-profit social marketing organizations, reinforcing my view that dedicated organizations, not commercial companies, will end up shouldering most of the burden for CSM.

Appendix 2

Colombia and Egypt—Two Case Studies

Two important programs that are not discussed in sufficient detail elsewhere are the relatively large social marketing programs in Colombia and Egypt. Colombia's CSM, which got under way in 1973, crossed the 5 percent success line in the mid-1980s and has provided services near or above 10 percent prevalence since 1992.

The Colombian project is particularly notable for having turned a real profit for several years consecutively. It has been operated from the start by PROFAMILIA, probably the most successful and best known of the IPPF affiliates (the founder of PROFAMILIA, Dr. Fernando Tomayo, was president of the IPPF from 1971–1977). Contraceptives were supplied free of charge by the IPPF until 1975, and then gradually phased out. Subsequently, PROFAMILIA operated under a special arrangement with several suppliers including the Ansell Corporation, a U.S. producer of condoms that has supplied it with the Tahiti brand, among others, for many years. Tahiti was still the leading PROFAMILIA condom in the mid-1990s.

Condoms are almost a sideline in Colombia, however. IUDs and orals comprise more than three-fourths of PROFAMILIA's CYPs (77 percent in 1995) and even Norplant implants contribute significantly to the total.

Prices for the largest-selling oral contraceptives in the PROFAMILIA program are around $1.60 per cycle to the consumer, making them substantially cheaper per CYP than condoms, and just within the Chapter 8 pricing guidelines. Orals are sold to 180 pharmaceutical wholesalers and also directly to more than four thousand pharmacies by PROFAMILIA staff. Orals are also sold at PROFAMILIA's forty family planning clinics.

PROFAMILIA's biggest seller (in CYP equivalence), however, is the Copper-T IUD. These are acquired from Finishing Enterprises (United States), and are sold to pharmaceutical distributors/wholesalers and retailers as well as hospitals, state government agencies, and PROFAMILIA's own clinics. Indeed, of the roughly 100 thousand IUDs sold by the Colombia CSM every year, nearly 80 percent are sold to these noncommercial outlets. PROFAMILIA makes a small but significant margin on pills and a generous margin on IUDs.

While the mix of contraceptives in the Colombia CSM project is both unusually varied and heavily weighted toward modern, "long-term" methods, the design of the project is traditional. PROFAMILIA, through its clinics, social marketing, and other family planning initiatives, has been the primary source of family planning services and information in Colombia for many years. It began providing these services in the mid-1960s when it was still very risky to do so, the Catholic Church being continually (though ineffectively) opposed. In part because of the pioneering efforts of this aggressive organization, PROFAMILIA has enjoyed certain advantages in the selling of contraceptives in the Colombian marketplace that it has been able to turn to financial gain as the project matured. Additionally, Colombia, with a per-capita GNP of $1,900 (1995), has an economy sufficiently advanced so that contraceptives may be sold at a modest profit and still fall within the CSM pricing guidelines for most low-income buyers.

Throughout its history, PROFAMILIA and its clinics as well as its CSM project have received substantial assistance from the IPPF and from USAID and other donors. PROFAMILIA also received technical assistance from SOMARC in the mid-1990s.

The Egyptian project, like that in Colombia, was started as a traditional social marketing project with supplies donated by USAID. The project was started by Family of the Future, a local organization affiliated with the Family Planning Association of Egypt but independent from it. FOF got things started in 1980 and managed the project until the early 1990s. Until 1986, FOF and the project were managed by Effat Ramadan, the founder of the organization.

The Egyptian CSM has been characterized from a very early date by its heavy emphasis on IUDs. In the first few years of operation, IUDs represented over 80 percent of Egypt's CSM CYPs. Even as other methods were added, IUDs continued to dominate. Sixty percent of the CYPs were provided by IUDs in 1995, for example. This focus was reflected in the pattern of distribution outlets served by the project that, in 1985, consisted of nearly 4 thousand pharmacies, an equal number of private doctors plus just over 300 hospitals and 370 other outlets. The Egyptian project, like Colombia's, has been marketing to family planning service providers (rather than just consumers) since its inception. This is an unusual characteristic for CSM programs.

The Egyptian CSM Project served a very substantial portion of the total Egyptian market, using donated contraceptives, into the early 1990s. By then, FOF had grown into one of the largest and most praised family planning projects in the world. In 1988 the project accounted for more than 40 percent of the CYPs provided through all sources in Egypt. Backed by a strong communication program and a distribution component that utilized the extensive network of doctors and pharmacies in Egypt, FOF aimed to protect 50 percent of the nation's couples by the year 2000. At the time, that goal seemed within its reach.

But a series of managerial disasters was looming. After Effat Ramadan stepped down as executive director in 1986, the project went through four executive directors in as many years. In April 1991 a new board of directors was elected, apparently determined to appoint yet another executive director who, in this case, would also be designated the treasurer of FOF. This new executive director, Dr. Mohammed Abd El Al, was widely believed to have his eye on the financial assets of the organization, and his simultaneous appointment as treasurer and executive director was seen as cause for concern.

Within one month the board ousted its own chairman, who did not belong to the same camp as the board majority that had appointed Abd El Al. Charges and counter charges were made, libel lawsuits were initiated, and the staff was plunged into new depths of confusion and uncertainty. The controversy over the composition of the board and especially Abd El Al's appointment became public knowledge with extensive coverage by television, radio, and the national press. Four years after the departure of its founding director, FOF found itself at an all-time organizational low.

Under pressure from USAID, which was concerned about the fate of several million dollars worth of donated contraceptives held by FOF, as well as more than a million dollars in cash that had accumulated from the sale of USAID donated contraceptives, the government's Ministry of Social Affairs (MOSA) stepped in, removed the new board of directors, and fired Abd El Al. As a protective measure, MOSA placed the CSM component of FOF under the nominal control of the Egyptian Family Planning Association in an attempt to detach all USAID-supported activities from FOF and from the legal actions that had already begun. Abd El Al was replaced by Dr. Khaled Abdel Aziz in mid-1991. Aziz quickly moved to get the organization back on track. However, Abd El Al had protested the manner of his firing in court. In late 1992 the court agreed with El Al and, on Christmas eve of that year, officially reinstated him as FOF's executive director.

The prospect of Abd El Al's return was anathema to most of the staff as well as to USAID and to MOSA who formally withdrew their support of the FOF/CSMP. At their urging, the now three-year supply of contraceptives was removed from the FOF warehouse in the dead of the night by a convoy of twenty-five trucks, so that there would be no product left when Abd El Al returned to his post. The contraceptives were temporarily hidden in Nasser City in a youth club assembly hall from which they were transferred two weeks later to a bonded warehouse. Meanwhile the $1.5 million balance in the project sales account, which belonged to USAID, was transferred to the Egyptian government, with USAID's approval.

At this point FOF was effectively dead. Nominally headed by an executive director whom neither the government nor the principal donor was prepared to accept, and without funds or contraceptives, there just was not much left.

It now fell to Jestyn Portugill, the resident SOMARC representative with Porter/Novelli, and to USAID to attempt to revive the project under a different aegis. It was decided to invite bids from commercial distribution firms for the sale and distribution of the remaining donated contraceptives and to work out a plan with the winners of the bid for product sales at social marketing prices, followed by complete commercialization of contraceptive (social) marketing in Egypt after depletion of USAID stocks. A consortium consisting of Middle East Chemical (MEC), the largest pharmaceutical distributor in Egypt, and MEDTEC was awarded the bid. MEC was to provide distribution of the contraceptives to pharmacies, and MEDTEC would handle detailing and selling to physicians for IUDs and promote oral contraceptives and condoms.

These roller-coaster events are reflected in sales (Figure A2.1). In 1993 contraceptive supplies were virtually unavailable, and CYPs plunged below levels of even a decade earlier. When the contraceptives were released, the pipeline was refilled in 1994 resulting in skyrocketing sales that year. Then in 1995–1996 the reorganized project, with gradually increasing prices under its commercial reconfiguration, brought CYPs back to a realistic but sadly reduced level.

WHAT NEXT?

Prices of the project's oral contraceptives, initially raised from 35 to 50 Egyptian cents, drifted higher to commercial rates. The Copper-T IUDs, sold for 3 Egyptian pounds in 1994, cost between 6.5 and 12 pounds (about $1.75 to $3.50) a few years later. Condoms too moved to higher (and increasing) price levels. On the bright side, the Depo-Provera injectable was added in the mid-1990s.

The extent of political/managerial disruption in the Egyptian project represents an extreme case. Few social marketing projects have suffered

Figure A2.1
Egypt CSM CYPs (000)

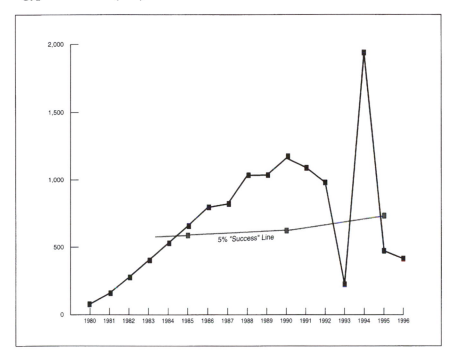

such turmoil. It is to be hoped that MEDTEC and its affiliates will market and sell contraceptives at rates that at least approach those attained by FOF in the late 1980s. However, I am not optimistic. SOMARC/Porter Novelli have been taken off the project, and USAID (in 1998) was no longer actively involved and was no longer even trying to collect sales information. When there is no party involved with an interest in and a commitment to maximizing family planning impact, sales, especially to low-income consumers, inevitably suffer.

Appendix 3

Birth Control Today—Methods and Practice

Given the many ways of preventing pregnancy, little correlation seems to exist between the particular methods used to do so and overall birth rates and other demographic trends. In the United States and Western Europe, birth rates dropped very sharply, most of the way to their present levels, before oral contraceptives, IUDs, and the other "medical" methods had been invented and before the practice of sterilization for contraception was widely known or practiced. These relatively low birth rates were almost certainly the result of practicing various combinations of condoms, rhythm, withdrawal, and abortion, methods which, taken together, were extremely effective.

Today's armamentarium is far more sophisticated and today's couples have far more options. In approximate order of importance, they are:

Sterilization. Contraceptive sterilization is by far the most widely used method of birth control (or at least of contraception) in the world today. About 140 million women and 40 million men (now living) have undergone sterilization procedures, and this method is over 99 percent effective.

Abortion. Abortion is not, of course, a contraceptive because it does not prevent conception. Nevertheless, it is probably the second most widely practiced form of birth control in the world, with an estimated 45 million abortions performed annually, about 40 percent of them illegally. Abortion has been very widely practiced in virtually all societies throughout human history. Today abortion most frequently is performed by vacuum aspiration of the uterus, using a hollow plastic tube which is inserted through the vaginal opening, through the cervix (mouth of the uterus), and into the uterus, from which is extracted, though suction, the products of conception. This procedure is highly effective up to about fourteen weeks of pregnancy. Later-term abortions are performed by scraping the walls of the uterus with a metal curette to remove the fetus and other material.

Oral Contraceptives. In the mid-1990s, probably 60 million women throughout the world are taking the birth control pill. The one most widely used contains a combination of two hormones—estrogen and progestin—that prevent ovulation, that is, the regular ingestion of the hormone in a kind of "imitation pregnancy" prevents the release of an egg from the ovary into the fallopian tube so that no egg is available to be fertilized.

The Condom. The condom has been in use for many years and is still very widely used throughout the world for both contraception and for the prevention of sexually transmitted disease. An estimated 50 million couples rely on condoms for birth control; many millions more use condoms to prevent disease, especially the transmission of HIV. Condoms are simple to use and appear to be easily understood by people of virtually all cultures and economic levels.

The IUD. The idea of placing something in the uterus to prevent implantation of a fertilized egg or to otherwise inhibit pregnancy is a very old approach to birth control, and dozens of varieties of intrauterine devices have been used over time. The present-day choices of IUDs include the Copper T, produced by several companies, and the Multiload IUD made by Organon. The Copper T is a "T"-shaped device, part of which is wrapped with fine copper wire that adds significantly to its contraceptive efficacy. Approximately 70 million women around the world (most of them in China) are using IUDs in the mid-1990s.

Injectable Contraceptives. Injectables contain hormones similar to those contained in the birth control pill except they are injected intramuscularly every two or three months, normally into the arm of the woman who wishes to remain free of pregnancy. The two most widely used are Depo-Provera, the brand name for depotmedroxy progesterone acetate (DMPA), and Noristerat (NET-EN), but others are becoming available, including a once-a-month injectable. About 12 million women rely on this method in the mid-1990s.

Norplant. Norplant delivers hormonal contraception through five matchstick-sized rods that are implanted into a woman's upper arm. Its contraceptive effect lasts for five years, and the rods can be removed at any time to restore fertility. In 1994, two million women had begun using this new method; by 1995 this number had more than doubled, with an estimated 3 million women using Norplant in Indonesia alone.

Traditional Methods. The so-called traditional methods of birth control are withdrawal and rhythm. Withdrawal refers to the removal of the penis from the vagina prior to ejaculation and, for some couples, it can be a very effective method of spacing pregnancies, though for many others it is not. Nonetheless, withdrawal is a time-honored technique that has contributed substantially to pregnancy prevention throughout history. If the withdrawal always occurred prior to ejaculation, it would be quite an effective method; in fact, many men are unable to predict precisely when their climax will occur, and for others withdrawal detracts from sexual pleasure, both of which render withdrawal less effective as a birth control approach. One criticism of withdrawal appears to be unfounded, however, that pregnancy often occurs as a result of the leakage of pre-ejaculatory fluid. In fact, such fluid contains a count of sperm so low as to be associated with infertility and does not likely often cause pregnancy.

Rhythm refers to periodic abstinence from intercourse during those periods of the menstrual cycle when a woman is most likely to become pregnant. It is notoriously unreliable as a method of birth control but can be improved somewhat by routinely measuring a woman's body temperature, which rises slightly just prior to ovulation. This approach is often referred to as the "Billings" method. Rhythm is the only method of birth control explicitly accepted by the Roman Catholic Church, on the grounds that it is "natural" (the rhythm method is also sometimes referred to as "natural family planning").

Rhythm is unreliable for a variety of reasons, including the fact that women's menstrual cycles sometimes vary considerably from month to month; because intercourse is often unanticipated; because women cannot always control when intercourse will occur; and because the method requires such long periods of abstinence—up to fifteen days per month for some couples—that many of its adherents simply do not practice it assiduously.

Appendix 4

Estimate of Lives Saved by Contraception

I have used two-hundred lives saved per ten thousand CYPs as the estimate of the impact of contraception on mortality throughout this book. The number is derived from the Alan Guttmacher Institute's calculations of March 6, 1996. These AGI data were published to demonstrate the impact of a major cut in U.S. government funds for family planning programs in developing countries. The AGI estimated that the funding reduction would result in a decrement of seven million CYPs (their exact figure was 6,946,568) with the following outcomes:

Current family planning users left unprotected	6,946,568
Proportion adopting traditional methods	40%
New users of traditional methods	2,778,627
Additional pregnancy rate with traditional methods	30%
Unwanted pregnancies from traditional use	833,588
Additional pregnancy rate for those unprotected	75%
Unwanted pregnancies from those unprotected	3,125,956
Total unwanted pregnancies from budget cuts	3,959,544
Percentage resorting to abortion	40%
Additional abortions	1,583,818
Percentage of pregnancies resulting in live births	47%
Additional unwanted births	1,860,986
Maternal mortality rate	410/100,000

Additional maternal deaths	7,630
Infant mortality rate	72/1,000
Additional Infant deaths	133,991

From this it follows that the provision of contraceptives sufficient for ten thousand CYPs (e.g., 1 million condoms or 140 thousand cycles of OCs sold through CSM) will result in saving 193 infant deaths and 11 maternal deaths:

$$\frac{6,946,568}{10,000} = \frac{133,991}{x} \; ; x = 193 \text{ infant deaths averted per 10,000 CYPs}$$

$$\frac{6,946,568}{10,000} = \frac{7630}{y}; y = 11 \text{ maternal deaths averted per 10,000 CYPs}$$

Note that the AGI estimate is based on an infant mortality rate (IMR) of 72/1,000 (i.e., 7.2 percent of all babies die in their first year) and maternal mortality of 410 maternal deaths per 100 thousand live births. In countries where these rates are higher (e.g., Sierra Leone where the IMR = 143; Afghanistan IMR = 163), the impact of birth control will be greater. In countries like the Philippines (IMR = 34) and China (IMR = 44), the impact on mortality will be less.

RANGE OF ESTIMATES FOR HIV TRANSMISSION PREVENTED BY CONDOM USE

The estimation of HIV transmissions prevented by condom use is even more complex than the assessment of the impact of contraceptive use on infant and maternal mortality. I should further state that Family Health International, who provided the following transmission probabilities from their AVERT model, do not endorse my extrapolations from their probability figures. However, as the basis for forming an estimate or, perhaps better, a *range* of estimates, I believe the following calculations are reasonable.

1. Probability of HIV transmission equals 0.15 percent for each coital act by a discordant (one partner is HIV positive; the other is negative) heterosexual couple with no genital urinary infections. If either partner has a GUI, the probability goes to 6 percent.
2. Comparable probability of male-to-male transmission is 1 percent with no GUI, 30 percent with GUI.
3. Assumptions:
    i. 95 percent of coital acts are heterosexual; 5 percent are male-to-male.
    ii. GUI is present in 15 percent of the population, both male and female.

4. Then each 100 unprotected coital acts by discordant couples will result, on average, in the following transmissions:

   i. 85 percent (no GUI) of 95 percent (heterosexual) = 80.75 percent have odds of 0.15 percent (average of male-to-female and female-to-male).

   ii. 15 percent (GUI) of 95 percent = 14.25 percent have odds of 6.0 percent.

   iii. 85 percent of 5 percent = 4.25 percent have odds of 1.0 percent.

   iv. 15 percent of 5 percent = 0.75 percent have odds of 30.0 percent.

      i. $80.75 \times .0015 = .12113$

      ii. $14.25 \times .06 = .855$

      iii. $4.25 \times .01 = .0425$

      iv. $.75 \times .30 = .225$

Total = $1.24 \times V$, where V (positives with positives are not discordant) = (1 minus the percentage of population that is positive).

5. If 5 percent of the sexually active population is HIV positive, then we have $1.24 \times .05 \times .95 = 0.059$ transmissions per 100 coital acts.

6. If 1 percent of the sexually active population is HIV positive, the number of transmissions per 100 coital acts drops to 0.0123; if HIV positivity is 10 percent, transmissions are 0.112 per 100 coiti.

If condoms are 90 percent effective in preventing transmission, we have the following transmissions prevented, per 1 million condoms sold/used:

HIV Positivity	Transmissions Prevented per Million Condoms
1%	111
5%	531
10%	1,080

Or, roughly, 100 transmissions prevented for every percentage point of HIV positivity in the target population.

I recommend interpreting these numbers as estimates ±50 percent, i.e., one million condoms sold will prevent between 50 and 150 transmissions in a population with 1 percent HIV positivity.

(Probability estimates from Family Health International, AVERT Model, 1998.)

Bibliography

Ahmed, G., W. P. Schellstede, and N. E. Williamson. 1987. "Underreporting of Contraceptive Use in Bangladesh." *International Family Planning Perspectives* 13, no. 4 (December): 136–140.

Andreasen, A. 1995. *Marketing Social Change.* San Francisco: Jossey-Bass.

Barberis, M., and P. D. Harvey. 1997. "Costs of Family Planning Programs in 14 Developing Countries by Method of Service Delivery." *Journal of Biosocial Science* 29, no. 2 (April): 219.

Barton, R., ed. 1950. *Advertising Handbook.* Englewood Cliffs, NJ: Prentice-Hall, cited in Simon, 1965.

Black, T. 1977. "The Baby Who Lived." *New Scientist* (January 20).

———. 1972. "Ten Institutional Obstacles to Advances in Family Planning." In *New Concepts in Contraception*, M. Potts and C. Wood, eds. London: Medical Technical Press.

Black, T., and P. D. Harvey. 1976. "A Report on a Contraceptive Social Marketing Experiment in Rural Kenya." *Studies in Family Planning* 7, no. 4 (April): 101.

Centers for Disease Control and Prevention. 1993. "Morbidity and Morality Weekly Report" 42, no. 30: (August 6).

Cernada, G. P. 1970. "Direct Mailings to Promote Family Planning." *Studies in Family Planning*, no. 53 (May): 16.

Chapman, S. 1996. Personal communication.

Ciszewski, R. L., and P. D. Harvey. 1994. "The Effect of Price Increases on Contraceptive Sales in Bangladesh." *Journal of Biosocial Science* 26, no. 1 (January): 25.

———. 1995. "Contraceptive Price Changes: The Impact on Sales in Bangladesh." *International Family Planning Perspectives* 21, no. 4 (December): 150.

Civilization. 1995. (November/December).

Coale, A., and E. M. Hoover. 1958. *Population Growth and Economic Development.* Princeton, NJ: Princeton University Press.

Cohen, J. E. 1995. *How Many People Can the Earth Support?* New York: W. W. Norton.

Darden, C. 1995. Personal communication.

Davies, J. 1978. Personal communication.

———. 1992. "Monthly Progress Report from Pakistan (January)." Washington, D.C.: Population Services International, unpublished report.

———. 1996. Personal communication.

Davies, J., and T. Louis. 1975. "Doctors and Community-based Pill Promotion in Sri Lanka." *IPPF Medical Bulletin* 9, no. 3 (June).

———. 1997. "Measuring the Effectiveness of Contraceptive Marketing Programs: Preethi in Sri Lanka." *Studies in Family Planning* 8, no. 4 (April): 82.

DKT International. 1997. "Social Marketing Statistics, 1996." (July).

———. 1998. "Social Marketing Statistics, 1997." (August).

Donald, M., and P. D. Harvey. 1992. "The Impact of Price Reductions on Condom Sales in Haiti." *DKT Reports/Findings*, no. 1 (September).

Finkle, J. L., and C. A. McIntosh, (eds.). 1994. *The New Politics of Population.* New York: The Population Council.

Fowler, F. J., Jr., and T. W. Mangione. 1990. *Standardized Survey Interviewing: Minimizing Interview Related Error (Applied Social Research Methods Series* Vol. 18) Newbury Park, London, New Delhi: Sage Publications.

Frost, J., and J. D. Forrest. 1995. "Understanding the Impact of Effective Teenage Pregnancy Prevention Programs." *Family Planning Perspectives* 27, no. 5 (Sept./Oct.): 188.

Fryer, P. 1965. *The Birth Controllers*, cited in Stycos, 1977.

Furstenberg, F. F., L. M. Geitz, J. O. Teitler, and C. C. Weiss. 1997. "Does Condom Availability Make a Difference? An Evaluation of Philadelphia's Health Resource Centers." *Family Planning Perspectives* 29, no. 3 (May/June): 123.

Gershman, M. 1987. "Packaging: Positioning Tools of the 1980s." *Management Review* 76 (August), cited in Government of Canada, 1995.

Government of Canada. 1995. "When Packages Can't Speak. Possible Impacts of Plain and Generic Packaging of Tobacco Products." Expert panel report prepared at the request of Health Canada, March.

Gupta, D. R. 1974. "Achieving a Social Objective Through Modern Marketing." Government of India Mimeo.

———. 1996. Personal communication, July.

Gwartney, J., and R. Lawson. 1997. *Economic Freedom of the World, 1997 Annual Report.* Vancouver, B.C.: The Fraser Institute (with several copublishers).

Gwartney, J., R. Lawson, and W. Black. 1996. *Economic Freedom of the World, 1975–1995.* Vancouver, B.C.: The Fraser Institute (with several copublishers).

Harvey, P. D. 1969. "Development Potential in Famine Relief: The Bihar Model." *International Development Review* 2, no. 4 (December): 7.

———. 1984. "Advertising Family Planning in the Press: Direct Response Results from Bangladesh." *Studies in Family Planning* 15, no. 1 (Jan./Feb.): 40.

———. 1991a. "In Poor Countries 'Self-Sufficiency' Can Be Dangerous to Your Health." *Studies in Family Planning* 22, no. 1 (Jan./Feb.): 52.

———. 1991b. "Intercept Data from Cameroon." DKT unpublished memo (November).

———. 1994a. "The Boss Who Won't Let Go." *ASBA Today* (Feb./March): 26.

———. 1994b. "The Impact of Condom Prices on Sales in Social Marketing Programs." *Studies in Family Planning* 25, no. 1 (Jan./Feb.): 52.

———. 1996. "Let's Not Get Carried Away With 'Reproductive Health'." *Studies in Family Planning* 27, no. 5 (Sept./Oct.): 283.

Harvey, P. D., and J. D. Snyder. 1987. "Charities Need a Bottom Line Too." *Harvard Business Review* 65, no. 1 (Jan./Feb.): 14.

Huber, S. C., and P. D. Harvey. 1989. "Family Planning Programs in 10 Developing Countries: Cost Effectiveness by Mode of Service Delivery." *Journal of Biosocial Science* 21, no. 3 (July): 267.

Hynam, C.A.S. 1966. "The Dysfunctionality of Unrequited Giving." *Human Organization* 25, no. 1 (Spring).

Indian Institute of Management. 1964. "Proposals for Family Planning Promotion: A Marketing Plan." (Unpublished).

———. 1965. "Proposals for Family Planning Promotion: A Marketing Plan." *Studies in Family Planning* 1, no. 6 (March): 7.

Johns Hopkins Communication Program. 1991. "Paying for Family Planning." *Population Reports* Series J, no. 39 (November).

Johns Hopkins University. 1990. "Condoms—Now More Than Ever." *Population Reports* Series H, no. 8 (September).

Kennedy, D. 1970. *Birth Control in America: The Career of Margaret Sanger*. New Haven, CT: Yale University Press, cited in Stycos, 1977.

Klein, M. 1990 "Censorship and the Fear of Sexuality." *The Humanist* (July/Aug.): 15.

Kodjo, K. L., J. M. Convisser, and C. Ferreros. 1991. "Dual Strategy in Zaire Promotes Condom Use for AIDS Protection." PSI, unpublished report.

Kotler, P., and E. L. Roberto. 1989. *Social Marketing*. New York: Free Press.

The Lancet. 1995. "STD Control for HIV Prevention—it works!" (editorial), August 26.

Lewis, M. A. 1986. "Do Contraceptive Prices Affect Demand?," *Studies in Family Planning* 17, no. 3 (May/June): 126.

Lissance, D. M. 1996. Personal communication.

Lissance, D. M., and W. P. Schellstede. 1993. "Evaluating the Effectiveness of a Family Planning IE&C Program in Bangladesh." *PSI Special Reports*, no. 2.

Manoff, R. K. 1985. *Social Marketing*. New York: Praeger Press.

Myers, J., 1995, Personal communication.

New York Times. 1996a. Review of *How Many People Can the Earth Support?* by J. E. Cohen. January 14, 12.

———. 1996b. "AIDS Epidemic, Late to Arrive, Now Explodes in Populous Asia." January 21, A-1.

———. 1996c. "Give Ukraine a Break." August 8, 26.

Ogilvy, D. 1963. *Confessions of an Advertising Man*. New York: Atheneum.

Opatow, L. 1984. "Packaging Is Most Effective When It Works in Harmony With the Positioning of a Brand." *Marketing News* 18 (February), cited in Government of Canada, 1995.

Piller, A. 1995. Personal communication.

Plata, S. 1996. Personal communication.

Population Action International. 1993. "Population Picks and Pans for '92." (April).

Population Institute. 1995. POPLINE (Nov.-Dec.).

Population Reference Bureau. 1991. "Family Planning Saves Lives." 2nd ed.

———. 1995. "1995 World Population Data Sheet."

Rangan, V. K. 1985. "Population Services International: The Social Marketing Project in Bangladesh." Harvard Business School, 9–586–013 (case study).

Reitmeijer, C. A., J. W. Krebs, P. M. Feorina, and F. N. Judson. 1988. "Condoms as Physical and Chemical Barriers Against Human Immunodeficiency Virus." *Journal of the American Medical Association* (March 25): 1851.

Ross, J. A., and E. Frankenberg. 1993. "Findings from Two Decades of Family Planning Research." The Population Council, New York.

Schramm, W. 1971. "Communication in Family Planning." *Reports on Population/Family Planning*. The Population Council, no. 7 (April).

Schuster, M. A., R. M. Bell, S. H. Berry, and D. E. Kanouse. 1998. "Impact of a High School Condom Availability Program on Sexual Attitudes and Behaviors." *Family Planning Perspectives* 30, no. 2 (March/April): 67.

Schwartz, J. B., J. S. Akin, D. K. Guilkey, and V. Paqueo. 1989. "The Effect of Contraceptive Prices on Method Choice in the Philippines, Jamaica, and Thailand." In *Choosing a Contraceptive: Method Choice in Asia and the United States*, A. Bulatao, J. A. Palmore, and S. E. Ward, eds. Honolulu, University of Hawaii, Westview Press.

Shelton, J. D. 1991. "What's Wrong with CYP?" *Studies in Family Planning* 22, no. 5 (Sept./Oct.): 332.

Simon, J. L. 1965. *How to Start and Operate a Mail-Order Business*. New York: McGraw-Hill.

———. 1981. *The Ultimate Resource*. Princeton, NJ: Princeton University Press.

Social Marketing Forum. 1987. No. 12: (Spring).

State Innovations in Family Planning Services Agency (SIFPSA). 1995. *Brochure*. Lucknow, India.

Stover, J., and A. Wagman. 1992. "The Costs of Contraceptive Social Marketing Programs Implemented Through the SOMARC Project." SOMARC, Special Study no. 1 (June).

Strossen, N. 1995. *Defending Pornography*. New York: Scribner.

Stycos, J. M. 1977. "Desexing Birth Control." *Family Planning Perspectives* 9, no. 6 (Nov./Dec.): 286.

Tribe, L. 1988. *American Constitutional Law*, 2nd ed. Mineola, NY: The Foundation Press.

United Nations Population Fund (UNFPA). 1992. *State of World Population 1992*. UNFPA/United Nations Population Fund, New York.

U.S. Centers for Disease Control and Prevention. 1992. "HIV/AIDS Prevention Training Bulletin" (July).

Wattleton, F. 1996. *Life on the Line*. New York: Ballantine.

World Bank. 1994. "Population and Income Change: Recent Evidence." World Bank Discussion Papers, no. 249.

———. 1995. "World Development Report 1995."

World Health Organization (WHO). 1995. "Health Benefits of Family Planning." WHO/FHE/FPP/95.11.

Zero Population Growth. (ZPG). 1996. Direct mailing, March.

Index

About the Author

PHILIP D. HARVEY is president of DKT International, a non-profit organization that oversees social marketing programs in eight countries in Asia, Africa, and Latin America.

DATE DUE

HIGHSMITH #45230

Printed
in USA